Sound Sentiment

The Arts and Their Philosophies,
a series edited by Joseph Margolis

Sound Sentiment

An Essay
on the Musical Emotions

Including

the Complete Text of

The Corded Shell

Peter Kivy

Temple University Press

Philadelphia

Temple University Press, Philadelphia 19122
Copyright © 1989 by Peter Kivy. All rights reserved
Published 1989
Printed in the United States of America

The paper used in this publication meets the minimum
requirements of American National Standard for Information
Sciences—Permanence of Paper for Printed Library Materials, ∞
ANSI Z39.48-1984

Library of Congress Cataloging-in-Publication Data
Kivy, Peter.
Sound sentiment : an essay on the musical emotions, including the
complete text of The Corded shell / Peter Kivy.
p.   cm. — (The Arts and their philosophies)
Bibliography: p.
Includes index.
ISBN 0-87722-641-5 cloth (alk. paper)
ISBN 0-87722-677-6 paperback
1. Music—Philosophy and aesthetics.   2. Music—17th century—
History and criticism.   3. Music—18th century—History and
criticism.   I. Kivy, Peter. Corded shell. 1989.   II. Title.
III. Series.
ML3845.K595   1989
780'.1—dc19   89-4336
                                                       CIP
                                                       MN

To the memory of Aaron Rosenberg,
who wrote and composed
under the name of Saul Aarons.

Contents

Foreword

When Peter Kivy mentioned, some time ago, that he had some intention of revising *The Corded Shell*, the entrepreneur in me saw at once a splendid opportunity to launch the series The Arts and Their Philosophies in a very strong and visible way. The more civilized part of me prompted a curiosity about how he would actually handle the revisions. I had no idea what he would do, when we first agreed to the thing, except a general sense of his intending to "respond to [his] critics." That was quite enough to go on. But I must say that Peter has now added what is very close to a second book only a little shorter than the first. Which is only a little more than splendid: a small windfall, in fact.

The Corded Shell was an extraordinarily successful book when it first appeared in 1980. Apart from winning the ASCAP–Deems Taylor Award, in 1981, it formed, together with Guy Sircello's *Mind and Art* (1972) and Alan Tormey's *The Concept of Expression* (1971), the serious center of very nearly all recent analytic discussions of expression in the arts, of musical expression in particular in Kivy's case. It has, since its appearance, come to be regarded as the indispensable locus for a promising theory of musical expression. In fact, together with a very small number of other recent discussions—Susanne Langer's, for instance —it is distinguished in being regularly contrasted with Eduard Hanslick's famous broadside, which set the general lines of the argument about musical expression pretty well down to our own day. Since *The Corded Shell*, of course, Kivy has made himself one of the preeminent contemporary philosophers of music.

In his having elected—in what in effect is more than a second edition of *The Corded Shell*—to change the title to *Sound Sentiment*, I myself find a pretty equivocation of accent in Kivy's well-known personal style that is not only a little sly but also a small clue about the double take of the new book. For the charm of what he's given us rests largely with the narrative of a man who had put forward a forthright claim favoring musical expression (in *The Corded Shell*) and now returns to ask himself whether his principal critics (or implicit critics) could have been right after all. Needless to say, he does not abandon his thesis; but that thesis has gained strength from having been so strenuously tested. In effect, Kivy pronounces his continuing verdict at the end of the new account: *sound SENTIMENT*, as far as favoring *SOUND sentiment* goes.

The message of *Sound Sentiment* remains very close to that of *The Corded Shell*. It rejects skepticism about musical expressiveness, and it opposes "musical emotivism" to "musical cognitivism" —that is, the view that expressive attributions are due to arousal in listeners of certain emotions as opposed to the view that we actually hear certain emotive or expressive qualities in the music. The account is tempered by the review of intervening criticism (including Kivy's own), and its effect is to strengthen the findings Kivy reached in *The Corded Shell*, by further careful analysis.

There is a pleasant candor in Kivy's discussion, both with regard to finality and to seemingly parallel cases (fiction, for instance), that marks the special reliability of his account. I think it can be said in a fair way that Peter Kivy is never simply dogmatic where he is most convinced. In any event, his thesis remains pretty much the same: that music, like the face, is "expressive of sadness," say, without (for that reason alone) reducing to "expressions of sadness." He calls this notion the "contour model of musical expressiveness."

The amusing frontal picture of a Saint Bernard dog starkly opening a monograph on musical expressiveness gives the entire argument its bite—if I may be allowed to express myself thus. Kivy would favor the joke: it's the sort of thing that surely occurred to him when he put *The Corded Shell* together. What is so appealing about Kivy's discussion is that the strenuous issues raised in the technical literature since at least the middle of the nineteenth century (running back to the ancients, actually) never outrun the good sense of his plain man's game and never require distortion in order to be scanned effectively.

He goes on to offer, in *Sound Sentiment*, some biological suggestions about our responsiveness to the expressive qualities in music. How scrupulously he proceeds here—and how pointedly, in a musical sense—may be judged from the second of these essays ("Newcomb's Problem"). But the biological speculation is offered in an entirely conjectural spirit.

In this essay, Kivy examines in careful detail what he regards as the most sustained and serious criticism of *The Corded Shell*: an essay by Anthony Newcomb that appeared in *Critical Inquiry* (1984). This leads him to a variety of deft responses on questions that fan out from a close review of musical examples to promising applications to literature and literary criticism. He continues his reexamination of himself in the following chapter ("And Nevertheless It Moves") in the company of what he takes to be the most salient efforts in the analytic literature, since 1980, to revive the "arousal" theory—that is, musical emotivism. He selects three exemplars from the philosophical discussion—what he calls "the stimulus model," "the representation model," and "the property model"—and gives us a running account of why they fail; that is, an account of the general strategies, not merely the instances.

What we have to bear in mind, through all of this, is the notable strength of the "cognitivist" thesis Kivy champions. Because the truth is that that thesis had been thought to be impossible or nearly impossible to defend, from Hanslick to our own time. What I think Kivy's argument—and similar arguments applied to visual and literary arts—leads us to acknowledge is the need for a fresher theory of the nature of artworks themselves, musical and other, as opposed to mere physical sounds and marks.

Kivy links these issues, incipiently, to biology at least. But that, I submit, cannot be the whole story if, say, in addition to our being discerning enough to see the sad contour of a face, the sad contour of a piece of music is also discerned *in the music*. What is needed, clearly, is an account of the sense in which music is the kind of phenomenon that can, in a conceptually apt way, take ascriptions of the sort in question and *manifest* or *possess* the properties in question. What Kivy had effectively shown, among other things, in *The Corded Shell* was that the "expression" theory (whether per arousal, representation, textual analogue, or individual psychological utterance) failed to capture the sense of the "expressive" possibilities of music—which an important tradition of musical theory spanning the views of Arthur Schopenhauer and Johann Mattheson (1739) down to Langer and Kivy himself has actually preserved. The truth is that the line of argument favored in that tradition is not central to, or well-formed in, Hanslick's attack on the "expression" theory—nor indeed is it in Edmund Gurney's *The Power of Sound* (1880). It is the essential feat of Kivy's contribution to have isolated and defended the thesis of expressive properties in music in what may well be the cleanest and most effective way the literature affords.

The final surprise of Kivy's new book is rather prettily predictable—with hindsight. Kivy is a formalist as far as "pure" instrumental music goes, very much in Hanslick's sense. Except that, having recovered the discernibility of expressive qualities *in* music, it proves quite easy for Kivy to reconcile formalism and "feeling" (in the final chapter.) There you have it. Kivy himself pretty well opposes (for instance, agreeing with Anthony Kenny's analysis of emotions) the fashionable theory that music arouses "the garden-variety emotions." But I think the force of the thesis Kivy means to support does not actually require that particular disclaimer; and the disclaimer itself obscures the difference between *music's* arousing emotions and one's emotions being aroused *on the occasion of listening to music.* It seems to me that the final answer to that question depends on a further analysis of the nature of musical "entities" or phenomena and of the causal relations music, as such, may enter into.

Kivy is quite right to resist the crude arousal theory; but there surely is another option. Indeed, Kivy himself favors that other option, for he affirms that "the better the music expressive (say) of anguish, the more intensely moving and the more enjoyable the music." Kivy also opposes the semantic and representational construals of expressiveness in music, of course. He is an "emotive formalist." But, for that very reason, he acknowledges the moving power *of* music.

What I think beckons Kivy on, what may well (I hope) be the subject of another sequel, is the intriguing question of the very nature of artworks—of music in particular—at least insofar as they are the kind of phenomena that can actually possess expressive qualities. This is a question that would lead Kivy ineluctably into the space of the very reality of the cultural world. Not that he opposes it but that his elegant account of expressive qualities has proceeded largely without benefit of its distinctive analysis.

It is always pleasant to read a book that promises to go on smoothly and effectively beyond its own back cover.

Joseph Margolis

Preface to The Corded Shell

The argument of this book, as well as its sources, bespeaks the author's long and enduring interest in the seventeenth and eighteenth centuries, and his conviction that although the writers on musical expression during that time were wrong about many things, they were profoundly right about something important, from which a satisfactory theory of musical expression might be built. It is my purpose here to bring out that profundity, and build that theory.

I hope though that my indebtedness to seventeenth- and eighteenth-century writers will not cause the opening chapters to be taken for a history of theories of musical expression in the Enlightenment. I have made no attempt to produce that. My selection of theories is a highly biased one, based not on any historical judgment but merely on what would be useful to my theory-making. The history of seventeenth- and eighteenth-century music aesthetics has yet to be written; and the present undertaking is not a contribution to that worthwhile project, except in a very tangential way. What this book is intended to be, and what I hope it is, is a contribution to our present understanding of the aesthetics of music. The part that is historical is to that end, and not an end unto itself.

A word about the musical examples: they are very much a part of the argument. If they fail to convince, the argument will founder; but if the reader fails to take them in, either by reading score, playing, or listening, the argument will literally, as well as figuratively, fall on deaf ears. In order, therefore, to make the music as accessible as possible to as many readers as possible, I have tried, first of all, to present as much of it as I decently could in piano, or piano and vocal score, so that anyone with facility at the keyboard could play it; second, to choose, whenever I could, familiar examples, easily obtainable on phonograph records. Few of my readers are likely to be able to read scores; and I have tried to take that into account. It is unfortunate but true that books cannot "sing" to as many people as they can "speak" to.

Like most writers and scholars, I have incurred various debts in the course of thinking and rethinking my work. Some I can acknowledge; but others, unfortunately, must go unmentioned because forgotten long ago in the process of assimilation that scholars, to compliment themselves, call "research."

My thanks are due to those who have offered suggestions and criticism in response to portions of this work that I have delivered as talks and lectures at the American Musicological Society, at various meetings of the American Society for Aesthetics, the New Jersey Regional Philosophical Association, at Columbia College, Rutgers University, the State University of New York at Binghamton, the University of Chicago, the University of Cincinnati, and the University of Wisconsin. I cannot thank them all by name. Those that I can are: James Bogen, Martin Bunzl, Seymour Feldman, Nelson Goodman, Lawrence Gushee, Fadlou Shehadi, Francis Sparshott, Alan Tormey, Bruce Vermazon.

I owe a special debt of gratitude to Wilson Coker and Francis Sparshott for reading the complete manuscript and offering many helpful criticisms and suggestions.

To Margot Cutter and Sanford G. Thatcher of Princeton University Press I am heavily indebted, in different ways, for seeing the manuscript through the process of publication, which often seems to the outsider one of the divine orphic mysteries. I owe "Sandy" something that is exceedingly hard to define: "encouragement" does not half describe it, but I will have to let it go at that. I owe Margot Cutter something no easier, perhaps, to define, but easier to name: "style."

I thank the editor of *The Music Review*, A. F. Leighton Thomas, for kind permission to reprint, in Chapter V, portions of my article, "What Mattheson said," which appeared in that journal, XXXIV (1973). And I thank Arthur Bloom for his beautiful execution of the musical examples, as well as for helpful advice on various musical points.

I am most grateful to Priscilla and Elliot Billings for their photograph of the lovable Lillian.

And, finally, I am deeply grateful to my wife, Lindley Hanlon, both for musical conversation, and for moral support when spirits flagged.

I thank them one and all, and absolve them from complicity in a work that in detail, or as a whole, may be displeasing to them.

New York City
November 1979

Preface to Sound Sentiment

A story is told of the great Morris Raphael Cohen receiving a perplexed undergraduate in his office with the following complaint: "I don't understand it, Professor Cohen. In Philosophy 1 you told us *P*. And now in Philosophy 2 you are telling us not-*P*. What's going on?" Cohen's reply is supposed to have been: "Well, young man, the difference between us is that between last semester and this, *I* have learned something."

In looking back on it, nothing I wrote in *The Corded Shell* makes me blush. But certainly I have learned a few things since 1980; and the opportunity of shepherding a second edition of the book into print makes me acutely aware of how many questions were left unanswered—indeed, unthought of—and how much of what I said might have been said differently today. Of course, I stand by my views, or I would not be allowing, indeed encouraging the publication of a new edition. And of course my views have been modified, improved, and corrected by criticism and by my own efforts to rethink the issues.

To drastically revise *The Corded Shell* in the light of recent philosophical developments since its publication seemed to me a dreary and self-defeating enterprise. The book would undoubtedly have been spoiled in the attempt. Better, I thought, to let it stand, and to bring it up to date by the tried-and-true method of supplementary essays. That is what I have done, and indeed I seem to have produced a monograph, in the process, almost as long as the original work itself.

I have tried in these supplementary chapters to avoid, as much as is possible, the all-too-familiar stance of the outraged author, totally misunderstood, and stubborn to the last. If I sometimes seem intransigent, it is not, I hope, because I am obstinate in error, but because I am strong in my convictions and anxious to persuade within the powers of rational discourse to do so.

Criticism of minor points, and criticism that I have thought too easy of refutation to raise any interesting questions, I have passed over in silence. Even so, these supplementary chapters cannot help but seem argumentative. Nevertheless, I believe that they advance the subject in a positive way, even though they do so by, for the most part, saying "nay." It only remains to say to all of my critics, both the answered and unanswered ones, that I am most grateful for the attention they have given my work. Better, I suppose, to be beyond criticism. Failing that, to be criticized is to be noticed. The third alternative is oblivion.

New York City
November 1988

Part One

The Corded Shell
Reflections on Musical Expression

What Passion cannot MUSIC raise and quell!
When *Jubal* struck the corded Shell,
His list'ning Brethren stood around
And wond'ring on their Faces fell
To worship that Celestial Sound.
Less than a God they thought there cou'd not dwell
Within the hollow of that Shell
That spoke so sweetly and so well.
What Passion cannot MUSIC raise and quell!

JOHN DRYDEN

The Saint Bernard Has a Sad Face

CHAPTER I

The Paradox of Musical Description

◊ 1 ◊ Description is often a form of flattery, which perhaps explains why we are so fond of describing works of art. When such description becomes interesting enough, or pretentious enough, it attains the status of "criticism." Then we begin to wonder what the use of it is, and whether it has been done well or ill.

Description of music is in a way unique. When it is understandable to the nonmusician, it is cried down as nonsense by the contemporary musician. And when the musician or musical scholar turn their hands to it these days, likely as not the nonmusician finds it as mysterious as the Cabala, and about as interesting as a treatise on sewage disposal.

Let me illustrate this peculiar state of affairs—this "paradox"—by presenting four very familiar kinds of musical description (from well-known and admired sources) in what I imagine is an ascending order of current respectability. I shall confine myself to these four critical types, but I need hardly remind the reader that this is far from being an exhaustive typology of musical description.

◊ 2 ◊ The first kind of musical description I have in mind I have dubbed (for reasons that will immediately become obvious) *biographical*, and my example is drawn from the writings of Robert Schumann.[1]

> Among the older artists, [Ludwig] Berger, like Moscheles, has not looked idly on at the new impulse given to pianoforte music. If old recollections sometimes overcome him, he lifts himself above them, and is yet active while daylight shines. After the long silence of this already elderly artist, who enjoys so wide a fame, considering the small number of his works, we should have expected something quite different from these studies [*Fifteen Etudes*, Opus 22]. We should rather have expected to find him restfully float-

ing on the stream of harmony, and rejoicing in the recollection of his long and successful labor. Instead of this, we are allowed to gaze upon a deeply agitated life, that seeks, with strong endeavour, to support itself at the high level of the day. Here and there we find gloomy expressions, mysterious hints, and then a sudden concentration of force, a feeling of approaching triumph,—all emanating, however, from a deeply poetic heart, and accompanied by artistic consciousness up to the moment when it becomes overwhelmed by its own impetuosity.

We all know what is wrong here. Schumann leads us to believe that he is going to describe some études by Ludwig Berger. Indirectly, I suppose, he does. But for the most part it is Berger, not his music, that gets talked about. When we listen to the études of Berger, "we are allowed to gaze upon a deeply agitated life, that seeks, with strong endeavour, to support itself at the high level of the day." We learn that his music emanates "from a deeply poetic heart" and an "artistic consciousness" which sometimes "becomes overwhelmed by its own impetuosity." We seem to hear a whole lot about Ludwig Berger, but little about his music. Some would say that we haven't heard anything about Berger either; that what we have really heard is Robert Schumann's Romantic babblings; that Berger's études cannot provide evidence for the claims about Berger that Schumann makes. I do not intend to examine here how much can be found out about the personalities of composers from their music. The important point for our purposes is not the validity or invalidity of Schumann's claims about Berger, but their obvious irrelevance. We came for a description of music, and we were given a description of the composer instead; that is our complaint.

◇ 3 ◇   The second type of description I will call, again for obvious reasons, *autobiographical*. And again I draw from a familiar source, this time the *Memoirs* of Hector Berlioz.[2] Needless to say, it is no mere coincidence that this second kind of description, closely related to the first, is, like the first, endemic to the Romantic movement in its fullest flowering.

I closed my eyes, and whilst listening to the divine gavotte [in Gluck's *Armide*], with its caressing melody and its softly murmuring monotonous harmony, and to the chorus, *Jamais dans ces beaux lieux*, so exquisitely graceful in its expression of happiness, I seemed to be surrounded on all sides by enfolding arms, adorable, intertwining feet, floating hair, shining eyes, and intoxicating smiles. The flower of pleasure, gently stirred by the melodious breeze, expanded, and a concert of sounds, colours, and perfumes poured forth from its ravishing corolla.

As our objection to Schumann was that while supposed to be talking about Berger's music, he ended by talking about Berger, so our objection to Berlioz is of a similar nature: again the wrong thing is being talked about, only this time it is not the composer but the critic. Gluck's music simply serves as a stimulus to Berlioz' reveries. He might just as well have taken a dose of laudanum as a dose of Gluck. About the reveries themselves one doesn't know quite what to say: whether they are charming or grotesque. I must confess that Berlioz' collection of arms, feet, hair, and eyes sounds more to me like a catalogue of spare parts than an enchanted garden. However that may be, the point is that we expect a description of *Armide*, and get, instead, a description of Berlioz' state of mind. That Berlioz' was a supremely interesting mind makes his autobiographical ruminations themselves supremely interesting. But it doesn't make them descriptions of music. The subject is Berlioz.

◇ 4 ◇   Let me move on, then, to what will appear, on first reflection at least, a far more respectable kind of musical description than the romantic effusions of Schumann and Berlioz. My examples of this genre are taken from what was, not too long ago, one of the most admired works of musical exegesis, Tovey's *Essays in Musical Analysis*.[3] I shall call this, simply, *emotive description*.

The first episode [of the second movement of the *Eroica*] is a regular trio in the major mode, beginning in consolation and twice bursting into triumph. Then the light fails and the mournful theme returns. . . . Above this enters at last, in a distant key, the beginning of a new message of consolation, but it dies away and the movement concludes with a final utterance of the main theme, its rhythms and accents utterly broken with grief.

Here follows [in the first movement of Brahms's First Symphony] a very beautiful passage of preparation for the second subject; a pathetic diminuendo, beginning angrily . . . and softening (while passing quickly through very remote keys) to tones of profound tenderness and pity. . . .

Tovey, it is clear, knows what he is supposed to be talking about: not Beethoven, not Brahms, and not Tovey, but music. If anyone has a quarrel with him, it is not over what he is talking about but over what he is saying about it. It is not Beethoven or Tovey that is consoled, triumphant, mournful, utterly broken with grief. It is the music. It is not Brahms or Tovey that is pathetic, angry, tender, pitying. It is the music.

But here the musically learned, and the philosophically hard-boiled, may immediately take issue. Two major objections are generally raised. For one thing, it will be argued, how on earth can these emotive predicates *really* apply to the *music*? Music broken with grief? Well if it is, shouldn't we try to cheer the poor thing up, as one wag has suggested? A composer can be triumphant, and his audience angry. But angry and triumphant music? If Beethoven's symphony is triumphant, shouldn't we give it the Victoria Cross, or chide it for being boastful? If Brahms's symphony is angry, shouldn't we try to mollify it, or stay well out of its way until it calms down? Surely Tovey could not intend these descriptions to apply to the music. Only sentient beings can have emotions. So he must mean, when he says that a theme is broken with grief, that Beethoven was broken with grief when he wrote it, or Tovey was broken with grief when he heard it. When he says that themes by Brahms are angry and tender, it must be a figurative way of saying that Brahms was feeling angry and tender when he wrote them, or that Tovey felt angry and tender when he heard them. If this is indeed the case, then we are right back where we started: with *biographical* or *autobiographical* description, both of which we have determined to be unacceptable. In other words, talk about emotions in music always seems to come down to talk about emotions in composers or listeners; and since the latter is not music description, emotive description *of music* is impossible.

But suppose it did make sense, the opponent of emotive description continues, to talk about music in emotive terms. There would still be the imposing problem of "objectivity": whether emotive descriptions can be "shared" intersubjectively. For we demand of genuine description not just that it not be nonsense, but that it be verifiable: that there be publicly accepted ways of telling whether or not a description is accurate. And this is just what the musical "purist" claims is lacking in emotive descriptions. As Edmund Gurney wrote in *The Power of Sound*, "it is often found that music which wears a definable [emotive] expression to one person, does not wear it or wears a different one to another, though the music may be equally enjoyed by both."[4] The musical purist assumes that there is universal disagreement over what emotive description correctly characterizes any given musical theme or composition. The reason, he insists, is that there is a lack of any agreed upon standard of correctness in these matters. Or, alternatively, he argues that the absolute disagreement over emotive character *proves* that there is no commonly accepted standard. It is purely a "subjective" matter that Tovey finds a Beethoven theme mournful, or a theme by Brahms pathetic. If one is looking for "scientific," objective criticism, one must look elsewhere, and shun the always tempting expedient of describing music in emotive terms. For when we yield to it, we end by either talking nonsense, or saying nothing that can be verified by anyone else. Such is the musical purist's view of the matter.

◇ 5 ◇ This brings us to our fourth and final descriptive type: what I shall call, for want of a better term, *technical description*. My examples, once again, are taken from well-known and musically impeccable sources:

> The rhythm of the theme of the last movement of Haydn's "Surprise" Symphony . . . has a much more patently iambic shape. In this case the initial groups, though both amphibrachs, are very different melodically and temporally, are in close proximity to each other, and are held together by a strong chord progression (I-V-I). Hence these two units tend to form a trochaic group on the second rhythmic level and constitute a single, unified anacrusis on the third rhythmic level.[5]

> In any case, the confrontation between D major and F minor [in the first and second movements of Beethoven's F-minor Quartet] stands as the most extreme between movements in any Beethoven work, bar none. The second key of the first movement already represented an enhanced dominant, D♭ (♭VI) in place of C(v). D♮ in the second movement represents an enhancement of the enhancement. Furthermore, this D-major *Allegretto ma non troppo* keeps importing B♭ , its own minor sixth degree—the same enhanced dominant relationship (♭VI) that is made so much of earlier. As a result, the joint between the second movement and the third can hang on the progression D-B♭ -B♮ , which is parallel to F-D♭ -D♮ between the first and second.[6]

Here, finally, is the purist's sought after goal, no-nonsense, objective, scientific description of music, without a taint of subjectivity or Romantic excesses. Either a rhythm is iambic or it is not. A chord is a five-chord or it is not. All knowledgeable perceivers are more or less in agreement about how such issues are decided. And if there are disputes and borderline cases, well, what discipline is without them?

Now there are those, I am sure, who genuinely believe that this is the only intellectually respectable way of describing music, and that describing music in emotive terms, after the advent of "scientific" musicology and modern musical theory, is about on a par with explaining natural phenomena on animistic principles or insanity in terms of possession by demons. Without agreeing with that opinion, I can certainly sympathize with it. Music critics may not have the patent on nonsense; but they have been mighty busy during the last two hundred years churning out more than their share of it. And the present day musician, music theorist, and musicologist feel an immense sense of relief when they can escape from this emotive flapdoodle into the healthy atmosphere of amphibrachs and enhanced dominant relationships.

But as enticing as this is to the musically learned, it leaves a large and worthy musical community completely out in the cold. Music, after all, is not just for musicians and musical scholars, any more than painting is just for art historians, or poetry for poets. It seems to me both surprising and intolerable that while one can read with profit the great critics of the visual and literary arts without being a professor of English or the history of art, the musically untrained but humanistically educated seem to face a choice between descriptions of music too technical for them to understand, or else decried as nonsense by the authorities their education has taught them to respect. Either description of music can be respectable, "scientific" analysis, at the familiar cost of losing all humanistic connections; or it lapses into its familiar emotive stance at the cost of becoming, according to the musically learned, meaningless subjective maundering.

The resolution of this musical "paradox" is not, obviously, to denegrate technical description. It has its virtues, and I am, by training and inclination, by no means blind to them. What needs doing, rather than to take cheap shots at technical language, is to make emotive description once again respectable in the eyes of the learned, so that it can stand alongside of technical description as a valid analytic tool.

◇ 6 ◇ One familiar philosophical strategy, at this juncture, might be to grant both the meaninglessness and the subjectivity of emotive description but claim that such "description" (it is, on this view, "description" in name only) nevertheless serves a useful critical purpose. It gets us to perceive something *else* in the work that really *is* there for us to perceive. "It seems reasonable for us to suppose," Arnold Isenberg concluded, in a highly influential essay on criticism, "that the critic is thinking of another quality, no idea of which is transmitted to us by his language, which he *sees* and which by his use of language he *gets us to see*."[7] This being the case, then, might it not also be that emotive description of music is, at the same time, both nonsense and respectable: respectable in that it is *useful* nonsense, nonsense capable of getting us to perceive, as Isenberg put it, "another quality," of which the describer is thinking, "no idea of which is transmitted by his language," since his language is emotive description, and emotive description both "subjective" and unintelligible.

With the claim that a music critic, in describing music emotively, may *sometimes* be getting us to perceive one thing by talking about another, I have no quarrel. Indeed, this is one way of looking both at *biographical* and *autobiographical* description: that is to say, in biographical description, the critic talks about something else, namely the composer, to get us to hear the expressiveness of the music, and in autobiographical description, the critic talks about something else, namely himself, to accomplish the same end. But I would balk at the stronger claim that emotive description of music is always talk by "indirection"; that emotive description is a kind of necessary conspiracy, in which the critic somehow trepans us into hearing what he wants us to hear, and, worse still, does it by talking nonsense, as if we were not ready for the awful truth, or capable of following a genuine argument. The position is counterintuitive, to say the least, and need not be resorted to in the first place. Emotive description of music does not have to be construed as an elaborate hoax.

This does not mean we reject the claim of Isenberg, and many others, that the point of criticism is to *get us to see* (or *hear*) things in the objects of criticism. We accept the end, rejecting only the means. Of course the music critic tries to get us to hear things in the music. But sometimes he does this by describing its expressive features. One of the points, clearly, of Tovey's describing a theme as "utterly broken with grief" is to get us, not to hear something else, but to hear that very thing: the grief of the theme. To hold that emotive descriptions of music are genuine, "objective" descriptions, is not to give over the role of the music critic of sharpening our musical perceptions. It is, I take it, a truism that the point (or a point) of description is to get us to perceive in the object that which we are describing in it. This the emotive description of music shares with the scientific description of the universe, the moralist's description of our depravities, and the accountant's description of his client's financial condition. They *all* are trying to "get us to see," and they *all* are *descriptions*.

But again the objection is heard: Emotive descriptions are "descriptions" in name only. For how can anything rightly be called a "description" if we have no objective standards by which to distinguish accurate descriptions from inaccurate ones? And anyway, it is quite unintelligible to describe music literally in emotive terms, because only sentient beings can literally be sad, cheerful, and so on.

It is this "paradox" of musical description that I hope the present monograph will help to resolve. We *can* have intellectually respectable description of music that is not remote from the humanistic understanding to which music itself has traditionally appealed. We *can*, in particular, have intellectually respectable description in the familiar emotive mode, of which Tovey's criticism is, perhaps, the finest modern example. But we can have this only if we can answer the musical purist's two principal charges: that emotive descriptions of music are unintelligible, and that they are congenitally "subjective." What follows is an answer to these charges, in the form of an account of how *some* emotive predicates can intelligibly apply to music, and why these are applicable intersubjectively. It is, in other words, what the eighteenth century called a theory of musical expression.

CHAPTER II

To Express and to Be Expressive

◇ 1 ◇   I am going to present here, as I have said, a theory of musical expression. My first task is to explain just what I mean by that.

If, under the proper circumstances, I am incited by anger to shout and clench my fist, I may correctly be said to have *expressed* my emotion; and the shouting and fist-clenching are correctly said to *express* or be *expressions of* my anger. It is extremely important to note that *one* necessary condition for shouting and fist-clenching to be expressions of my anger is that I actually be angry; and unless I am indeed angry, it is incorrect to say that I have expressed anger or that my shouting and fist-clenching are expressions of it. Let this stand as the paradigm of emotive *expression*.

But contrast this with another case. The Saint Bernard has a sad face (see illustration). We do not mean to say by this that the Saint Bernard's face *expresses* sadness. For certainly the Saint Bernard is not *always* sad. And for her face to always be appropriately described as expressing sadness, that is just what would have to be the case: the poor creature would have to be in a continual state of sadness. When, therefore, we describe the Saint Bernard's face as a sad face, we are not saying that it expresses sadness, but, rather, that it is *expressive of* sadness.[1] Let this stand as the paradigm of being *expressive of* φ, where "φ" is the name of an emotion or mood (like "anger" or "melancholy").

Now we have all been tempted, at one time or another, to describe a song or a tune, a theme or a symphony in emotive terms. We have said that a song is sad, or a tune gay; a theme angry, or a symphony brooding. And we read these kinds of descriptions of music everywhere: in the "lowest" as well as the "highest" forms of musical criticism, on the "blurb" of the record jacket and the essays of Tovey. Composers, great and not so great, have described their music in emotive terms, and musicologists (in their weaker moments, anyway) have done so as well. When we, or the composers, the critics, or the musicologists, say that a tune is sad, are we all saying that it *expresses* sadness or that it is *expressive of* the emotion? Is it the clenched fist, or the Saint Bernard's face?

◇ 2 ◇   There is good reason, I think, for rejecting the notion that when we say, "The music is sad," we need be, or very often are saying, "The music expresses sadness." For if music expresses sadness, then it must stand in the same relation to someone's sadness as my raised voice and clenched fist stand to my anger when I am correctly said to be expressing anger, in the paradigm of emotive expression. The obvious candidate is the composer, whose sadness his music is supposed to express. And therein lies a well-known difficulty.

J.W.N. Sullivan, the popular biographer of Beethoven, was much inclined to this sort of thing, seeing in Beethoven's music the mirror of the man—the expression of the passions of Beethoven's soul. In a characteristic passage, he wrote:

> The courage and resolution we find in the first movement [of the *Hammerclavier* sonata] is curiously austere. . . . Those cold harmonies, so characteristic of Beethoven's later work, no longer convey the warm human confidence of a man who knows that victory lies at the end. There is expressed a stark, bare resolution, courageous enough, but uncoloured by any joy in conflict. . . . The man who wrote this music is already a great solitary. He has abated nothing of his courage, but it has become more grim. Suffering, it would appear, has hardened him; never again, one would think, can this man melt. . . . The slow movement is the deliberate expression, by a man who knows no reserves, of the cold and immeasurable woe in whose depths, it would seem, nothing that we could call life could endure.

And so on.[2]

This passage, clearly, is rife with suggestions that music—Beethoven's music, at least—is not *expressive*, but *expresses*: that the music stands to the emotions as the clenched fist to my anger, not as the Saint Bernard's face to sadness. I do not say this merely because Sullivan unabashedly uses "expression" rather than "expressive of," as, for example: "There is expressed a stark, bare resolution, . . ." or "The slow movement is the deliberate expression . . . of the cold and immeasurable woe, . . ." and so forth. Musical discourse is full of talk about music *expressing* this and that and the other, where it is perfectly clear from the context that *expressive of* is what is meant, there being no suggestion that the composer is supposed to be giving vent to feelings or emotions. But the passage before us gives every indication of Sullivan's meaning exactly what he says when he says "express." For the emotive qualities of the music are seen to project the state of mind of the composer. Beethoven's music in the *Hammerclavier* does not *express* warmth and confidence just because Beethoven is no longer warm and confident but "a great solitary," never again to "melt." Again and again, here and elsewhere, Sullivan explains the expression of music in terms of the evolving state of mind of the composer. And if the present passage does not make this clear enough, we can call Sullivan into the witness box once more, this time stating a general principle: "The function of the kind of music we have been discussing is to communicate valuable spiritual states, and these states testify to the depth of the artist's nature and to the quality of his experience of life."[3]

I hold Sullivan's view up for scrutiny for two reasons: to disassociate myself from this kind of view; and to make it unmistakably clear that I am not setting up a man of straw.

The theory of musical expression I intend to outline here is an account of how it is that music can be *expressive of* the emotions; it is not a theory of how music can *express* them. That is because music does not, I think, ordinarily express them (although sometimes it can and does). I want to present a theory of what is going on when we describe music in emotive terms, in the absence of any suggestion that it is expressing the composer's emotions, or anyone else's. For we describe music emotively even when it is perfectly clear that the music is not (and cannot be) expressing the emotions we ascribe to it, or when we have no way of knowing whether it expresses those emotions because we have no way of knowing what emotive state the composer was in when he wrote it. That is to say, many, and perhaps most, of our emotive descriptions of music are logically independent of the states of mind of the composers of that music, whereas whether my clenched fist is or is not an expression of anger is logically dependent upon whether or not I am angry. It is unthinkable that I should amend my characterization of the opening bars of Mozart's G-minor Symphony (K. 550) as somber, brooding, and melancholy, if I were to discover evidence of Mozart's happiness and untroubled state of mind during its composition. But if my characterization were really to the effect that the opening bars of the symphony *express* somber, brooding melancholy, that is exactly what I would have to do, just as I must cease to characterize a clenched fist as an expression of anger if I discover that the fist clencher is not angry. This is a matter of logic.

◇ 3 ◇   But it is vital here to enter certain cautions and caveats.

First, I am not necessarily denying the psychological generalization—which perhaps might be true, although I doubt it—that sad music is often composed by sad composers, and happy music by happy ones. If this generalization is true—and I know of no evidence that it is—it is not enough to make it true that sad music often expresses sadness, or happy music happiness. The fact—if it were a fact—that composers who are sad tend to compose sad music, or composers who are happy, happy music, would not, of itself, make their music the expression of their sadness or happiness.

Second, there are things that music might express, or be expressive of, other than emotions: ideas, for one; points of view, for another; and so on.[4] I do not want to take a stand on whether music does, or really can express, or be expressive of such things. I merely confine myself to the question of how music can be expressive of what we call "emotions" and "moods."

Third, I do not want to claim that music cannot or does not express emotions. Indeed, I am inclined to think it sometimes does; and it is often important to know this. It seems fairly clear, to instance a case in point, even when we separate the abundance of fiction from the modicum of biographical fact, that parts of Mozart's *Requiem* (K. 626) express the composer's terror of death, and are not merely expressive of terror. Now some would argue that whatever interest that may hold for the biographer or psychologist, it holds little for the listener or critic. That is a large question in the philosophy of criticism, which there is no need to go into here. For terror will be heard in the "Dies irae" of the *Requiem* whether or not the music is indeed expressing it. And it is this terror—the terror that the music is expressive of—that is the subject of this study. I am interested here in understanding one of the important ways music can be expressive of emotions, and not in denying it can express them, or denying the critic a legitimate concern with that expression, or even in denying that sometimes what someone means to say by "The music is sad" is "The music expresses sadness" (which indeed seems to be just what Sullivan means). None of this do I want to deny.

Fourth, there may be ways music is expressive of emotions other than the ways I will be expounding.[5] I am inclined to believe that the account of musical expressiveness given here covers the central cases: those cases that have been central to the experience and criticism of Western music since the first flowering of polyphony. I shall not argue for that belief, but leave it to the musical reader to decide how wide a swath I have cut. It would be folly, though, to claim, without argument, that what follows is an account of the *only* ways music can be expressive of the emotions, or the only ways it can be intelligibly described in emotive terms. I make no such claims here.

In part, my theory is an explanation of why there is wide agreement (and I simply assume from the outset that there is) about what emotive characterizations at least broadly fit many parts of many musical works. There surely are disagreements over delicate shades of emotive "color." (Are the opening bars of the G-minor Symphony "melancholy," or "brooding," or perhaps just "serious" and "earnest"?) But our judgments usually fall into predictable bounds. (No one, to my knowledge, has ever been tempted to characterize the opening bars of the G-minor Symphony as "spritely" and "good humored," or Papagano's "Der Vogelfänger bin ich ja," in *Zauberflöte*, as "somber," "brooding," or "melancholy.") I hope my theory will provide an explanation for this. And to the extent that my explanation will be an historical one, based on certain facts about music and its evolution in the West, this monograph will be philosophical only in a borderline sense.

In part, however, my theory will be an attempt to give some kind of partial account of the aesthetic discourse in which we emotively characterize music. And to that extent it will be more like what goes under the head these days of "the philosophy of art" or "aesthetics." The theory is, to be sure, heavily "psychological," in a nonformal sense. But at this particular time in the history of philosophy in general, and the philosophy of art in particular, no excuse need be made for that; for psychology is back in the philosophical limelight.

Perhaps, having said this much, I should now just get on with it, and let the reader decide what kind of theory is presented here, and where this book is to be shelved. In the long run, it does not matter, since, as I believe Whitehead once said, the universe is not divided into departments.

CHAPTER III

Speaking and Singing

◇ 1 ◇   At the outset of the seventeenth century, in a misguided attempt to revive what was thought to be the authentic performance practice of Greek tragedy, a new musical style came into being whose "emergence . . . has often been regarded as the most important turning point in the entire history of music."[1] It is, essentially, the birth, in the modern era, of solo song: that is, "solo melody with a chordally conceived accompaniment."[2] Solo singing, to an instrumental accompaniment, often the lute, was a familiar part of the musical scene in the Renaissance. But in such performances, there was no *musical* distinction between the accompaniment and the vocal line. The musical texture was polyphonic throughout, with the solo voice singing one of the obbligato parts. And what contrast there was between the solo voice and accompaniment was due merely to the obvious fact that one of the parts was sung and the others played. Indeed, if the word "accompaniment" suggests something less than musical equality, it is a misnomer when applied to solo singing in the Renaissance. However, in the waning years of the sixteenth century, and the beginning years of the seventeenth something quite different begins to appear: a kind of *parlando*, or "recitative," called by its early practitioners "monody," or the *stile rappresentativo* (that is, the style of the actor or declaimer), in which a solo voice intones a text, accompanied by a simple bass line, supplied with numbers and other signs indicating what chords are to be filled in by the accompanying keyboard instrument (the so-called *basso continuo* of the musical Baroque).

The emergence of the *stile rappresentativo* was as much the result of theorizing as it was of the pure creative impulse. A product of a group of Florentine intellectuals known as the *Camerata*, "Monody counts among the few musical innovations in which theory antedates practice."[3] Paramount in the minds of the composer-theorists that made up this musical "salon" was "the affective approach to the words and the virtuoso embellishments."[4] What we have, then, in early monody, is a musical style that directly reflects a preconceived theory of musical expression. I shall call this theory, for reasons that will soon become obvious, the "speech theory" of musical expressiveness.

Pietro de' Bardi, son of the original patron of the Florentine *Camerata*, has provided us with a valuable account both of its founding and of the theoretical foundations on which its music was based. Jacopo Peri, who is credited by tradition with having written the first opera, *Dafne* (in 1597), "found a way," Bardi tells us, "of imitating familiar speech by using few sounds. . . ."[5] Peri himself, in the Foreword to his opera *Euridice* (first printed in 1601), gives us a more expansive description of his "discovery."

> I knew . . . that in our speech some words are so intoned that harmony can be based upon them. . . . And having in mind those inflections and accents that serve us in our grief, in our joy, and in similar states, I caused the bass to move in time to these, either more or less, following the passions. . . .[6]

In the same vein, Giulio Caccini, whose name is also closely associated with the early days of the *stile rappresentativo*, boasts in the Dedication of his *Euridice*—the first printed opera (1600)—that "In this manner of singing I have used a certain neglect which I deem to have an element of nobility, believing that with it I have approached that much nearer to ordinary speech."[7] And again, in the Foreword to his collection of monody, *Le nuove musiche*, of 1602, Caccini explains: ". . . I have endeavoured in those my late compositions to bring in a kind of music by which men might, as it were, talk in harmony, using in that kind of singing, as I have said at other times, a certain noble neglect of the song. . . ."[8]

What Peri and Caccini were doing was evolving a kind of musical declamation which, by following the rise and fall of the speaking voice, as it expresses the emotions of the speaker, resulted in a musical line distinctly nonmelodic in nature. That is what Caccini means by saying that in this kind of composition he has "used a certain neglect," "a certain noble neglect of song." He has, in other words, made the vocal line follow closely the declamation of the text as it would be if it were spoken, keeping it from breaking out into florid, melismatic melody. This musical technique survived in "recitative," the mainstay of musical "conversation."

Let us look, by way of illustration, at the opening of *Arianna's Lament*, the only surviving portion of Claudio Monteverdi's opera *Arianna* (1608). It is, perhaps, the most celebrated example of early monody—still an enormously affecting piece, and so much so at its first performance that, we are told, "all the listeners were most profoundly stirred and none of the ladies remained without tears."[9] It begins, "Lasciatemi morire!" (Let me die!):

EXAMPLE 1:
Monteverdi, *Lamento d'Arianna*

Clearly, Monteverdi has an idea of how someone in a heightened emotional state, as the abandoned Arianna must be imagined to be in, might declaim these words. And he has let the fall of the musical line reflect it:

La-scia-te-mi mo-ri-re!
—
—
— —
— — —

And one can well imagine a similar fall of the voice, in the English, if it were declaimed in a passion:

Let me die!
—
—
—

Making allowance for the aesthetic demands of the musical line, the representation of speech, in musical tone, is quite striking.

Now the point I want to bring out here is this. The musical line can be, and was, thought of as a kind of musical icon, resembling a piece of human emotive expression. In practice as well as in theory, music of a certain kind is seen to be a resemblance of human expression. And what we must now ask ourselves is whether this, in and of itself, is the explanation that the speech theory offers of how music can be *expressive of* the emotions. Is the musical setting of "Lasciatemi morire" expressive of grief simply in virtue of its modeling the speaking voice expressing grief, or is there more to it than that?

◇ 2 ◇ There seem to be two distinct speech theories, really, that grow out of the musical speculations of the *Camerata*. The duality lies in the vagueness of certain statements concerning the relationship of the emotions "represented" in music and the emotions "felt" by its auditors. The new style of singing, Bardi tells us, has made music "capable of moving the passions in a rare manner, . . ."[10] and Caccini, in *Le nuove musiche*, makes a similar claim: the *stile rappresentativo*, he says, "may fitly serve to the better obtaining of the musician's end, that is, to delight and move the affections of the mind"; for "exclamation is the principal means to move the affection. . . ."[11]

One very obvious interpretation that can be put on such statements is that what is being talked about here is the *arousal* of emotions. The musical line of "Lasciatemi morire" resembles an expression of grief, but, in so doing, *arouses* grief in the listener. And, indeed, just such an arousal theory did gain wide currency in the late seventeenth and early eighteenth centuries.

Sprinkled, for example, throughout the manuscripts (from c. 1695-1728) of Roger North, the English musician and musical theorist, is a speech theory of musical expression which puts the mechanism of arousal in musical resemblance to the speaking voice, but puts musical expressiveness itself in the arousal of the emotion, not in its resemblance. In other words, music for North is expressive (say) of sadness in that it *arouses* sadness, not in that it resembles its expression, the resemblance merely being the means to the end of arousal. So North writes in one place:[12]

And as to all of Musick, besides the bare pleasing the sence, it must be referred to a power, by similar sounds, of bringing to our minds or memorys the state of joy or greif, or of less important affections, as may be conforme to what wee hear. As for instance, who can hear the miserable clamor of one in affliction, without compassion? And whence that, but from a sensible reflection or memory of the same or like circumstances? And Musick by its sounds doth the same, and thro' the same operation of mind. . . . I have instanced in greif, but the case is the same in all the various states of humanity; for by hearing certain sounds that are like what men commonly use by way of expressing their then present condition, our minds are affected accordingly.

Melody resembles passionate speech, and the listener is affected with the appropriate passions. The composer "is to consider what manner of expression men would use on certain occasions, and let his melody, as near as may be, resemble that." And, in consequence, "an hearer shall put himself into the like condition, as if the state represented were his owne."[13]

We can see this view articulated still more clearly in the first quarter of the eighteenth century in the highly influential philosophical treatise on aesthetics—perhaps the first such—by Francis Hutcheson: *Inquiry Concerning Beauty, Order, Harmony, Design* (1725). Hutcheson writes:

> There is also another charm in music to various persons, which is distinct from harmony and is occasioned by its raising agreeable passions. The human voice is obviously varied by all the stronger passions; now when our ear discerns any resemblance between the air of a tune, whether sung or played upon an instrument, either in its time, or key, or any other circumstance, to the sound of the human voice in any passion, we shall be touched by it in a very sensible manner, and have melancholy, joy, gravity, thoughtfulness excited in us by a sort of *sympathy* or *contageon*.[14]

I shall call this the arousal speech theory of musical expressiveness. And by that I will mean the theory which states: (1) music is sad (or cheerful, or whatever) in virtue of its arousing sadness in the listener; (2) it arouses sadness by resembling, musically, the speaking voice when it expresses sadness; for (3) the listener recognizes the likeness and feels an appropriate emotion by a kind of empathy, or fellow-feeling, much as I might be saddened by the sadness of a friend.

The theory in whatever form it appears, that musical expressiveness lies in emotive arousal, is not a tenable one; and the serious objections to it are not by any means new. To begin with, there is the obvious objection that the most unpleasant emotions imaginable are perceived in music; and if that meant our *feeling* those emotions, it would be utterly inexplicable why anyone would willfully submit himself to the music. *Tristan und Isolde* is full of music expressive of deep anguish. None, I would think, except the masochists among us, would listen to such music if indeed it were anguish-producing. Nor, if one considers the *range* of emotions that *Tristan* is expressive of, would it be thought possible that the concertgoer could, unless he or she were some kind of supercharged mannic-depressive, experience them in five hours. Again, there is, in the behavior of concert- and playgoers, strong evidence to show that they are not experiencing the emotions they perceive. Peppermints and ice cream are both sold at the Royal Shakespeare, even when *King Lear* is on the bill; for we don't lose our appetites when we perceive the storm of emotions in the play, as we surely would if we *felt* them. (Could Cordelia eat peppermints?)[15] Indeed, it is quite compatible with my perceiving the most intense and disquieting emotions in a work of art that I not myself be moved in the least— which often happens when the work of art in question happens to be poor, and even when it is not.

These specific objections point to a more general one, which sums them up. Expressive predicates, when applied to art works, do not apply to them after the manner of dispositional ones. Sadness is a quality of the music, not a power of the music to do things to the listener. As Richard Wollheim aptly puts it, the main objection to the arousal theory of aesthetic expressiveness "is that it removes what we ordinarily think of as one of the essential characteristics of the work of art from among its manifest properties, locating it . . . in its hidden or dispositional endowment."[16] Or, in the more Puckish phraseology of O. K. Bouwsma, "the sadness is to the music rather like the redness to the apple, than it is like the burp to the cider."[17]

◇ 3 ◇   What is it, then, in the speech theory, that might suggest a plausible account of musical expressiveness? That part of the theory which construes "*X* is sad" as "*X* arouses sadness" we reject. But there is, nonetheless, the rather intriguing notion that music can resemble the passionate speaking voice, and the listener *recognize* the resemblance. If we lop off the unsound limb, we may very well, with a little further constructive surgery, end up with at least part of a healthy theory. Indeed, one wonders whether, at least in the case of the speech theory, any surgery is necessary at all, if the theory is sympathetically interpreted with the avoidance of the arousal component in mind. This is what I meant earlier when I suggested that there really were *two* speech theories lurking in the speculations of the *Camerata*. Let us look again at some of these earlier statements, with a view to extracting this second theory from them.

Recall, Bardi tells us that the monodic style is "capable of moving the passions in a rare manner, . . ." and Caccini that it "may fitly serve to the better obtaining of the musician's end, that is, to delight and move the affections of the mind," that "exclamation is the principal means to move the affections. . . ."[18] But perhaps we were too quick to assume that the principal end of the composer, namely, the arousal of the passions and affections, is identical with the task of imparting expressiveness to the music; or that the emotion that the composer is said to arouse is necessarily identical with the one the music is said to be expressive of.

If I express grief, it may arouse pity. If music is expressive of grief, might it not also arouse pity rather than grief, according to Bardi, Caccini et al.? Might we not, then, be able to interpret the speech theorists as saying that the expressiveness of music serves a further end, the moving of the passions and affections, not that the expressiveness lies in the arousal? What we would then have is a theory which holds that: (1) music is sad (or cheerful, or whatever) in virtue of its representing the expressive tones and other expressive characteristics of the human voice; (2) the listener recognizes and identifies these musical "icons"; (3) this recognition, in turn, triggers an emotion in the listener, not necessarily the one represented in the music. I will call (1) and (2) together the cognitive speech theory of musical expressiveness. It is not, I think, without adherents in the eighteenth century. Let me suggest a possible one.

Thomas Reid, the late eighteenth-century philosopher, closely associated with the movement known as the Scottish Philosophy of Common Sense, had an elaborate and sophisticated theory of human expression, which not only formed the basis for a philosophical account of the fine arts, but for a philosophy of mind, an analysis of perception, and a theory of knowledge as well.[19]

Reid, among many others of his contemporaries, believed that there was a natural, unlearned language of the passions and emotions, understood universally. And, he believed, "It is from the natural signs of the passions and dispositions of the mind . . . that painting, poetry, and music derive their expression. . . ."[20]

In the case of music, Reid seems to have held a version of the speech theory, a rather outmoded theory, it should be added, at this late date in the century. Melody, he believed, was often "an imitation of the tones of the human voice in the expression of some sentiment or passion. . . ."[21] When it was, the music was expressive of the passions and sentiments. But the question arises, of course, Wherein did Reid think the expressiveness lies? In the arousal of the passions and sentiments? Or in their "imitation"?

It would be dishonest to claim that Reid is completely free of the taint of the arousal theory. His statements are not altogether unambiguous. But there is at least one passage very suggestive of what I have called the cognitive speech theory. In the passage of which I speak, from his manuscript *Lectures on the Fine Arts* (1774), Reid states:

> There is something in music called expression and with which we are pleased. . . . [T]his expression is nothing but the fitness of certain sounds to produce certain sentiments in our minds. The first mother among mankind understood that the first time her son cry'd, he was in pain. . . . It is so ordered by the constitution of our nature that such sounds should produce such sentiments in us.[22]

Expression in music, then, consists in the "fitness of certain sounds to produce certain sentiments in our minds." This fitness of sounds makes them part of the natural language of the passions; and music, when it resembles them, becomes a natural language of passions itself. But notice. The cash value of the phrase "produce certain sentiments in our minds" is explicated by the example of a mother who "understood that, the first time her son cry'd, he was in pain." She did not feel pain; she *understood* that her son was in pain. The pain was produced not in the sense that she was made to feel pain, but in the sense that the concept of pain was communicated to her in the form of knowledge that her son was in pain. And since musical expression is being compared to *this*, it seems clear that music expressive of sadness does not produce the affection in us in the sense of making us feel sad, but in the sense of conveying to us the concept of sadness. We recognize that the music is expressive of sadness. It is worth noting that "sentiment" in Reid's time, as in ours, means not only "feeling," but "opinion." So when sounds are said to produce "sentiments" in us, we may perfectly well understand that to mean that they produce "opinions"—in the case at hand, opinions about emotions.

Reid, then, was maintaining here a version of what I have been calling the cognitive speech theory of musical expression: *cognitive* because the expressiveness of music lies in our recognition of the emotions, not in our feeling them; a *speech* theory because what we recognize is a kind of musical "iconography" of passionate speech.

What, then, is the legacy to us of the seventeenth- and eighteenth-century speech theories? What use can we make of these speculations? I would urge that what we can salvage from them is the suggestion that the major operator in musical expressiveness—or at least *one* major operator—is a musical resemblance of some aspect of human expression; and, further, that at least one such aspect is human speech. The origin of this theory, as a specific aesthetic program, in support of a specific musical style, must not be misunderstood. It does not confine the explanatory power of the speech theory to any specific period, necessarily, or any specific form of musical composition. The speech theory is not, in other words, merely an account of vocal monody in the seventeenth century, however its early propounders intended it. It applies, on the contrary, to *any* music in *any* period of music history, that bears the required analogy to human utterance which the *Camerata* consciously cultivated: an isorhythmic motet, a Renaissance madrigal, a Classical symphony, a Mahler song—what you will. To be sure, the speech theory alone is not an adequate account of musical expressiveness, even of the kind we are discussing: first, because not all such musical expressiveness lies in musical resemblance of expressive behavior; second, because human speech is not the only aspect of our emotive life that music can resemble. But we have, here, a good beginning. Music as "speech-icon" will be part of the theory of musical expressiveness to be outlined in this study. More, however, will be needed to make it work.

CHAPTER IV

A "Physiology" of Musical Expression

◇ 1 ◇ Although the *Camerata* was responsible for the creation of a vocal style, and a predominantly vocal form, the history of music from that time until the end of the eighteenth century was characterized by the steady, inexorable growth of instrumental music, and instrumental technique. As the complexities of the instrumental line, and the virtuosity of the performer increased, it became less and less possible to understand musical expressiveness as *solely* the function of an analogy to the impassioned speaking voice. No more expressive melody can be imagined than the ornate cantilena—typical of its kind—that Bach gives to the oboe in the second movement of the first Brandenburg Concerto:

EXAMPLE 2:
Bach, *Brandenburg Concerto No. 1*

Yet one would have to stretch a point to account for the expressiveness of this musical "lament" in entirely the same manner as the *Lamento d'Arianna*. There is, to be sure, a kind of "whining" or "wailing quality" to it, not unlike the quality Bach gives to the vocal line of the Evangelist, in the *St. John* and *St. Matthew Passions*, when he wants to imitate Peter's weeping, after the denial of Christ.

EXAMPLE 3:
Bach, *St. Matthew Passion*, Part II

And so there is, here, at least a strong suggestion of human *utterance*, although not human *speech*. Nevertheless, the complexity of the musical line is such that the allusion to human utterance can only be part of the expressive story. Such instrumentally conceived music required a far different account of musical expressiveness than the speech theory could provide, a different mechanism of expression than the rising and falling of the speaking voice. And the burgeoning mechanistic world view of the Enlightenment pretty much assured that the expressive model would be a *mechanistic* one.

Two "mechanisms" were available, and exploited by writers on musical expression, in the eighteenth century, as alternatives to the speech theory. One was the ubiquitous "association of ideas," which loomed so large in British psychology, moral philosophy, and aesthetics in the period. The other was the equally influential Cartesian psychology, which flourished on the Continent. In the present chapter, I want to examine an example of each, both chosen from British sources, and both out-and-out arousal theories. Their weaknesses will be highly instructive, and some hidden strengths will prove valuable to what follows.

The first is, in the main, a correct account of how music can, and sometimes does, arouse emotions. But since the arousal of emotions, we have argued, has nothing to do with the expressiveness of music, it is an incorrect theory of musical expression. The second is a completely incorrect account of how music arouses emotions; and in that it is an arousal theory also, it is, *eo ipso*, an incorrect theory of musical expression. But, when properly laundered, it has some materials of a correct theory; and it is these materials that we want to get at.

◇ 2 ◇ Let us look first, then, at the association of ideas as a theory of musical expression. It arises from the trivial and true observation that we tend, other things being equal, to think of B, after perceiving or experiencing or thinking of A, if, in the past, we perceived or experienced A and B together; or tend to feel a certain way, all things being equal, when we perceive or experience or think of A, if we felt that way in the past when we perceived or experienced A. All of this was common property in the seventeenth and eighteenth centuries, and was exploited philosophically by Hobbes, Spinoza, Locke, Hume, and others, before it froze into a psychological and philosophical doctrine in the latter part of the eighteenth century, in David Hartley's associationism.

Sights and sounds, tastes and smells, can, we all know, remind us of events or places, and make us feel a certain way, if they are associated with events, or places, or experiences in our pasts. "Thus music," Charles Avison writes in *An Essay on Musical Expression* (1752), "either by imitating these various sounds in due subordination to the laws of *air* and *harmony*, or by any other method of association, bringing the objects of our passions before us . . . does naturally raise a variety of passions in the human breast. . . ."[1]

Avison's view seems to be something like the following. Music can arouse images in our minds in either of two ways: first, by imitating the sound of a real object (say, a babbling brook, or a singing bird); or, second, by "association" (as I might be reminded of Vienna by hearing a song that I first heard there). When the image is brought to mind in either of these two ways, *it* in turn arouses in us whatever feeling or emotion may be associated in our minds with that image: happiness, if you were happy in Vienna, fear if you were afraid there, and so on. Avison seems to assume, however, that the image will have pretty much the same effect on everyone—an assumption which his theory needs, but which is completely unjustified, and a major flaw in it as an account of musical expressiveness.

I suggested at the outset that theories such as Avison's were correct (or at least plausible) accounts of the way music arouses emotions. For indeed we do find ourselves emotively aroused by music in specific ways; and we can, more often than not, ferret out a reason for it not unlike the kind Avison suggests. Strictly speaking, it is not the music that (directly) arouses our emotions, according to Avison, but the images and remembrances of things past which the music stimulates. By and large I think Avison is correct; at least it seems to be confirmed by my own experience of what is essentially the "our song" phenomenon. Mahler's *Knaben Wunderhorn* never fails to make me feel a bit off color when I hear it nowadays, even the "happy" parts, because it is associated with a particularly unhappy period of my life which it invariably calls to mind. No one should doubt that music can and does arouse emotions in this way. What we deny is that this has anything to do with musical expressiveness. And the fact that so much of the power music does have to arouse the emotions is due to private, idiosyncratic associations is itself additional reason for rejecting the arousal theory altogether as a theory of musical expressiveness. Surely, we intend to say something "public," something "objective" about music when we ascribe expressive properties to it. But if "The music is sad" merely means "The music makes me sad," we would be doing no such thing. For the power of some particular musical composition to cause sadness in me, unlike, say, the power of acid to burn my flesh, is not a power that it has over all "normal" people. It is a power the music has acquired by having played a special role in my private affairs; and is no part of music's "public," "objective" aesthetic surface.

Perhaps it will be insisted that contemporary thinkers have better things to offer in the way of an arousal theory than the tired old association of ideas, with its undesirable implications of subjective and private significance. There must be some new combination of the latest results in psychology, physiology, and the psychology of music to show how sounds in general, and musical sounds in particular, interact with the human organism to produce emotional reactions of the appropriate kind. Perhaps there may be, but I do not know about them; and I think a little preliminary reflection on the possibility suggests that this is a blind alley. This is not to suggest, it must be emphasized, an a priori attempt to dismiss any advance in the psychology of aural perception. It is, rather, to argue that such advances are simply answers to a set of questions that are different from the question of musical expression.

That sound stimuli have an effect on a human being's affective states is beyond question. It also seems beyond question that when sound is in the form of music, it possesses at least some of whatever stimulative potency it inherently has, or has acquired; and what its inherent or acquired potency is, is of course a question for the psychologist of perception, among others, to answer. I think it must be something along these lines of speculation that a recent, and well-informed musical theorist, Wilson Coker, has in mind when he writes:

> when we perform or listen to music, the tone of the musical gestures—the attitudes they carry—affect us. . . . If the tone of the gesture appears aggressive or angry, our most natural tendencies of response are a physiological mobilization for fight or flight.

Such responses are "primitive," "instinctual," "unselfconscious."[2]

Now the point I want to make here is not that such a view may be mistaken—although indeed it may be, since no evidence is offered for the claim that there is "physiological mobilization for fight or flight" or whatever, when we listen to music. Indeed, built into the claim is an antidote to the most obvious counterevidence. Clearly, we do not fight or flee. So all that can safely be claimed under the circumstances is that we "physiologically" prepare to. To further guard against counter-evidence, we are told that this is "unselfconscious," thus thrusting aside any introspective claim to the contrary. What then *is* or *can be* the evidence for the claim that we physiologically prepare to fight or flee or whatnot? None, apparently. All we are told is that these are our most natural tendencies of response. But that is a manifest begging of the question. For our most natural response to "angry" music would indeed by preparation for fight or flight only if what we meant by "angry" music were music that made us angry. Our "most natural response" to "angry music," where by "angry" we mean "expressive of anger," on the contrary, would be to sit tight and listen to the music—which is just what we do.

But again the point is not that the view may be mistaken. Suppose that it were true: suppose that there is some unconscious psychological reaction to musical sounds that can correctly be described as "emotion" or "affect." All the advances in contemporary philosophical psychology suggest that such an "emotion" could not be fear, or anger, or sadness, or any of those (and Coker is quite well aware of that). Such emotions are not merely physiological reactions to stimuli, like changes in body chemistry. They are concept-laden modes of attention and attitude that cannot logically exist in the absence of appropriate objects and attendant circumstances; and even when they are neurotic or pathological (or unconscious), this is so. We are not just angry, or frightened, or sad: we are angry *at* someone, frightened *by* something, sad *about* some state of affairs. Having these emotions involves believing as well as feeling. We are certainly not angry *at* the music, or frightened *of* it, or sad about *sounds*. There is not the object or context for us to feel emotions such as these in the concert hall or opera house. But it is *these* emotions—anger, fear, sadness, and the like—that we ascribe to the music. Whether such "primitive," "instinctual," "unselfconscious" affects as Coker describes are aroused by musical sounds is questionable; there seems to me to be no hard evidence that they are. But granted even that such evidence is forthcoming, it would indicate the existence of affective states other than the kinds we refer to in describing music emotively, for the reasons stated above. And that is why I could claim with some confidence that whatever physiological and psychological discoveries are made with regard to sound as an affective stimulus, it will answer questions unrelated to the problem of musical expression as it has been traditionally understood, and as I understand it here. This is not a matter of empirical discovery but merely a matter of the "logic" of concepts.

If music, then, arouses the full-blooded emotions—fear, anger, sadness, and the like—and I believe it can and sometimes does, it arouses them in something like the good old-fashioned way Avison suggested: through the association of ideas. For that route can supply the context and objects necessary for such concept-laden mental states. (When the *Knaben Wunderhorn* makes me sad, my sadness has an object: the unhappy events in my life which, by association, it recalls to me.) And the association of ideas, as I have already argued, is irretrievably private and idiosyncratic—not the publicly negotiable medium we require for an account of the expressiveness of music that would satisfy the contemporary musician and "scientific" musicologist.

Here, perhaps, the musical skeptic will argue that we are begging the question right from the start. If you begin with the unexamined assumption that musical expressiveness *is* a public, objective matter, you will have to reject the arousal theory, with

its associationist implications, as a completely unacceptable account. But, the skeptic will insist, the very reason to accept the
arousal theory is just that it is unabashedly "subjective." Indeed,
we do nothing more (the skeptic goes on) when we predicate
sadness of the music than project our feelings onto it, mistaking,
as enthusiasts are wont to do, a "subjective" state for an "objective" property. This is an old story: the aesthetic (and Humean)
skeptic's accustomed line.

To a degree, the skeptic is right. It *has* been assumed from the
outset—as a working hypothesis, at least—that expressiveness is
a public, "objective" phenomenon. But my intention is not to let
the matter rest there. Rather, the whole direction of this study is
toward a rational justification of the assumption of expressive
objectivity. All that can be said here and now to the skeptic, however, is: "Wait and see." If, at the end, we have provided a plausible account of musical expressiveness as a public, "objective"
property, then the musical skeptic has all the answer he will
need.

◇ 3 ◇   Let us return, then, from the associationist theory
to the Cartesian. I should say, straightaway, that I mean "Cartesian," at this point, in spirit rather than in letter. For in the work
we are about to examine, Daniel Webb's *Observations on the Correspondence between Poetry and Music* (1769), the philosopher's name
does not once appear, nor is there any direct evidence that Webb
was aware of Descartes' physiological and psychological speculations. Rather, Webb tends to cite classical authors as his exemplars. Nevertheless, the theory *is* so Cartesian in outline that the
name is not misapplied as a description of the doctrine, even if it
is misleading as to the doctrine's source. In the next chapter, we
shall look at another theory, Johann Mattheson's, which is
Cartesian in a more literal sense. But it is important to have before our minds at that point a theory like Webb's, with which to
contrast it. For the two are crucially different in one respect:
Webb's is an arousal theory, and Mattheson's is not. And because
the majority of such theories were arousal theories as well—in
fact, *all* that I know about, with the exception of Mattheson's—
Mattheson has, quite unjustifiably, been tarred with the same
brush.

Webb begins with the explicit assumption that music arouses

emotions, and the implicit one that this is the sense in which music "expresses" the emotions. The problem of musical expression then becomes for him the problem of how arousal takes place. He writes: "Though the influence of music over our passions is very generally felt and acknowledged; . . . yet we find ourselves embarrassed in our attempts to reason on this subject, by the difficulty which attends the forming of a clear idea of any natural relation between sound and sentiment."[3]

The associationist account is dismissed summarily with the puzzling observation that some emotive responses to sounds are clearly innate and unlearned, as, for example, some of the responses of infants:

> I have observed a child to cry violently on hearing the sound of a trumpet, who, some minutes after, hath fallen asleep to the soft notes of a lute. Here we have evident marks of the spirits being thrown into opposite movements, independently of any possible associations of ideas.[4]

Of course it would have been as absurd for the associationists to deny that blowing a trumpet in a baby's ear would scare it witless as it was for Webb, apparently, to be put in the position of having to maintain that the same emotions I have now when I hear "Deutschland Über Alles" would have been aroused in me in the cradle. Webb seems to have confused here the thesis that *sound* can arouse emotions without prior associations with the thesis that *music* can. The associationists need not have denied the former. It is a very nice question whether, in some individual case, we are reacting to sound or to music; and which alternative you choose may well serve to tacitly beg an aesthetic question. Susanne Langer has argued, in an attempt to defend her denial that emotive arousal has anything to do with emotive significance in music: the "somatic influences seem to affect unmusical as well as musical persons, . . . and to be, therefore, functions of *sound* rather than of *music*."[5] And here one is tempted to suspect that the arousal of emotion being attributed always to sound and never to music has as its only justification the prior assumption that music cannot arouse emotions, which looks very much like making it true by stipulative definition: "You can't have been responding to the *music*, because you responded with an emotion." In any case, Webb looked elsewhere for the mechanism of musical arousal than the association of ideas.

Music, when performed, is a perturbation of a physical medium. And Webb's problem as he sees it—a distinctly Cartesian one—is what causal connection there can be between the motion of this physical medium and the human emotions: "between," as Webb puts it, "sound and sentiment." Webb answers his question with an assumption very like that of Descartes in *The Passions of the Soul*: that there is a physical medium diffused throughout the human body, which, by its motions, arouses emotions in us, and which, in turn, is put in motion by the emotions. So the perturbation by the external world of what I shall henceforth call, after Descartes, the vital or animal spirits, causes emotions to arise; and its perturbation by the emotions, fear let us say, will result in some appropriate movement of the body— flight, or defense, or whatever. Here is Webb's hypothesis in his own words:

> As we have no direct nor immediate knowledge of the mechanical operations of the passions, we endeavour to form some conception of them from the manner in which we find ourselves affected by them: thus we say, that love softens, melts, insinuates; anger quickens, stimulates, inflames; pride expands, exalts; sorrow dejects, relaxes: of all which ideas we are to observe, that they are different modifications of motion, so applied, as best to correspond with our feelings of each particular passion. From whence, as well as from their known and visible effects, there is just reason to presume, that the passions, according to their several natures, do produce certain proper and distinctive motions in the most refined and subtle parts of the human body. . . . We are then to take it for granted, that the mind, under particular affections, excites certain vibrations in the nerves, and impresses certain movements on the animal spirits.[6]

Webb is suggesting, then, a physical medium, not directly observable (a "theoretical entity," the contemporary philosopher might want to call it), whose existence we assume to account for what we can observe; and the structure of this "theoretical entity" is assumed, as part of its explanatory power, to be similar in some vital respect to the structure of our emotions as revealed in our ordinary descriptions of them. Along with what is quite implausible, here, there is also something, as we shall see in a moment, that is quite intriguing and suggestive.

Where, then, does music fit into this picture? "I shall suppose," Webb writes, "that it is in the nature of music to excite similar vibrations, to communicate similar movements to the nerves and spirits."[7] That being the case, whatever motions music imparts to the vital spirits will necessarily result in the arousal of the emotion appropriate to those motions, much as the direct stimulation of my brain, if it results in the appropriate stimulation of my optic nerve, will make me have the same visual sensation I would have had if I had been looking at a bright light. "When, therefore, musical sounds produce in us the same sensations which accompany the impressions of any one particular passion, then the music is said to be in unison with that passion; and the mind must, from a similitude in their effects, have a lively feeling of an affinity in their operations."[8] And so we can compile, as it were, a kind of pharmacopoeia of musical stimuli, by which the composer and listener can name his or her own poison.

> All musical impressions, which have any correspondence with the passions, may, I think, be reduced under one or other of these four classes.
>
> If they agitate the nerves with violence, the spirits are hurried into the movements of anger, courage, indignation, and the like.
>
> The more gentle and placid vibrations shall be in unison with love, friendship, and benevolence.
>
> If the spirits are exalted or dilated, they rise into accord with pride, glory, and emulation.
>
> If the nerves are relaxed, the spirits subside into the languid movements of sorrow.[9]

Now we have not spent all this time examining Webb's account only to reject it out of hand. Nevertheless, reject it we must, before we can think of extracting anything of value from it. For it is clearly defective on at least three counts. As a "physiology" of the human emotions it is, needless to say, hopelessly outmoded. As an account of how music arouses emotions, its general approach is quite wrong, even given a reasonably correct physiology, since it sees the power of music to arouse emotions as an intrinsic, "natural" property of sounds, rather than an acquired response of listeners to them. And, finally, being an arousal theory of musical expression, it falls prey to all of the objections we have already raised against such accounts.

What, then, *is* intriguing about it? It is, I would suggest, the tantalizing notion that music bears resemblance to the "structure" of our emotions in a wider field than the speech theory could accommodate. In that the propounders of the speech theory had observed the affinities of melody with impassioned speech, they opened up the possibility that music could be thought of as, somehow, an emotive icon, rather than simply an emotive stimulus. But speech is, after all, only one aspect of a person's emotional life, albeit a very important aspect. And as impassioned speech does not exhaust the possibilities of human emotive experience and expression, so the affinities of melody to impassioned speech do not begin, as we have seen, to exhaust the possibilities of musical expressiveness. Webb's account, for all of its errors, widens our horizons.

What is particularly suggestive throughout Webb's little book is his allusion to the language in which we ordinarily describe the "feel" of our emotions—their phenomenological structure, if you will. Thus Webb thinks it very important to point out that "we say, that love softens, melts, insinuates; anger quickens, stimulates, inflames; pride expands, exalts; sorrow dejects, relaxes. . . ." But beyond the fact that this is perhaps the way our emotions "feel," it is also the way our emotions manifest themselves, more or less, in our *behavior*: what Webb calls the "known and visible effects" of the passions, and not only in our *linguistic* behavior. The feeling of love may not only be described as "soft," but "softens" our countenance; anger is not only violent in feeling, but violent in action; in experiencing pride, we not only experience an expansive feeling, but we become expansive in gesture and carriage; sorrow not only depresses our spirits, but subdues our behavior. And music, Webb wants to say, reflects all of this in some way. Had he not been, from the outset, a prisoner of the arousal paradigm, he might have seen a more viable relationship of music to the emotions than that of stimulus to emotive response, with the resemblance of music to the vital spirits as merely the mechanism of the thing. We can, of course, reconstruct Webb's theory accordingly, to meet our needs. In fact, there is no need to do so. Such a theory already existed in Webb's own time, propounded some thirty years before by the composer and highly influential musical theorist, Johann Mattheson. As I have already observed, Mattheson is generally taken to be offering nothing more than the usual arousal theory. I shall argue in the next chapter that this is a misreading of what he actually said. What we are disappointed not to find in Webb, we can find in his predecessor: namely, an elaborate iconography of musical expression, far more thoroughgoing and expansive in its "vocabulary" than the speech theory could hope to be by consideration of the human voice alone.

CHAPTER V

An "Iconography" of Musical Expression

◇ 1 ◇ I am going to examine, in the present chapter, some passages from Johann Mattheson's most well-known and influential book, *Der vollkommene Capellmeister* (1739); and I can sum up the theory that I hope to extract from it as follows:

(i) Music is not primarily a stimulus; and its emotive expressiveness is not manifested in an emotional response.

(ii) Music, in its structure, bears a resemblance to the "emotive life"; and the primary aesthetic response is a cognitive response: a recognition of the emotive content present in it.

We must now determine how Mattheson stands with regard to these claims, beginning, for convenience, with the second.

◇ 2 ◇ It is at first very obvious that Mattheson, like Webb, believes the structure of music to resemble something very closely related to the emotions as he construes them, namely, the motion and structure of the Cartesian vital or animal spirits. The passage in which this is established is crucial, and must be quoted at some length.

> 55. Those who are learned in the natural sciences know physically, as it were, how our emotions function. It would be advantageous to the composer to have a little knowledge of this subject.
>
> 56. Since, for example, joy is the result of an *expansion* of our vital spirits, it follows sensibly and naturally that this affect is best expressed by large and expanded intervals.
>
> 57. Sadness, on the other hand, is caused by a *contraction* of those same subtle parts of our bodies. It is, therefore, easy to see that the narrowest intervals are the most suitable.
>
> 58. Love results from a *diffusion* of the spirits. Thus, to

realize this passion in musical composition, it is best to use intervals of that nature. . . .

59. Hope is caused by an elevation of the spirits; despair, on the other hand, a casting down of the same. These are subjects that can well be represented by sound especially when other circumstances (tempo in particular) contribute their share. In such a manner one can form a concrete picture of all the emotions and try to compose accordingly.[1]

The leading idea here, as in Webb, is the formal analogy between certain parts of the body, namely, the vital spirits, and the intervalic (harmonic and melodic) structure of music. Whether it follows from this that, for Mattheson, musical structure bears an analogy to the structure of what I called at the outset the "emotive life" is a question that cannot be answered until we determine what we take the phrase "emotive life" to mean exactly, and what precisely the relationship is between it and the vital spirits.

Susanne Langer quotes with approval a statement of the musical psychologist, Carroll Pratt, to the effect that *music sounds the way emotions feel*.[2] We can take a partial cue as to how we will construe the phrase "emotive life" from this. The structure of music is congruent with my emotive life; and this, according to Langer, is roughly equivalent to saying that music sounds the way my emotions feel. Thus my emotive life can, in part at least, be taken to be the succession of my emotions as I experience them. Music, according to Pratt and Langer, bears a resemblance to the subjective phenomenology of my emotive life—with the "feel" of my emotions. But we need not stop here; we need not construe "emotive life" quite so narrowly as this. For as in the case of Webb, we think of the character of the vital spirits in Mattheson's version as being not merely related to the way we describe the "feel" of our emotions, but to the way we describe our behavior under their influence. The emotive life for Mattheson is, by all means, the way our emotions "feel"; but it is also, I would suggest, the way we express them in gesture, facial configuration, posture, and so forth. It is all of the behavior with which the emotions are associated, and which helps define them. We have already determined that, according to Mattheson, music resembles the vital spirits in some structural way. If we can show that the motion and structure of the vital spirits bear a resemblance to the emotive life, as construed above, we will have shown at the same time that music resembles the emotive life (assuming the relation of resemblance to be transitive).

Descartes was quite unequivocal with regard to the relation he postulated between the emotions and the animal spirits. It was strictly causal: the passions, he wrote, "are caused by some particular movement of the animal spirits."[3] Of course, Descartes never claimed to have directly observed anything like what he called the animal spirits, any more than Freud claimed to have observed the ego and id, or Bohr electrons and nuclei. These are theoretical constructs, as we suggested they also were for Webb, contrived to account for certain observed phenomena—a "model," tailor-made to organize data. And what is immediately evident about Mattheson's vital spirits, as about Webb's, is that they are tailor-made to account for the ways we commonly describe the feel of our emotions. Joy is commonly described as an *expansive* feeling; and thus the *expansion* of the vital spirits is postulated as its cause, the assumption apparently being that the cause must have a structural similarity to its effect. (As Descartes would put it, the cause must be adequate to its effect, which is to say there must be something common to both.) Again, we talk about being *bouyed up* or *uplifted* by hope; and hope is said to be caused by an *elevation* of the vital spirits. So I think it abundantly clear that Mattheson, like Webb, conceived of the vital spirits as resembling the emotions-felt; for it was the resemblance which, apparently, was to constitute the *modus operandi* of the causal connection. We are therefore in a position to conclude that, for Mattheson, music resembles the emotive life, since music resembles the motion and structure of the vital spirits and the motion and structure of the vital spirits the emotions-felt and expressed.

◇ 3 ◇ We have thus far established that Mattheson concurred with half of claim (ii); but in order to establish his concurrence with its whole substance, we must establish not only that he believed music to be structurally similar to the emotive (for Webb, after all, believed that too). We must establish, further, that he, unlike Webb, believed the listener's response to music to be primarily a cognitive one: a recognition of its emotive content. In so doing, of course, we will at the same time establish that Mattheson also concurred with the substance of claim (i), denying implicitly that the primary response to the emotive content of music is an emotive response; which is not to say, as we shall see, that Mattheson denied any aesthetically significant emotive effect whatever to music.

Now there is one passage that, on first reflection, suggests that Mattheson was in fact presenting an arousal theory of musical expression, very much like Webb's. In introducing his whole discussion of emotive content, Mattheson wrote: "This part examines the effects of well disposed sounds on the emotions and the soul."[4] With such views as Webb's before us as exemplars, would it not be reasonable to conclude from this that Mattheson intended the resemblance of music to the vital spirits as an explanation of how music causally interacts with them, thus arousing the emotions which it is said to be expressive of? The interpretation is an inviting one, as such theories were so common in the eighteenth century. And I think a good many have accepted the invitation—which, like the spider's, is deceptive. For if we read on we find that the emotions music is expressive of are usually not the emotions it arouses (or is intended to arouse), any more than the emotions I express are usually the ones I arouse (or intend to arouse).

The composer's primary office, according to Mattheson, is a moral one:

> to represent virtue and evil with his music and to arouse in the listener love for the former and hatred for the latter. For it is the true purpose of music to be above all else a moral lesson.[5]

This ethical commitment of the musician, which one associates with such "Enlightenment" composers as Mozart, Haydn, and Beethoven, was apparently widespread in the Baroque period as well. We find it, for example, in the friend of Mattheson's youth, George Frideric Handel, who upon being told by Lord Kinnoul that *Messiah* was "a great entertainment," is supposed to have replied: "My lord, I should be sorry if I only entertained them; I wished to make them better."[6]

So the emotions the composer arouses are only two in number: *love* and *hate*—love of virtue and hatred of vice. Or perhaps a less evangelical way of putting it would be to say that the composer's role, as moralist, is to engender in his listeners a positive attitude toward virtue and a negative one toward vice.

He may do this in part by making his music expressive of all
sorts of *other* emotions: joy, hope, anger, fear, and so on. But the
only emotions he intends to arouse—and they are "emotions" in
only the broadest sense of the word—are moral approbation and
disapprobation. And these are not—and probably could not
be—the emotions his music is expressive of. Let me illustrate
this.

Suppose I am setting to music a religious text extolling the
Christian virtue of charity. The poet has provided me with some
sort of verse to the effect that at the Day of Judgment all gener-
ous souls will be rewarded with eternal *joy* in heaven while all
selfish pinchpennies will go to the other place and suffer eternal
sadness. Each time I set the word "joy" I follow Mattheson's advice and use "large and expanded intervals"; likewise, each time
I set the word "sadness" I use "the narrowest intervals." According to Mattheson's account, my music is now expressive of joy
and sadness. But if I have been successful, I have *aroused* in my
listeners a love of Christian charity and a hatred of selfishness.
My listeners recognize the joy and sadness my music is expressive of, and this helps them to grasp the moral lesson I am trying
to inculcate. Love of virtue and hatred of vice are aroused: but
only through the cognitive process of grasping the moral lesson;
and part of that complex cognitive process is the cognitive response to the expressiveness of my music. It is this kind of cognitive response to the emotive resemblance in music that, I imagine, Manfred Bukofzer had vaguely in mind when he described
Baroque music as "a sort of indirect iconology of sound."[7]

Mattheson, then, held that music somehow resembles our individual emotions, felt and expressed, and that the primary response of the listener to the emotive "content" of music is a cognitive response, not an affective one. Thus Mattheson accepted
both claims (i) and (ii); and this, I think, makes him a pivotal
figure in the history of modern music aesthetics whose importance has yet to be recognized. He should, I think, occupy, by
rights, the place of honor accorded to Schopenhauer by Susanne
Langer—but not for the reason Langer adduces.

◇ 4 ◇   Langer has singled out Schopenhauer as the earliest precursor of *her* theory of musical "meaning":

The best known pioneer in this field is Schopenhauer; and it has become something of an accepted verdict that his attempt to interpret music as a symbol of the irrational aspect of mental life, the Will, was a good venture, though of course his conclusion, being 'metaphysical,' was quite bad. However that may be, his novel contribution to the present issue was certainly his treatment of music as an impersonal, negotiable, real semantic, a symbolism with a content of ideas, instead of an overt sign of somebody's emotional condition.[8]

I would suggest, however, that Schopenhauer does not point forward to the semantic theory of Langer so much as backward to the resemblance theory of Mattheson (by which I mean to pay him a compliment). I say this for two reasons: first, because what Schopenhauer can be seen as doing is, essentially, appropriating Mattheson's theory (or one very much like it), merely substituting a "metaphysical" object of resemblance for a "physiological," "psychological," or "expressive" one; second, because in adopting Mattheson's theory almost across the board, he accepts along with it that which Langer is at such pains to disavow, namely, the notion that music can be rightfully described in terms of specific emotions—joy, anger, sadness, and the like.

Music, Schopenhauer tells us, "is . . . a *copy of the will itself*, . . ."[9] the will being here, of course, not the human will but the metaphysical will of which the world is the "representation." Thus music stands to the metaphysical seat of the emotions, the will, for Schopenhauer, as it stands to the physiological seat, the animal spirits, for Mattheson. For Mattheson, music resembles the motion and structure of the animal spirits which, in turn, bear resemblance to the human emotions as felt and expressed. For Schopenhauer the equation is the same, except that a substitution has been made for the middle terms. And for Schopenhauer, as for Mattheson, music stands to the emotions in such a way as to be identifiable in specific emotive terms. It is not expressive of individual emotions in the sense of my emotions, or your emotions, or the composer's; rather, it represents emotion types or essences: as *The Thinker* might be seen to represent not Plato's thoughts, or Aristotle's, but thought in itself. Nevertheless, what it represents are individual emotions in the sense of emotions that can be individuated, not emotion "in general," a point, I think, which, in the wake of Langer's philosophy of music, has tended to become obscured. Schopenhauer writes:

> Therefore music does not express this or that particular and definite pleasure, this or that affliction, pain, sorrow, horror, gaiety, merriment, or peace of mind, but joy, pain, sorrow, horror, gaiety, merriment, peace of mind *themselves*, to a certain extent in the abstract, their essential nature, without any accessories, and so also without the motives for them. Nevertheless, we understand them perfectly in this extracted quintessence.[10]

Schopenhauer may have been largely ignorant of the theoretical aspects of music; or perhaps he saw no point in redoing what had been satisfactorily done before. Whatever the reason, he seems simply to have appropriated for his philosophical purposes what was ready to hand in one of the most widely consulted musical reference works of the eighteenth century: that is to say, Mattheson's *Der vollkommene Capellmeister*. (The reputation of this work was such that Beethoven was still consulting it as a text in 1802, putting Mattheson's influence well within reach of Schopenhauer, whose *Die Welt als Wille und Vorstellung* was first published in 1818.)[11] And it is a sign of his philosophical genius that he made so distinctively an eighteenth-century concept of musical expressiveness into so distinctly a Romantic one, with a sleight of hand so sure, deft, and utterly economical that the tracks have been covered ever since. The musical metaphysic that has always seemed so ideally suited to *Tristan und Isolde*, and its century, is, in reality, far more the work of the Baroque era than the Romantic. But it suited both. And if I am right, this is as it should be; for my argument right along has been that it is in the seventeenth and eighteenth centuries that we are to seek for the most suggestive insights into the nature of musical expressiveness. It is now high time to make good this claim by putting these insights together into a coherent whole.

CHAPTER VI

A *"Physiognomy" of Musical Expression*

◇ 1 ◇ What Langer, Schopenhauer, Mattheson, Reid, and the *Camerata* share is the discovery that music is *expressive* rather than *expression*; that we recognize emotions as features of music rather than feel them as a result of its stimulation. Langer parts company with her predecessors in that they believe music is expressive of individual emotions—grief, melancholy, joy, and the like; whereas she believes it is expressive in a nonspecific sense: "For *what music can actually reflect*," she insists, "*is only the morphology of feeling. . . .*"[1] It is clear, I think, that the practice of music criticism is on the side of those who hear in music identifiable human emotions, for such emotive characterizations of music are the critic's stock and trade. And it is my own view that this practice reflects a common musical experience—it certainly reflects mine. But it would be a mistake to dismiss views like Langer's out of hand, since they are supported by some persuasive arguments that must be answered before we can move on.

There are, I think, two familiar arguments likely to persuade someone that if music is expressive at all, it is not expressive of individual, specifiable human emotions. The first of these arguments will be familiar to musical readers because of its exploitation by such formalists as Eduard Hanslick and Edmund Gurney; but it is a common enough argument in philosophical circles as well, being of the well-known form: "There is no general agreement about whether or not any particular X is φ; therefore, φ cannot be an 'objective' property of Xs." As Hanslick states the argument:

> Now, how can we talk of a definite feeling being represented when nobody really knows what is represented? Probably all will agree about the beauty or beauties of the composition, whereas all will differ regarding its subject.[2]

The second argument, also a familiar type, is a refinement, really, of the first, and it is to the effect that as there are no

"rules," "conventions," or other established criteria for determining whether or not any individual X is φ, φ cannot be an "objective" property of Xs. What sort of "rules" or "conventions" are
in question depends of course on the nature of the objects and
properties under discussion. In Langer's case, the properties are
discrete "meanings," and so the argument is couched in semantic terms. "The purely structural requirements for a symbolism,"
she argues, "are satisfied by the peculiar tonal phenomenon we
call 'music.' " "Yet it is not," she insists,

> logically speaking, a language, for it has no vocabulary. . . .
> [T]ones lack the very thing that distinguishes a word from a
> mere vocable: fixed connotation, or 'dictionary meaning.'[3]

The argument from disagreement, which Hanslick and Gurney place so much weight on, is, to begin with, a non sequitur, at
least as it stands. For it simply does not follow from the mere fact
of disagreement over whether Xs are or are not φ, that they are
not one or the other. I suspect, however, that what propounders
of such arguments have in mind is not that music cannot bear
emotive descriptions simply because there is disagreement over
what description fits a given piece some of the time, but that
there is *too much* disagreement for emotions to be "objective
properties" of music. Unfortunately, as might be expected, no
one seems to have the slightest idea how much is "too much";
and so the argument comes to nothing, merely begging the
question by assuming there is "too much," without ever justify-
ing the assumption.

In addition, the notion of "disagreement" is left enticingly
vague. What, one would like to know, exactly is the disagreement about, of which there is "too much"? Is it about fine shades
of meaning? Or are the parties to such putative disputes so wide
apart that it is a case of "black" versus "white"? As I suggested
earlier, the assumption of the present study is that there is general agreement about gross distinctions; and that, I think, is all
that is needed. That two critics should disagree about whether a
theme is expressive of "noble grief" or "abject sorrow" does not
worry me much. It no more shows that the theme is not expressive of a specifiable emotion than would a dispute over whether
a swatch were cerulean or aquamarine prove that it wasn't blue.

Imagine that two people should disagree about whether the
Saint Bernard's face is expressive of "deep brooding melancholy" or "petulant childish disappointment." What is important

for our purposes is the general agreement on all hands that the face of the Saint Bernard is expressive of sadness and not joy. That is the kind and degree of agreement required for the theory of musical expressiveness to be presented here—no less, but certainly no more. And it seems to be beyond reasonable doubt that listeners and critics agree at least to that extent. Why such agreement exists will become more apparent, I trust, as the general conclusions of this study begin to emerge.

I cannot leave off the discussion of Hanslick, however, without one more observation. It is revealing, I think, of the utter confusion that surrounds the question of aesthetic disagreement—as to its degree, and its implications—that Hanslick thinks there is general agreement about whether or not a piece of music is beautiful ("Probably all will agree about the beauty or beauties of the composition . . .") and general disagreement about whether or not it rightly bears some emotive epithet (". . . whereas all will differ regarding its [emotive] subject"). For the most familiar, and oldest skeptical argument in aesthetics (it can be found in the ancient world) is to the effect that there is *too much* disagreement over whether or not objects are "beautiful" to allow that "beauty" can be an "objective" property. But Hanslick, wrapped up in his own particular brand of aesthetic paranoia, is willing to argue that there is general agreement over beauty and not over expressive qualities. I doubt that this proves anything substantive about beauty or expressiveness. It should convince us, though, to count the "argument from disagreement" for nought. Not only can we not agree about the degree and extent of aesthetic disagreement; we can't even agree about where there is disagreement and where there isn't.

◊ 2 ◊   The second argument cannot be given here the full answer that it deserves. For that answer will also devolve on the general conclusions that we reach concerning musical expressiveness. But we can at least begin to probe the question.

Langer suggests that in order for a theme (say) to be expressive of a specific emotion φ, there must be some semantic rule, or dictionary definition, to the effect that themes of this sort "mean" φ. This can be generalized, I suppose, for all properties. A predicate "φ" names an "objective" property, we might argue, if and only if there are agreed upon, public criteria whereby we can determine beyond reasonable dispute whether or not something is φ.

Of course, a semantic theory of musical expressiveness puts rather stringent requirements on what would constitute adequate criteria. If, to say that theme *X* is expressive of emotion φ is to say that *X means* φ, then there must be some meaning-rule, some "dictionary definition" to the effect that theme *X* (or something in it) *means* φ, the way the manual of arms tells you that a certain bugle call means "Retreat." And although it is not inconceivable that a musical culture should possess such meaning-rules, and such a musical art, there is no such musical semantics in the Western musical tradition; and it is that tradition we are trying to understand.

But to say emotions in music are recognized rather than felt as a result of its stimulation is not necessarily to commit oneself to a semantic theory of musical expressiveness. We recognize the sadness in the Saint Bernard's face, but need not say that the Saint Bernard's face *means* sadness. (One might, at this juncture, go in the direction of Nelson Goodman's analysis of expression, whereby the Saint Bernard's face is literally expressive of sadness, and metaphorically sad, since it is the creature, not its face that "feels" emotions: and go on to say, with Goodman, that the expressive "object" exemplifies what it is expressive of, and hence symbolizes it, exemplification being a symbolic function.[4] I am inclined to think that this move toward expressiveness as symbolism, unlike Langer's, is consistent with the view being put forward here.)

To be sure, our "reading" of sadness in the Saint Bernard's face is dependent upon "conventions," tacit "rules," and commonly accepted, public "criteria" of expression. But we hardly expect such precepts to be set down in dictionaries and grammars. And the failure to show that music is a "language" (which it isn't) is not necessarily a failure to show that music is expressive of particular, identifiable human emotions.

◇ 3 ◇   We must now go back over the seventeenth- and eighteenth-century sources to see if we can put them together into something plausible. Perhaps it would be well to state briefly, to begin with, what a plausible account of musical expressiveness would be like. First, emotions, we will want to say, are recognized in music much as we recognize the sadness in the Saint Bernard's face. Second, just as it is specifically sadness that the Saint Bernard's face is expressive of, our account must show how it is that music is expressive of the various human emotions that critics and listeners recognize in it. And, finally, we shall want to be able to state, with satisfactory explicitness, what the conventions, criteria, or rules are for the application of emotive terms to music. For we will not have made out a persuasive case for our claim that music really possesses such emotive qualities unless we can convince ourselves that there are public criteria for applying the terms which supposedly name them.

Let us determine, then, to begin with, just what we are recognizing when we recognize sadness in the Saint Bernard's face. We are not, it must be remembered, recognizing *that* the Saint Bernard is sad; for the Saint Bernard's face being expressive of sadness is invariant with the emotional state of the Saint Bernard: it does not express the Saint Bernard's sadness. Nevertheless, it does have something to do with the way *we* normally express sadness. That we normally frown, let our mouths droop, and assume a "hang dog" expression when we are sad of course makes the face of the Saint Bernard seem peculiarly appropriate to the expression of sadness. And were there a place, or a planet where creatures with faces like ours "frowned" and let their mouths droop to express their joy, their Saint Bernards' faces (if they had Saint Bernards with faces) would be described by them as expressive of joy. Perhaps, too, their willows wouldn't weep even though they drooped.

Thus, what we see as, and say is, *expressive of* φ is parasitic on what we see as, and say is, *expressing* φ; and to see X as expressive of φ, or to say X is expressive of φ, is to see X as appropriate to expressing φ, or to say that it is appropriate to such expression. It is in this way that the expressiveness of music is like the expressiveness of the Saint Bernard's face. And all that is right, all that is insightful in seventeenth- and eighteenth-century theories of musical "expression" adumbrates or anticipates this point.

The members of the *Camerata* and their spokesmen saw the melodic line of their monody as resembling the rise and fall of the human voice in impassioned speech. Surely there is that to be heard in a melodic line, and is something accurately described as "expressive" of some given emotion in the sense of "appropriate" to its expression, as the face of the Saint Bernard is seen as appropriate to the expression of sadness. We can now see, in some detail, how certain musical figures are expressive of certain specifiable emotions. The opening of the *Lamento d'Arianna* is a perfect icon in sound of the fall of the human voice when it expresses sadness in declaiming "Let me die!," or something of the kind, just as, to take a fresh example, the opening phrase of the well-known air from *Messiah*, "Rejoice Greatly, O Daughter of Zion!" resembles the voice rising in joy:

EXAMPLE 4:
Handel, *Messiah*, Part I

We see sadness in the Saint Bernard's face in that we see the face as appropriate to the expression of sadness. And we see it as appropriate to the expression of sadness because we see it as a face, and see its features as structurally similar to the features of our own faces when we express our own sadness. We hear sadness in the opening phrase of the *Lamento d'Arianna* in that we hear the musical sounds as appropriate to the expression of sadness. And we hear them as appropriate to the expression of sadness (in part) because we hear them as human utterances, and perceive the features of these utterances as structurally similar to our own voices when we express our own sadness in speech. We hear joy in the opening phrase of Handel's air for the very same reasons.

Mattheson, and others like him in the eighteenth century, widened our musical perspective in a necessary way, pressed on to it, no doubt, as I have suggested before, by the growth in complexity and variety of instrumental music. For although the speech theory outlined above, which (so far as I know) was formulated for the first time by the *Camerata*, is correct as far as it goes, it does not go nearly far enough. The likeness of some musical lines to the structure of speech will hardly account for all of the instances of expressiveness in music, as we have already seen. And views like Mattheson's, although predicated upon false theories of human psychology, nevertheless open up possibilities for expressive resemblance beyond what is afforded by the speech theory. They do so because the vital spirits of the Cartesian psychology are thought of as covering the whole range of emotive phenomena: how we feel, how we move, how we hold ourselves, as well as how we speak under the influence of any given "passion of the soul." We have in Mattheson's theory, it will be recalled, the following equation: music resembles the motion and structure of the vital spirits, and the motion and structure of the vital spirits resemble our subjective experience of the individual emotions—joy, sadness, hope, fear, and so on. We shall now do two things with this equation: first, construe the motion and structure of the vital spirits as resembling not the "feel" of our emotions (which seems to me to be an imponderable and, perhaps, without the requisite "structure,")[5] but with their behavioral repertoire—movement, gesture, posture, and so on; and second, we shall let the middle term drop out of the equation altogether, since the vital spirits are about as likely a part of the emotive life as phlogiston is an element in combustion. What we are left with, then, and what we will take to be Mattheson's legacy, is the notion that *music, in many respects, resembles our expressive behavior.* And if we add to this the already established resemblance of music to emotional speech, we now have a way of dealing with a vast array of emotive behavior in musical terms. We have here the means of expanding the "resemblance" powers of music beyond the confines of human utterance.

To illustrate our widened horizons, let us return to a musical example previously alluded to: the oboe solo that opens the second movement of Bach's first Brandenburg Concerto. We saw early on that it was not plausible to construe this expressive line as a speech-icon, in the manner of the *Lamento d'Arianna.* But imagine it, now, in terms of expressive gesture: as a "choreography" of expression. Think of the motions a player or conductor might make in performing it; or the way a dancer might move to it. What I am suggesting, then, is not that this musical line can be conceived of as a speech-icon—it cannot—but rather that it is an emotive icon of another kind, resembling not the vocal expression of sadness but its expression in bodily gesture and posture. As we see sadness in the Saint Bernard's face because we see its features as resembling those of our own appropriate to the expression of sadness, we hear sadness in this complex musical line, we hear it expressive of sadness, because we hear it as a musical resemblance of the gesture and carriage appropriate to the expression of our sadness. It is a "sound map" of the human body under the influence of a particular emotion.

Another example or two might drive the point emphatically home. Compare the exuberant joy of the "Pleni sunt coeli" of the *Mass in B minor* with what might be described as the confident but more subdued joy of "I know that my Redeemer liveth" from *Messiah*:

EXAMPLE 5:
Bach, *Mass in B minor*

EXAMPLE 6:
Handel, *Messiah*, Part III

The bodily motion and gesture which the former "maps" is one of tremendous expansiveness, vigor, violent motion—it is "leaping" joy. Whereas the latter suggests, rather, a dignified public declaration of faith: a speaker firm, confident, stepping forward, gesturing expressively, but with a certain circumspection, a reserve commensurate with the divine mystery of the text—something of the sort.

◇ 4 ◇ It is, to be sure, a rather big and important step from the speech theory to the wider horizons of the general resemblance of music to human expressive behavior. For we move here from the literal to the sinaesthetic and metaphorical. The similarity of certain musical lines, when sung or played, to inflections of the human speaking voice, are obvious and unproblematic. When the Evangelist, in Bach's *St. Matthew Passion*, describes Jesus as crying aloud, we hear the cry as surely as we see La Gioconda's smile or Olympia's body.

EXAMPLE 7:
Bach, *St. Matthew Passion*, Part II

The music quite literally sounds like a cry: Bach has made it impossible for the tenor to sing it in any other way. But when we say that a musical line "maps" or resembles the bodily manifestations of human emotions, we are no longer on such firm, literal ground. We *hear* music, it might be objected; but we don't *hear* human posture and movement.[6]

Nevertheless, to be bull-headedly literal is not always to be safer and closer to the demonstrable truth. (Metaphors are not false simply by virtue of being metaphors.) And to confine the resemblance possibilities of music to the "sounds like" phenomenon alone would be to fly in the face of the human propensity to blur the distinctions between the senses, and their "proper" objects. Don't we *see* Laocoön's cry? Don't we hear the melodic line droop in the oboe solo of the first Brandenburg? Let us see if we can make this musical sinaesthesia a bit more intelligible.

The most obvious analogue to bodily movement in music is, of course, rhythm. And it is an embarrassing commonplace, but nonetheless true, that in all sorts of ways, the rhythmic movement of the human body in all kinds of emotive expressions is mirrored by and recognized in music. To state the most common of the commonplaces: *of course* funeral marches are slow and measured, as sadness slows and measures our expression of it; *of course* rapid rhythmic pulses in music are suggestive of rapid behavior under the influence of the lighter emotions; *of course* jagged and halting rhythms have their direct analogue in human expressive behavior.

But beyond the obvious part that rhythm plays in musical expressiveness—and I think it is considerable as well as obvious—there is the way we inevitably describe music in terms of motion: particularly "rising" and "falling." It is mistakenly thought, perhaps, that this is not a metaphor that cuts very deep—not a description of the way we hear music, but merely the way we see it on the written or printed page. For by an accident of convention, "high" pitch is at the top of the page in Western notation, and "low" pitch at the bottom.

But the metaphor is much more firmly entrenched than that. The "rise" in pitch, like the raising of a physical body against gravity, requires, at least in a great many of the most familiar cases, increased energy. And the rise of pitch, both in natural organisms and machines, betokens a rise in energy level. The faster the wings beat, the shriller the sound; likewise, the more energy expended, the higher the engine's whine. The rise and fall, the ebb and flow of the musical line is by no means simply a function of its position on the printed or written page, to be seen and not heard. The languid fall of the oboe in the first Brandenburg is not simply a fall in virtue of starting at the top of the page and ending closer to the bottom. To claim that is to overlook the intimate relation of pitch to energy, and energy to motion.[7] Granted that the relationship between the rise and fall of the musical line and the physical motion of the human body is not as transparent or unproblematical as its relation to the rise and fall of the speaking voice and other human utterances, to confine resemblance in music, or in the visual arts, for that matter, to such obvious relations of resemblance as "sounds like" or "looks like," would be to make resemblance as we know it to exist quite impossible. "For," as Nelson Goodman has rightly said, "the forms and feelings of music are by no means all confined to sound; many patterns and emotions, shapes, contrasts, rhymes and rhythms are common to the auditory and the visual and often to the tactual and the kinesthetic as well."[8]

◇ 5 ◇   I have now completed sketching what amounts to one aspect of a double-aspect theory. I have argued that music is expressive in virtue of its resemblance to expressive human utterance and behavior. Numerous objections to this view will, I am certain, immediately present themselves to the reader; and vagaries will demand suitable clarification. In the following chapter—a continuation, really, of the present one—I want to fill out my sketch more amply, by dealing with some of these pressing objections, and clarifying some concepts that will at this stage of the argument seem fuzzy and ill-defined.

CHAPTER VII

The "Physiognomy" Defended

◇ 1 ◇   At this juncture, I imagine, it will be protested that either I am recommending we indulge in all kinds of literary fantasy while listening to music, which is a bad, unmusical thing to do, or else I am committed to an entirely false "psychology" of music, since no mature musical listener ever does hear music in the way I am suggesting, although we do hear it as expressive.

In response to the first objection, let me say, straightaway, that I am not recommending a way of listening to music. I am attempting to describe a way we in fact do listen to it. That leaves the second objection to be contended with. But I think if what I am saying is properly understood, it will cease to have the fanciful, and even childish appearance it may now present. I am not saying anything childish, Romantic, metaphysical, or psychological (in any theory-laden sense). I think I am saying something commonplace, commonsensical, and well known, if not, perhaps, well understood.

It is a hard psychological fact that we tend to "animate" what we perceive. Tie a piece of cloth around the handle of a wooden spoon and a child will accept it as a doll; more to the point, *you* will see it as a human figure. This is not something you can choose to do, or refrain from doing. We apparently have no more control over it than we have over the way we see the Müller-Lyer illusion or the straight stick bent in water (which is why it is so easy for the animated cartoon to get us to see a plane, or automobile, or train as a "creature"). Put three lines on a circle,

and you will inevitably see it as a face. Why? Not simply because it resembles the features of a human countenance. After all, it also resembles many other things. Nevertheless, we do not usually see it as any of those other things, but as a face. It has been suggested that we tend to see things in this way because this way of seeing has survival value. For danger, more often than not, comes from things that have faces (and jaws). However that may be—whatever the proper explanation—that we do see faces and figures in perceptual patterns or ambiguous drawings, and not usually the other things they may even more closely resemble, seems to be an irrefutable, brute fact. And if that much is granted, I think it will be allowed that I am hardly making a very outré claim when I assert that we hear music as speech, utterance, gesture, bodily movement, and so on.

What I am arguing, then, is that we tend to "animate" sounds as well as sights. Music may resemble many other things besides human expressions. But just as we see the face in the circle, and the human form in the wooden spoon, we hear the gesture and the utterance in the music, and not another thing. I do not suggest, of course, that this is an entirely conscious, or self-conscious phenomenon. On the contrary, it is so natural as to go for the most part unnoticed. But only a moment's reflection on the way we talk about music will reveal, I think, how deeply "animistic" our perception of it really is. A musical theme is frequently described as a "gesture." A fugue subject is a "statement"; it is "answered" at the fifth by the next "statement" of the theme. A "voice" is still what musicians call a part in a polyphonic composition, even if the part is meant to be played on an instrument rather than sung by a voice. Violins as well as sopranos are instructed to sound *sotto voce*. A pianist is advised to cultivate a "singing" tone. A good woodwind is said to "speak" easily. And it is an age-old observation that instruments in musical ensembles seem like partakers in a conversation. Literature and musical criticism are rife with such descriptions. My own particular favorite is this passage from Thomas Mace's musical miscellanea, *Musick's Monument* of 1676, in which the author describes some of the ensemble music of his day as follows: "We had for our *Grave Music, Fancies* of 3, 4, 5, and 6 *Parts* to the *Organ*; Interpos'd (now and then) with some *Pavins, Allmaines, Solemn, and Sweet Delightful Ayres*; all which were (as it were) so many *Pathettical Stories, Rhetorical, and Sublime Discourses; Subtil, and Accute Argumentations.* . . ."[1] In short, our descriptions, and perceptions of music are redolent with animistic, anthropomorphic implications.

Richard Wollheim observes that "when we endow a natural object or an artifact with expressive meaning, we tend to see it corporeally: that is, we tend to credit it with a particular look which bears a marked analogy to some look that the human body wears and that is constantly conjoined with an inner state."[2] Adding the sound dimension to the visual, Wollheim's observation essentially captures what I have in mind here as an account of musical expressiveness. We must see a visual pattern as a vehicle of expression—a face or a figure—before we see expressiveness in it. Likewise, we must hear an aural pattern as a vehicle of expression—an utterance or a gesture—before we can hear *its* expressiveness. But there is no more problem with the latter case than the former. Indeed, far from being difficult to hear or see things as animate, it is, apparently, difficult *not* to. Exactly why this is the case is fortunately no part of the present study to determine. It suffices for our purposes to have acknowledged the fact.

◇ 2 ◇   The question may of course be raised whether it is a good thing to perceive music this way, and whether, if possible, we should not overcome our tendencies to hear "anthropomorphically." Maimonides suggests that thinking of God in human terms is only an early and unsatisfactory stage in our theological thinking which should be put aside along with other childish things in our maturity.[3] Might it not be the same with music?

To begin with, *can* we hear music antiseptically? Some people claim to, and I suppose we should take their word for it. I suspect, though, that the most plausible way of looking at it is as a matter of selective attention. A listener can, I think, decide to focus on the expressive qualities of music, or to focus on some other aspect instead. Whether one can totally extirpate one's perception of musical expressiveness I tend to doubt, but am prepared to believe if brought to it. I have never been able to get the two lines of the Müller-Lyer illusion to look equal (without artificial aids). But I know someone who claims to have done so. And I cannot hear music without hearing sadness as well as sounds— which is not to say that I am always thinking to myself "My how sad!" while listening to the second movement of the *Eroica*.

As to whether we *should* deemphasize the expressive, it might be useful, in answering this question, to ask ourselves first why a theologian should urge us to cleanse our theological thinking of anthropomorphic overtones. The answer, clearly, is that God does not possess those characteristics; and if we continue to believe that he does, we continue to believe a falsehood. I would suggest that behind the musician's misgivings is the same kind of premise: expressive properties do not really belong to music but are the result merely of fantasy and irrelevant association. Therefore, to continue to hear and describe music expressively is to mishear and misdescribe.

The theme of this study, however, is that expressive qualities are genuine "objective" qualities of music, and that there are objective criteria for applying expressive terms; further, that there is an intelligible way to understand how this all comes about. The argument, therefore, that hearing music expressively is to hear it falsely will not serve to support the prescription that we ought to subdue our musical "anthropomorphism," however the analogous argument may serve the theologian.

Nevertheless, that leaves open the question of whether there might not be some good reason or reasons to adduce for proscribing expressive hearing of music. That emotive *descriptions* of music might well serve a valuable function in music analysis and, when absent, be a considerable impoverishment, I have already urged in the opening chapter.

◇ 3 ◇ I think it would be useful, at this point, to contrast the view being put forward here with that of Langer, to which it bears some obvious affinities; for it might well be objected that what is here being presented is simply a rehash of her well-known view, and open to the same well-known objections. Both Langer and I claim that music bears some resemblance to the "emotive life," and that, one way or another, therein lies the explanation of its expressiveness. But there we part company. Langer claims that the "isomorphism" (her term) of music with the emotive life makes music symbolic of it, which I do not claim. I claim instead that music is expressive of individual, specifiable emotions, at least within certain limits, whereas she denies this, claiming only that music is a symbol of the emotive life as a whole, and cannot be symbolic—therefore cannot be expressive—of the individual emotions, since that would be tantamount to its being a "language" of the emotions, which it obviously is not.

As has been pointed out in the literature before, the step from "isomorphism" to "symbol" is a fallacious one.[4] It does not follow that because music is isomorphic with the emotive life, it is symbolic of the emotive life, although being isomorphic with the emotive life might be a necessary condition (not a sufficient one) for something's being a certain kind of symbol of the emotive life. This particular criticism cannot be brought against the position being advocated here; for I do not claim that music's resemblance to expressive behavior makes music symbolic of anything.

I have, indeed, admitted that a different symbolic account, Nelson Goodman's, which construes being expressive of the individual emotions as being symbolic of them in a special way, might well be consistent with my own view. But it should be noted that this is not to grant Goodman his conclusion. For it no more follows from Goodman's characterization of expressive objects (if true) as metaphorically φ (where φ is an expressive property) that they exemplify φ, and hence symbolize it, than it follows from Langer's characterization of music as isomorphic with the emotive life that it is symbolic of the emotive life. We need an *additional* argument to conclude that something exemplifies φ than merely that it is literally or metaphorically φ. The tailor's green swatch (to use one of Goodman's examples) is not a sample of green, does not exemplify green, is not (hence) a symbol of green merely in virtue of being green. It must also function, by some sort of agreement, in some sort of system, as a sample, as an exemplification, hence as a symbol. Not everything that is green so functions, which is why not everything green is a sample, exemplification, symbol of green. And it appears to me there is no clear evidence to suggest that expressive art objects do function as samples, exemplifications, symbols of their expressive properties. It does not appear to me that the second movement of the *Eroica* functions, in the art world, as anything like a sample or exemplification of sadness. We do not trot it out, either formally or informally, literally or metaphorically, as a sample of sadness, in anything like the way the tailor trots out his swatch of cloth. If we do, it must be shown.

But even though I have not made the illicit move from resemblance to symbol, it might be argued that I have committed myself to an analogous, and equally illicit move from resemblance to expressiveness; for although resembling emotive expression might perhaps be a necessary condition of the kind of expressiveness I am talking about, it is not, one could rightly insist, a sufficient condition. If A's resembling B were a sufficient condition for A's being expressive of B (or expressive of something related to it), then music would be expressive of *everything* it resembled: the waves of the ocean, and, for all I know, the rise and fall of the stock market or the spirit of capitalism.

The answer to this objection is simply that music might well be expressive of other things that it resembles, or things related to them, but only if certain other conditions were satisfied. One of these conditions, a "logical" one, is that it makes sense to say of the thing, "The music is expressive of *that*." One would hardly say that a kidney-shaped swimming pool is expressive of kidneys, or organs. A second condition, a frankly empirical one, is just that there be some psychological link between the music and what it expresses. Music is expressive of the emotions not just because it resembles expressive behavior, or that it, in addition, makes sense to say that something is expressive of emotions, but, as has been argued above, because *we*, for whatever reason, tend to animate our perceptions, and cannot but see expressiveness in them, any more than we can help seeing expressiveness in the Saint Bernard's face. For beings who do not do this, music will no more be expressive of the emotions than expressive of the stock market or the spirit of capitalism. But it is an empirical law that ultimately decides the issue. And it may well be that if fish had music, it would be expressive of the medium in which they live and move and have their being.

Langer, I suspect, was driven to deny that music is expressive of the individual emotions because she began with the assumption that music was expressive in virtue of being symbolism (and symbolism in virtue of being "isomorphic" with its object). She went from there to the conclusion that since there were no semantical rules connecting music with the individual emotions, it could not be symbolic of *them*. So it then became necessary to devise a kind of symbol that did not require such semantic credentials. And when music emerged as such a symbol, it could only be, in the absence of those rules, a pale ghost of the emotions: symbolic of them but not any one of them, rather like that peculiar kind of humanitarian who loves humanity, but can't stand people.

Langer's view was appealing to many musical people because it seemed to save the cherished link between music and the emotions (not to say that she also spoke of music with a keen musical, as well as philosophical, intelligence). But if you don't save the link to particular emotions, you don't really save the appearances; for our talk about music, both in high as well as low places, is talk about music's relations to the particular human emotions, not just to some abstract "emotion in general."

The advantages of the present account, then, seem to be these. It shows how the resemblance of music to expressive behavior results in the emotive expressiveness of music, but why its resemblance to other things does not make it expressive of those or related things. And it saves the link between music and the individual emotions, without construing music as a "language" of the emotions, which it is not, in any but a remote metaphorical sense, much overworked, in my opinion.

◇ 4 ◇   Finally, a cautionary note might be sounded here with regard to my (very deliberate) choice of the word "resemblance" to characterize the relation between music and expressive behavior. Two other tempting descriptions, "isomorphism" and "representation," have been rejected for reasons which it would be useful to put on the table as an aid in limning in the notion I have in mind.

As is well known, Langer made extensive use of the concept of isomorphism in her aesthetical writings in general, and in her musical ones—notably *Philosophy in a New Key*—in particular. I have avoided this word for two reasons, the first the rather obvious one that it would help to keep my view from being confused with one to which it bears some superficial resemblance. Secondly, and more importantly, the concept of isomorphism is at once too technically specific and (as a result) too abstractly general for my purposes.[5] It is overly specific because it suggests scientific, even mathematical notions of a rigor I do not pretend to in this work. And because of that, the notion, in some of its forms anyway, is so wide as to open the floodgates to all sorts of unwanted relationships. In the sense, for example, in which the program on a magnetic tape is "isomorphic" with the formulation of a ring nebula, the opening of Mozart's G-minor Symphony is isomorphic with all sorts of expressive behavior, I imagine, but hardly expressive of all those emotions the behavior might express. Isomorphism may be a necessary condition for the kind of expressiveness I am talking about. It is never a sufficient condition.

The temptation to treat music, in its expressive aspect, as a "representation" of expressive behavior is considerable, particularly when one extracts one's view, as I have done, from the seventeenth-century speech theories, and such eighteenth-century theories as are based on the relation of music to the Cartesian *esprits animaux*. For, seeing their theories as an extension of the "art-as-representation" doctrine, the seventeenth- and eighteenth-century theorists naturally tended to couch their views in representational terms. The members of the *Camerata* were clearly recommending that the composer "represent" impassioned speech in the vocal line, as Mattheson was recommending that the composer "represent" what he imagined to be the structure of the vital spirits. I have allowed myself to fall into the same mode of speech (innocently, I shall now insist) when I have been tempted to describe music as an "icon" of expressive behavior.

But I am as anxious not to represent my view of musical expressiveness as implying that music is a "representation" of expressive behavior as I am to avoid the notion that music is expressive simply because it is isomorphic with such behavior. One reason is that I can thus avoid taking a stand on whether or not music *can* at times be a representational art, as this has been denied of late.[6] (As a matter of fact I think it can, but do not wish to argue the point here. This is obviously not to be confused with the question of whether music is *primarily* a representational art, which, pretty clearly, it is not.)

My primary reason, however, for not employing the concept of representation is because representation, in my view, implies conscious intent on the part of the composer; and that, it seems to me, is lacking, more often than not. That is to say, for it to be true that some piece of music represents something or other, it must be true that the composer intended the music to represent it; but in most cases, where music is expressive of some emotion, the composer more than likely had no intentions whatever of representing expressive behavior, nor, for that matter, need he even have intended his music to be expressive at all.

It has been argued recently that representation is a completely "natural" concept, requiring no act of human intention, cognition, or attention. "It is the relationship," writes Dennis W.

Stampe, "that obtains between the moon and its image reflected on the surface of a pond, and it would do so were no minds ever to have existed; even had there been nothing that could count them, the number of rings in the stump of a tree would represent the age of the tree."[7] It would cost me nothing in terms of loss to the basic shape of my argument to agree with this view, and to adopt "representation" as the operative concept in musical expressiveness. But I have some nagging doubts that Stampe is correct in his contention. One treats the reflection in the pond, or the rings of the tree stump, not, it seems to me, as representations but *as if* they were representations—which is quite a different thing. They are "as if" representations: representations with quotation marks. Consider, for example, the following borderline case. I walk into an unfamiliar room, blunder about while looking for something, and accidentally set off a camera which takes my picture. Is the picture a "representation" of me? Clearly, I did not intend to represent myself on film, nor was the camera placed there with that intention. Nevertheless, I think we would tend to say that the photograph, though accidental, is a "representation." Consider, however, the related (and somewhat gruesome) case of the images of people's shadows that the blinding flashes of the atomic blasts are said to have left on the walls and sidewalks of Hiroshima and Nagasaki. Are these "representations" of the people whose outlines they recorded? I think we would tend to say that they are not. What, then, is the relevant difference between the two cases, since neither involves the intention to represent, and both involve the "recording" by well-understood natural processes of a person's image on a flat surface? The crucial difference, I would suggest, is that cameras were designed intentionally to make representations whereas atomic bombs were not. So in the former case we can trace at least a tenuous connection between the recording of the image and the human intention to do so, and in the latter case we cannot. In the interest of caution, therefore, I prefer to treat the absence of human intention to represent as ipso facto the absence of representation, and avoid the word in my discussion.

There are, of course, composers (like Peri and Cacinni) who actually did set out to represent the impassioned speaking voice in their music, in order to make their music expressive; and *their* music can be thought of as a "representation" of expressive behavior, if any music can. There are, however, those composers who have set out with the intention of writing expressive music and have quite consciously chosen expressive materials, without intending to represent expressive behavior, even though, as I claim, the materials they chose are expressive in virtue of their resemblance to such behavior. These composers were simply choosing, by musical instinct or musical culture, those musical materials which they knew were expressive of this emotion or that. Brahms knew how to write a *Tragic Overture* without having a "theory" of musical expressiveness, and certainly without intending to "represent" expressive behavior (or anything else). Finally, there are the cases in which music is expressive of the emotions neither with the composer's intending to represent expressive behavior nor with his intending to write expressive music at all. I don't suppose we will ever know what mental "chemistry" brought to Mozart's consciousness the wonderfully expressive opening of the great C-minor Serenade for winds (K. 388). But there is no evidence that he intended the music to be expressive of the dark emotions it is indeed expressive of (and which are so little in keeping with the social setting of the woodwind "divertimento"). His intention was to write a first movement, and doubtless to fulfill a commission—the expressiveness just came unbidden.

Thus, in spite of the fact that there are *some* cases in which composers intended, I believe, to write expressive music by writing music representative of expressive behavior, I advance the view here that expressive music only *resembles* expressive behavior. For in most cases it no more *represents* it than the face of the Saint Bernard represents a sad countenance. But what more, it may be asked, can I say about the nature of resemblance? My reply is: What more need be said? One thing I cannot do—and need not—is present a philosophical analysis of the concept of resemblance. I use the word, I hope, in the (or an) ordinary way, and throughout my book will try, as I have been doing, to illustrate my claim with musical illustrations. And if I am using the word, and its cognates, in the ordinary way, it will be consistent with any philosophical analysis of the concept that turns out to be the correct one.

◇ 5 ◇   We now have a fair idea of how a large part of the materials of music can be expressive of the individual human emotions. (I will not say "all" for reasons that will soon become apparent.) I have argued that they are expressive in the way the Saint Bernard's face is expressive of sadness; and I have shown in some detail what that way is. Thus, we have essentially covered two of three points outlined at the beginning of Chapter VI. I have given an explanation of what we recognize in music when we recognize its expressiveness, and have explained how it is that we recognize not just expressiveness "in general" but expressiveness in its particularity—how we recognize the sadness of the *Lamento d'Arianna* and the joy of Bach's "Pleni sunt coeli." A final question remains: What justification can we give for the assertions we make about the expressiveness of music? If I assert "The opening of the 'Pleni sunt coeli' is joyful," what rational support can I give for my assertion in the event of a disagreement? What, in other words, are the criteria to which I can appeal?

If we return to the face of the Saint Bernard, once again, and ask ourselves what we would do to justify our assertion that *it* is expressive of sadness, we very likely would answer that it surely involves pointing out "sad-making" features of the face, and, perhaps, reminding our questioner of how *we* normally express our own sadness. Beyond this, it is difficult to say what else we could do, if the sadness were not then acknowledged. Does this constitute a "proof" that the Saint Bernard's face is sad? Not, clearly, in the way in which one proves a theorem in geometry, or establishes a scientific hypothesis. But I don't think it too much to claim that we possess public criteria of expressiveness, *just because we possess public criteria of expression.* Just because I can be said to know—though perhaps not with "logical" certainty— when someone is expressing sadness (i.e. when he or she is sad), I can also be said to know that the Saint Bernard's face is sad and not happy.

What, now, of the musical cases? It is my contention that the same criteria for expressiveness in the Saint Bernard's face— namely, criteria that are parasitic on the public criteria of human expression—hold for musical expressiveness as well. So the skeptic of Hanslick's stripe is answered, to the extent, at least, that he is not willing to play the skeptic across the board with regard to expressiveness and expression. Aesthetic skepticism is, as it were, a second-order kind. The aesthetic skeptic usually does not argue that since we know nothing at all, we know nothing aesthetic by consequence. Rather, he argues that aesthetic assertions are deficient in some additional way, different from those deficiencies that the philosophical skeptic descries in our inductive policy, our sense perception, our knowledge of the external world, of other minds and their feelings. He argues that even if induction, sense perception, and so forth, are immune from skepticism, our aesthetic beliefs are not, being "subjective," or something of the kind. But *that* skepticism is answered, in the case of musical expressiveness, when we show (as I think I have done) that the criteria for ascribing joy or sorrow to a melody are the same as those for ascribing sadness to the Saint Bernard's face; and that all of these, therefore, are the very criteria that apply to human expression in general. If the criteria of human expression are public, objective, immune from philosophical skepticism, so too are the criteria of expressiveness in music; and the purist who casts a skeptical shadow on our emotive descriptions of music is defeated. (I shall return to this question in the final chapter.)

◇ 6 ◇ If I am, at this point, satisfied that I have given a correct account of a kind of musical expressiveness, as far as it goes, I am by no means satisfied that it goes nearly far enough. I think it is correct—but not complete. Let me begin to suggest where that incompleteness lies with a musical example from one of Bach's better-known cantatas, No. 131, *Aus der Tiefe rufe ich, Herr, zu dir*, a relatively early work, setting Psalm 130. The concluding double fugue sets out, in its two contrasting subjects, two contrasting segments of the text: "Und er wird Israel erlösen" ("And He will redeem Israel"); and "aus allen seinen Sünden" ("from all their sins").

EXAMPLE 8:
Bach, Cantata 131: *Aus der Tiefe rufe ich, Herr, zu dir*

The musical technique is a familiar one, for which the form of the double fugue is ideally suited. The composer invents two contrasting melodic lines which are expressive of two contrasting emotions, but which can combine contrapuntally, thus ministering at the same time both to textual and musical exigencies. The joy of salvation Bach represents in a series of sixteenth-note runs on the word "erlösen"—rapid musical movement being an obvious analogue to rapid bodily movement under the influence of the "lighter" emotions. And the "darker" passions surrounding the concept of sin he characteristically represents with a chromatic figure. Now the question is, *Why* should chromaticism be immediately recognized as expressive of sorrow, pain, sadness, and the like, as it consistently is in our musical tradition? Why should the use of half-steps in our harmonic system impart the character of grief and sorrow? Are half-tones any more isomorphic with the darker emotions than whole tones? The answer clearly seems to be, No. Thus our account, so far, fails entirely to explain one very common expressive feature of our musical culture.

A second, and no less obvious feature also still eludes us. And that is the contrast between major and minor, which has dominated Western music for over three hundred years. Everyone recognizes, that by the alteration of one note down a half-step in the "Marseillaise,"

EXAMPLE 9:

the composer of the sound track can tell you that France is in trouble, before the director shows you Hitler's legions goose-stepping down the Champs Elysées. Or, to take a sublime example, instead of a ridiculous one, consider the wonderful moment in the finale of the Ninth Symphony when, just before the outburst of the full orchestra and chorus, Beethoven tinges the theme with grief by giving it a minor harmonization (in measures 205 and 206):

EXAMPLE 10:
Beethoven, *Symphony No. 9*

Why should the change merely of one note in a melody of itself change the whole character from joy to sorrow? Does the minor third bear any more resemblance to behavior expressive of grief than does the major; or the major bear any more resemblance to behavior expressive of joy? Just to ask the question is to see its absurdity. Neither the major nor the minor third bears any resemblance to either. And again we find a ubiquitous element of musical expressiveness for which, as yet, we have no satisfactory account.

It is clear, then, that we must cast a wider net if we are to gather in all of the expressive elements we want to. The face of the Saint Bernard has taken us as far as it can. We must now take a new look at musical expressiveness to find what it is that thus far has evaded us.

CHAPTER VIII

Contour and Convention

◇ 1 ◇   It is not too dangerously speculative to assert that the theoretical interest in musical expression coexists with a practical interest in the "proper" setting of text to music: "proper," that is to say, in a particular sense. For it is not a coincidence that the earliest speculations on musical expressiveness with which we began—namely, the writings of the Florentine *Camerata*—were not merely intended as a theoretical account of how music can be expressive of the particular emotions, but as a "manual" of practical instructions as to how one is to "match" the expressiveness of the music to the expressiveness of the text which it accompanies.[1] "Proper," then, we take to mean "expressively appropriate."

The intimate relation of theories of musical expressiveness to methods of setting texts to music suggests that we might augment our understanding of musical expressiveness by taking a closer look at the problem of text-setting. That is what I propose to do at the outset of the present chapter—the goal, of course, being to extrapolate from the latter to the former. (I shall return to the relation between music and text, and look at it from a different angle, in Chapter X.)

Let me begin with a couple of well-known problems in the aesthetics of opera. The last act of *Le Nozze di Figaro* opens with an exquisite little aria in F minor for Barbarina. She sings (in Dent's translation): "Oh how dreadful! have I lost it? Oh, wherever can it be?" (See Example 11 on the next page.) She has lost a pin that Almaviva, in one of his endless intrigues, has given her to return to Susana; yet the music, as many have remarked, seems out of all proportion to the situation—more appropriate to the loss of a lover than the loss of a pin. The main "weeping" figure is reminiscent, for example, of one of the subsidiary themes in the first movement of Beethoven's *Pathétique* (also in F minor in the recapitulation). (See Example 12.) And the same motive can be identified in the weeping figure of the "Willow" song in Verdi's *Otello*. (See Example 13.) In *these* instances the figure seems ap-

EXAMPLE 11:
Mozart, *Le Nozze di Figaro*, Act IV

EXAMPLE 12:
Beethoven, *Sonate Pathétique*, Op. 13

EXAMPLE 13:
Verdi, *Otello*, Act IV

EXAMPLE 14:

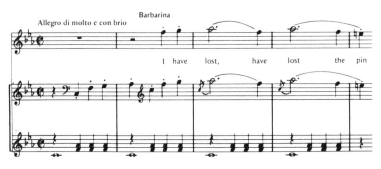

propriate. To underscore this, imagine the *Pathétique* as accompaniment to the loss of a pin. (See Example 14.)

Dent (as so often happens in such cases) attempts to show that the inappropriateness of Barbarina's music serves a higher purpose in the drama. "The opening of Act IV brings at once a complete change of temper," he writes. "Hitherto the whole intrigue has been hardly more than a game of scoring points, with a game-player's amused satisfaction at every trick won; and now Barbarina—the last character one would expect to do so—sets the tone of sinister anxiety with the strange key of F minor."[2] But even if Barbarina's "cavatina" is meant to draw a moral beyond itself, this would depend upon the disparity here; for the musical setting cannot draw us (as Dent would have it) to look for its appropriateness elsewhere unless we fail to find its appropriateness *in situ*.

The situation might usefully be compared to one in which, having stepped on someone's foot, instead of saying "Excuse me," or "I'm sorry," I say "In God's name forgive me, I beseech you," or "What agonies of grief and self-mortification I am suffering." It is not that the wrong sentiment has been expressed. It *is* customary to ask forgiveness or express contrition if you step on someone's foot. But you must use the accepted formulae: the ones that custom has made suitable to the occasion. "Excuse me" for foot-stepping; "In God's name forgive me" perhaps for accidentally shooting your best friend. It is not that Mozart has provided music inappropriate to grief. But there are conventions here as well; and musical figures, like figures of speech, may be sanctioned by custom for the expression of one kind of grief or another. Whatever the reason, Dent's or some other, Mozart chose for Barbarina's expression of grief over the lost pin a musical figure closely associated with grief far more serious than that; and this is engraved in our musical consciousness. It is the recognition of this sin against conventional usage that, despite the beauty and perfection of Mozart's music, makes us feel a disparity between text and tone.

◇ 2 ◇   My second example is a notorious one in the history of music: Orfeo's lament for the twice-lost Euridice, "Che farò senza Euridice," in Gluck's opera.

EXAMPLE 15:
Gluck, *Orfeo ed Euridice*, Act III

Eduard Hanslick long ago felt the inappropriateness of music to text, and he was not the first. It had, in his day, already become a well-known curiosity in opera aesthetics. Hanslick wrote: "We, for our part, are not of opinion that in this case the composer is quite free from blame, inasmuch as music most assuredly possesses accents which more truly express a feeling of profound sorrow."[3]

This is a different case from the previous one. Here it is not merely a question of the right sentiment inappropriately expressed, but the wrong sentiment entirely: "Thank you," when you should have said "Excuse me." Indeed, stylistic anomalies aside, Orfeo's sentiments seem much more appropriate to Barbarina's music than to Orfeo's.

EXAMPLE 16:

To quote Hanslick again, "Boyé, a contemporary of Gluck, observed that precisely the same melody would accord equally well, if not better, with words conveying exactly the reverse, . . ." that is, a celebration of Euridice regained instead of a lament for Euridice lost.[4]

Now there have been attempts to defend the appropriateness of Gluck's setting, as there have been of Mozart's. One of the more recent, by Deryck Cooke, in *The Language of Music*, is particularly relevant to my purposes in that it defends Gluck just by trying to find a musical "figure of speech" in Gluck's aria that *does* customarily accompany expressions of grief. Cooke writes, in this regard, that "Che farò senza Euridice" "is a well-known crux in the problem of musical expression. How can such a simple, diatonic, major melody express grief?" The answer is, according to Cooke, that Gluck has made use of another conventional device, the dissonant appoggiatura, to express the grief which is belied by the simple, diatonic, major tune.[5] You may disagree with Cooke, as I do, that Gluck has succeeded in counteracting the effect of such a conventional expression of joy with the dissonant appoggiatura. (More of the appoggiatura a little later.) But I am in thorough agreement with Cooke that the match or mismatch of music to text is to be explained, in part at least, in terms of the conventional musical tags which, since the very beginnings of the modern musical tradition in the West, have been used by composers, sometimes consciously, more often not, as the appropriate accompaniment of the words they have set. The musical characteristics conventionally associated with joy and sorrow are as easily identifiable and as consistently applied as halo on saint.

It is important to realize fully just how "second hand" the materials of composition are. When a composer invents a theme, he does not create it anew from individual tones, like a statue from a formless lump of clay, even if, like Beethoven, he struggles to mold his themes to his special purposes. His musical materials are, to a larger degree than one suspects, ready made, and have been used and reused. He does not begin with individual tones, any more than the writer begins with individual letters or words. His musical materials are hoary with age, and layered with tradition.

I have emphasized—perhaps even exaggerated—this ready-made character of the materials of music because I think it is not fully appreciated by most philosophers of art. This was suggested to me recently in rereading a passage from Dewey's *Art as Experience* in which literature and music are compared. Sounds, which Dewey construes as the medium of literature, are, he tells us,

> not sounds as such, as in music, but sounds that have been subjected to transforming art before literature deals with them. . . . The art of literature [as opposed to the art of music] thus works with loaded dice; its material is charged with meanings they have absorbed through immemorial time.[6]

Literature, then, is a kind of second-order art for Dewey, since it makes use of linguistic entities that can already be thought of as at least minimal art objects. Whereas music, on the other hand, is an art, so Dewey claims, that begins from scratch with natural materials, untouched by human artifice, that only first become art in the hands of the composer.

Nothing could be farther from the truth. Music, no less than literature, "works with loaded dice"; no less than literature it is made from "sounds that have been subjected to transforming art" before the artist ever lays hands on them. It is all the more important to drive this point home emphatically when a philosopher of Dewey's stature believes the contrary.

I have spoken, so far, only of music with text. And the question naturally arises as to whether the same musical "conventions" are responsible, too, for at least some of the emotive characterizations of "pure" instrumental forms. As I indicated at the outset of the present chapter, I am quite prepared to extend these conclusions to "pure" music as well. For it seems to me altogether plausible that if we recognize the appropriateness or inappropriateness of tone to text in part by our recognition of the used and reused musical "tags," with their four-hundred-year-old accretion of emotive associations upon their heads, we recognize, in part, by the same means, the appropriateness or inappropriateness of our emotive descriptions of instrumental compositions. The same feature that we recognize as appropriate to a deeper melancholy than Barbarina's regret over the loss of a pin will, in a symphony or sonata, be recognized as imparting a profound melancholy where it occurs.

◇ 3 ◇ What seems to be emerging, at this point, is *another* theory of musical expressiveness, quite different from the one outlined in the first five chapters. I shall henceforth call the first thesis, the "contour" theory (or model) of musical expressiveness because it explains the expressiveness of music by the congruence of musical "contour" with the structure of expressive features and behavior. The thesis which has been sketched in the beginning of the present chapter I will call the "convention" theory (or model) of musical expressiveness because it explains the expressiveness of music as a function, simply, of the customary association of certain musical features with certain emotive ones, quite apart from any structural analogy between them. I shall argue, in the remainder of Chapter VI, that the two theories *together* account for central cases of emotive expressiveness in music, sometimes one, sometimes the other, sometimes both together. They are, indeed, as we shall see, inextricably bound up together.

The two musical examples we have been discussing, Barbarina's cavatina and Orfeo's lament, provide two contrasting cases; and if we go back over them now, with the contour theory in mind, we will be able to see just how the convention model and the contour model operate vis-à-vis one another.

We have, in Barbarina's little arietta, two dimensions: a quality and an intensity. No one doubts that the music possesses a melancholy quality, due to the "weeping" or "sighing" figure, and the minor tonality. And the *quality* of melancholy is appropriate to Barbarina's unhappiness over the lost pin. It is the second dimension, the intensity, that disturbs; for the intensity is out of proportion to the depth of melancholy that the loss of a pin would be expected to produce. Leaving the minor key aside for the time being, we can now see, in Barbarina's cavatina, how the contour model, and the convention model join forces in explaining the phenomenon of musical expressiveness. That the sighing figure of Barbarina's music is expressive of sadness is accounted for, as the description "sighing" or "weeping" figure immediately suggests, by the analogy to human expression—by, that is, the contour model. But the intensity of sadness that it is expressive of is due, rather, to the fact that the figure has been associated, since time out of mind, with intense rather than transient and shallow grief: the intensity, that is to say, is accounted for by the convention thesis.

One might compare the "iconography" of the "weeping" figure to that of the English bulldog. The face of the bulldog is expressive of dogged determination and pugnacity in virtue of its visage resembling the human visage when expressing those traits. But that it is expressive of the English character is, of course, due to the "convention" that makes the bulldog England's national totem. Likewise, there are two forces at work in Barbarina's music, a "natural" and a "conventional" one; and the expressiveness of the music is a result of *both*. Of course, to the extent that expressive behavior may itself be "conventional"— relative, perhaps, to a given culture—the contour model relies on "conventions" as well. But whereas the conventions of the convention model are musical conventions only, the conventions of the contour model are expressive conventions of which the musical are a special case.

Now Orfeo's lament, as we have seen, is a different case. It does not misfire along the intensity dimension, but along the quality one. Deeply felt melancholy is called for, it would seem, by the dramatic situation; but the music is not expressive of melancholy at all, let alone intense melancholy. Why? Well, the *musical* reason is clear enough. Gluck gives Orfeo a diatonic (that is, nonchromatic), major tune in a moderate tempo, even a little on the allegro side of moderato—all characteristics of happy rather than sad music. It could be transformed, easily enough, into a sad (and bad) melody simply by altering just two of the parameters: tempo and mode. (Indeed, it is often taken at an impossibly slow tempo to try to put the melancholy in that Gluck left out.) Thus:

EXAMPLE 17:

The musical answer to our question, then, is clear and unequivocal. Three musical features, rapid tempo, major key, diatonic melody are responsible for the happy quality of Orfeo's lament. But the question which goes beyond pure musical practice—the question: Why do these features impart the quality?—remains partially unanswered. Tempo, of course, can easily be subsumed under the contour thesis. For tempo is very much an identifying characteristic of expressive behavior; and it hardly needs pointing out that the grief-stricken plod, while the joyful skip and run. And, by the way, whatever grief is imparted by the dissonant appoggiatura,

EXAMPLE 18:

also falls under the contour model. For the dissonant appoggiatura, which Gluck always uses to such good effect, is just our old friend, the "sighing" or "weeping" figure, in its simplest form.

◇ 4 ◇ What, then, of the major mode and the diatonic character? It seems to me that the only plausible answer must be that of the convention thesis: they are merely the customary accompaniments of happy emotions, and are recognized as such where they occur. It is important to note, however, that although the conventional musical "tags" such as certain chords, for example, are not of themselves analogues of any expressive behavior—how could a static event like the sounding of a chord be?—their "syntactical" function in a broader musical context is quite another matter. Take, by way of illustration, the "anguished," "restless" character of the diminished triad. By itself, a diminished triad has no such quality—it stands as an ambiguous cipher.

EXAMPLE 19:

But in its context, during a long period in the history of our musical tradition, it is an "active" chord; it has to go somewhere, lead to something. In this tradition, as a cadential chord, it does not make a well-formed formula, but an incomplete sentence.

We can now see why the diminished triad can, in a proper musical context, present an anguished quality that can be accounted for on the contour model. It has no contour of itself, any more than a single tone has aesthetic form. But when it occurs as part of a musical "sentence," it helps give contour to the melody it underlies; and the contour it imparts can be seen to resemble expressive behavior of a particular kind. It imparts a "restless," emotionally distracted quality because it is inserted at a place where the melodic line has come to an apparent resting place; and because it is not, syntactically, a "resting" chord but an active one, it contradicts the resting implication of the melodic line and forces it to continue, even as the restless, emotionally distracted person sits down in one place only to feel impelled by disquietude to get up and go somewhere else at once.

The diminished chord, in its "anguished" position, gives a melody the "fidgets."

Bach's recitatives abound in this syntactical use of the diminished chord to underlie the dark emotions of a text, as for instance:

EXAMPLE 20:
Bach, Cantata No. 78: *Jesu, der du meine Seele*

If we compare this with a slightly altered version, in which the diminished chord is replaced with a G-major triad, we can easily see what is happening.

EXAMPLE 21:

Example 21 comes to rest, making an acceptable (if not strong) cadence, and supporting the cadential implications of the tenor's line. But example 20 does not come to rest at all, defying the direction of the tenor line toward G major; it is not a well-formed formula, musical "grammar" dictating that something else must follow. Example 21 is a complete musical sentence, but example 20 is not. Hence the active, restless contour that the diminished chord imparts to the melodic line.

◇ 5 ◇ Such considerations suggest a possible scenario for the origin of the association between the minor triad and the darker side of the emotive spectrum. The syntactic role that the minor triad once played may have been very similar to that of the diminished triad in the period 1700-1900. It was once, I am suggesting, an active, dissonant chord, and was not considered suitable as a final resting place for a complete musical section, the last word being reserved for the major, a hypothesis that is supported by a look at musical style in the seventeenth century. For it is common in seventeenth-century music for a movement predominantly in a minor tonality to end in the tonic major. But the minor triad has not had that syntactic function for a long time: certainly there are only vestiges of it in the high Baroque (the so-called "picardy third"), and a cadence on the minor in late classical style was no more "active" than one on the major.

But if the minor triad was once an active chord, like the diminished, it could also have contributed, when it was so heard, to an expressive contour of a restless kind. Thus at a certain period in music history the minor third, through its syntactic function, might well have been accommodated on the contour theory of expressiveness. And to the extent that we can recapture the syntactic function in our listening to early Baroque music, to the extent, that is, that we can hear the minor triad as active, we can hear the restless expressive contour, and thus, one would think, heighten our appreciation of one of the parameters of the music, namely, its expressiveness. As we normally hear the minor triad today, however, it is the smile without the cat. The expressive contour no longer accrues, due to the altered musical syntax. What remains is the deep-seated convention, associating the minor third with the expressive behavior it could once help to "map."

It is inviting to suppose that many musical features, expressive by convention, were once more than that: were once heard as resembling identifiable expressive behavior, or at least ingredients in such structures. I am inclined to believe it is the case. Thus we at least have a one-term theory of the origin of musical expressiveness (of a certain kind) in the West, even though we require a two-term theory to account for its expressiveness at any given time (except perhaps in the musical Garden of Eden). In addition, the two models do not now stand apart as a makeshift expedient, an ad hoc dualism that has been patched together to repair a failed monistic account. We can now see a *connection* between what is expressive by contour and at least some of what is expressive by convention.

◇ 6 ◇   To conclude the present chapter, let me try to pull together the strands of theory that have emerged from the preceding remarks, and knot them into a coherent story. We can think of our musical tradition as a patchwork of features of (at least) the following kinds:

(i) Those that resemble expressive behavior of some kind, and thus are heard as expressive of something or other because heard as appropriate to the expression of something or other: for example, the "weeping" figure of grief or the falling line of "Lasciatemi morire."

(ii) Those that do not, themselves, present an expressive contour but contribute, in certain contexts, to the forming of one: for example, the "restless" diminished triad.

(iii) Those that are no longer heard as resembling expressive behavior, but which are expressive by custom or convention, such as, for example, the chromatic scale in some of its melodic manifestations.

(iv) Those that never were of themselves heard as resembling expressive behavior, but which once contributed, by virtue of their musical syntax, to such resemblance, and now, by virtue of a change in their syntactical function, are expressive by custom or convention merely: for example, the minor triad in general, and the minor triad in certain familiar contexts.

Add to this the genetic hypothesis that all expressiveness by convention was originally expressiveness by contour, either as the thing itself, or as ingredient, and we have the complete sketch of our theory of musical expression. And we must turn now to the development and examination of its implications.

CHAPTER IX

Breaking the Culture Barrier

◇ 1 ◇   Talk about something being such-and-so by "convention" immediately suggests cross-cultural comparisons; for "conventions," of course, are notoriously culture bound. If, then, there are features of music that are expressive by "convention," rather than by "nature," would we not expect to find other music—in other cultures—where the expressive features are quite different from our own, and the expressive character quite opaque to us? And would not the finding of such music, with such features, lend support to the claim that these features are indeed only expressive within a framework of specifically musical expression-conventions?

Consulting the findings of the ethnomusicologist in this regard is, therefore, very tempting indeed. But it is frought with danger as well, because it is so very easy, as has been demonstrated time and again, to misinterpret what the customs and conventions of an alien culture tell us, just because it is an alien culture, and we so prone to carry implicit suppositions to our cross-cultural observations which color with our own cultural stain the very data that are supposed to be free from it. Because these ventures are so chanceful, I do not intend to push any hard conclusions in the following brief sally into alien musical territory. I would like simply to probe a bit, and tease out some problems.

A word, first, about the dichotomy I suggest at the outset, between being expressive by *nature* and by *convention*. By natural expressiveness is meant, of course, expressiveness by contour. But expressiveness by contour is not, by any means, expressiveness completely free of convention: expressiveness to the "naive ear." At least two kinds of convention can be seen to govern it. For we cannot hear the expressiveness (say) of the *Lamento d'Arianna* unless we can, to begin with, hear it as music; unless, that is, we are educated musical perceivers who have been initiated into the musical culture of which Monteverdi is a part. And that involves, among other things, having internalized a parcel of musical conventions. In addition, we must, of course, be initiates into whatever conventions may govern expression of emotion in our culture. The expressiveness of "Lasciatemi morire" depends not only upon the contour of the melodic line, but upon the resemblance of that line—a falling line—to the falling of the speaking voice in the grief-striken expression of the words. But *if* the falling of the speaking voice in grief is an expressive *convention*, and not a biologically determined feature of expression, a listener who has not internalized that convention will not recognize the expressiveness of the musical line, however accomplished that person is as a musical perceiver. For although the listener will hear the musical contour, he will not perceive the resemblance to expressive behavior, because the expressive behavior in question will be unknown to him—not part of his repertoire. Thus, in calling expressiveness by contour "natural," we only mean to say that its "conventional" aspect is relative to a wider set of conventions than merely the specific conventions of musical expressiveness, not that it is natural in the sense of perceptible to some hypothetical "naive" listener, free of everything but the requisite biological equipment for hearing. There is no such expressiveness in music, whether or not there is anywhere else.

To understand this point fully, it is important to keep in mind the distinction between hearing a musical composition, X, and hearing a collection of sounds which are made in the performance of X. To hear the sounds that a soprano, 'cello and harpsichord make in performance of the *Lamento d'Arianna* is not necessarily to hear the *Lamento d'Arianna*. My dog, for all that I know, may be able to hear the whole range of sounds made in a performance of the *Lamento*. Yet there is a perfectly obvious sense of "hear" in which we would not want to say that my dog "heard" Monteverdi's work (although there is another perfectly obvious sense in which we might want to say he had). Let us suppose a non-Western listener, completely uninitiated into Western musical culture, "hears" a performance of X, some musical composition. He does not hear X, in a certain obvious sense, but he hears a collection of sounds that has quite a different significance for him from the significance it has for the Western ear. These sounds may, indeed, be heard by him as expressive of emotions, if their configurations resemble his emotive behavior, or happen, by chance, to conform to some of the expressive conventions of his musical culture. But he has not heard X; so he has not heard the expressive properties of X. And we are interested here only in the expressive properties that the musical composition has, not the ones that the collection of sounds involved in its performance might have, if heard by someone completely untrained in Western musical listening.

◇ 2 ◇   Having made the above disclaimers and caveats, I can now contrast natural with conventional expressiveness in music without being misunderstood. In terms of this contrast, a thesis in ethnomusicology emerges from our theory of musical expressiveness, the validation or invalidation of which bears directly on that theory's plausibility.

What we want to test is the plausibility of our dual account of expressiveness. Now *if* expressiveness in music were entirely natural, we might expect that a Western listener would be able to perceive the expressiveness of any of the world's music; and if we could find a musical style, outside of our own culture, that we could determine, on independent grounds, was expressive, we could test the natural hypothesis by listening to that music and verifying our ability or inability to perceive its expressive qualities. If we could not perceive the expressiveness, we could at least conclude that the experiment had rendered the natural hypothesis less probable, and the conventional hypothesis more probable, although we could not, I think, declare the experiment conclusive. Contrariwise, if we *could* hear the expressiveness, we could conclude that the natural hypothesis had been supported and the conventional one damaged though not perhaps demolished.

If, on the other hand, expressiveness in music were entirely conventional, the opposite would obtain. Failure to hear the expressiveness of an alien music independently determined to be expressive would render the conventional hypothesis more likely and the natural hypothesis less; success in hearing the expressiveness, the reverse—i.e. support for the natural hypothesis and lack of it for the conventional one.

Things are not quite so straightforward with the actual hypothesis in hand, however; for it construes expressiveness in music partly as natural and partly as conventional. Failure to perceive the expressiveness in an alien music would cast doubt on the natural component of the hypothesis; but success would not cast doubt on the conventional part; for the result would be compatible both with there being *no* features expressive by convention and with there being such features which, of course, we fail to perceive because we are unable to "read" the conventions. Our theory would seem to imply, then, that given an alien music, like our own in being expressive, the expressive qualities should, in part, be apparent to us—those, that is, that are natural ones.

But we have forgotten that even natural expressiveness is convention-bound—bound, for one, to the conventions which may govern expression-behavior in a culture, and bound, for another, to the musical conventions that are the prerequisite for intelligent, appreciative listening. Thus, failure to "read" the expressiveness of an alien music independently determined to be expressive, does not, of itself, cast doubt on the natural moment in our theory; for it may well be, and, I strongly suspect, is very likely, that we are failing not only to read the conventions of musical expressiveness of that music, but are failing to read the very musical conventions that make it possible to hear the sounds as music in the first place. And if we cannot hear the music as it is meant to be heard, we cannot perceive the natural expressiveness that is there, any more than someone who cannot hear "inner voices" can perceive the natural expressiveness lent to a string quartet by a particularly expressive passage in the viola. Perhaps this can best be brought out by the consideration of a concrete example.

◇ 3 ◇   The music of northern India—and I am thinking here, particularly, of the *rāgas*—seems to be music in which expressiveness plays a very substantial part. The term *rāga* refers both to an improvised musical composition, and to the germinal "theme," or tonal series which forms its musical "subject." For our purposes, what is important about these structural germs is that, as Walter Kaufmann tells us in *The Rāgas of North India*, "Each of a large number of '*rāgas*' has its own characteristic mood (*rasa*)."[1] Kaufmann goes on to compare these moods or emotive states both to the ethos of Greek music and the eighteenth-century doctrine of the affections, suggesting, into the bargain, a kind of "experiment" in listening that we might do well to consider. He writes:

It is hardly necessary to point out the resemblance of *rasa* to the *ethos* of ancient Greece, or to similar phenomena in the music of the Renaissance and Baroque periods of the West, particularly to the *Affektenlehre* of the late eighteenth century. In order to prove that the use of a fixed scale does indeed create a certain *rasa*, an experiment is suggested: we select a scale which may consist of any number of degrees. Let us assume that it has five notes, C E F# A B (c). . . . If we improvise with these five tones for a while, we can observe that a certain mood is created which, although quite distinct, can hardly be described in words. If, after the *rasa* has been established, we suddenly use a foreign note, for instance E ♭ or F, we notice . . . how severely it destroys the previously established sentiment.[2]

This is just the sort of "experiment" one imagines might test the nature-convention hypothesis. (Kaufmann, incidentally, seems committed to some kind of "nature" theory of expressiveness; for his suggestion here is that a somewhat naive Western listener—his work is addressed to Western ears—will immediately detect the change in *rasa*, that is, emotive character, that a slight change in *rāga* will effectuate.) Notice, though, that Kaufmann's experiment is, to begin with, fraught with vagaries. One always tends to suspect a claim about expressiveness when it relies on expressive qualities that "can hardly be described in words," the indescribable being so often a license for the unintelligible.

To determine if our hypothetical listener is hearing a change in mood and not just a change in music—that is, a change in *rasa* and not just in *rāga*—we must ask for a verbal response that will indicate what the mood was before, and after, the musical change. If we do not get that much, we will always suspect that the report of "a change from one indescribable mood to another" may simply report a change in how the music sounds; and not every change in musical sound is a change in musical mood, *unless* one makes it so by stipulative definition, in which case the reported change in mood tells us nothing. Curt Ducasse once argued essentially that every difference in perception is, ipso facto, a difference in "import of feeling," no matter how trivial: "a determinate one in each case, peculiar to the given situation and for which no specific name exists. . . ."[3] Kaufmann seems to be following Ducasse's example, which assures that every change in *rāga* will result in a change in *rasa*, at the cost, however, of utterly trivializing the notion of *rasa*, as Ducasse has trivialized the notion of feeling. In his eagerness to demonstrate the relation between *rāga* and *rasa*, Kaufmann intends, apparently, to *make sure* that his "experiment" will work, stipulating that a change in sound is a change in mood; you heard a change in sound, therefore, you heard a change in mood. If you accept that, then you reduce to nothing the claim that the *rāgas* of northern India bear expressive qualities; for all it means, by fiat, is that they bear musical ones. But this is hardly what an Indian means when he says that a certain *rāga* is tranquil, any more than it is what we mean when we say that the slow movement of the *Eroica* is expressive of grief.

Let us be more circumspect. Suppose we play to the untutored Western ear a *rāga* of specifiable emotive expression—say, the *Shri rāg*, which, Kaufmann tells us, "is mysterious, gentle, and often depicts the meditation of love and the nostalgic and prayerful mood of early evening."[4]

What can we conclude if, as I think is likely, the *Shri rāg* does not have for us, at least at the outset, the emotive significance it has for its Indian audience? To conclude that we are not reading its emotive conventions seems safe enough. But is it? To begin with, we are very unlikely to be reading *any* of its musical conventions; or, to speak more plainly, we are likely to be hearing the sounds but not the music. To the uninitiated ear, every *rāga* presents about the same mood: a kind of exotic stupor. (To quote a line from a detective movie: "It don't make no more sense than Chinese music.") And it is easy to see why, if we reflect for a moment on the nature of Indian music. To quote Kaufmann once again:

> The art music of India has evolved entirely within the realm of monophonic modality and, with the exception of some instances of contemporary popular and film music, has not been noticeably influenced by the polyphonic and harmonic tendencies of Western music. . . . This Oriental emphasis upon the horizontal extension of music has created an art exceedingly rich in scales, motives, melody formulas, and subtle refinements which, up to recent times, has found comparatively little appreciation in the West.[5]

Not the least of these "subtle refinements" (and one which greatly troubles the Western ear) is the introduction of intervals smaller than the half-tone (which is the narrowest interval in Western scales and modes), and the glissando up or down to a pitch, which, although a minor coloristic feature of Western music, is seldom used for anything but humorous effect.[6]

The Western ear, nourished on horizontal or (at least) vertical polyphony (i.e. harmony) will naturally tend to read Indian music harmonically or polyphonically and, of course, fail. Being prepared, as well, to hear microtones as nothing more than mistakes or "exotic" colorations, it will utterly fail to hear them as they must be heard in such music: as a vital structural component. It is natural, I suppose, that if music does not develop vertically, it will, if it develops at all, develop horizontally. Natural or not, that is what Indian music clearly did. And the Westerner, from the beginning attuned to a music that, to the contrary, has developed vertically, will listen vertically, and hear a "lack"; in addition, unable to listen horizontally in the appropriate way—unable, that is, to make structural sense out of microtones—he will fail to hear the melodic richness which makes monophonic music full in spite of its purely horizontal nature.

But if the Western ear falls so far short of hearing what animates the art music of India, how can it read even the natural expressiveness that might be there? Natural expressiveness is expressiveness by virtue of musical contour. Musical contour, in Western music, is achieved by a vector of horizontal *and* vertical forces. But musical contour in Indian music is the function of but one moment: the horizontal. (I exclude from consideration, here, the part played by rhythm both in Western and Indian music—it is, of course, an important part in both.) And if one is not prepared to hear the full complexity of the horizontal, one can scarcely hear the musical contour that may contribute to the expressiveness of a monophonic musical tradition like the Indian. What passes before the Western ear as trivial, or goes in fact unnoticed, may be of the very essence of a monophonic composition.

We can now see that the failure to hear the expressiveness of the Indian *rāga* is just as likely to result from the failure to hear the natural expressiveness of the musical contour as from the failure to read expressive musical conventions. Thus, failure to perceive expressive qualities does not, of itself, render the natural thesis any less likely. We cannot expect the Western ear to

hear, *ab initio*, the expressive contour in Indian music, any more
than we can expect an Australian aborigine to see expression in
Rembrandt's sketch of a face—not because he fails to read the
expressive conventions, but because, to begin with, he fails to
read the pictorial ones.

How are we to know if we have failed to hear what is to be
heard in the Indian *rāgas*? It will not do for us to assume that we
have failed simply because we have failed to hear the expressiveness. That smacks of an outright refusal to countenance any
evidence damaging to the theory of natural expressiveness. If
we have successfully heard the musical contour of a piece, and if
its expressiveness is, in part, a function of the resemblance of
that contour to some item of expressive behavior, as our theory
claims, then we should be able to "read" the expressiveness when
we can "read" the contour, given only that the expressive behavior is in our repertoire. If we cannot, the theory is falsified, or at
least rendered less probable. If there is no criterion of successful
perception of contour, independent of successful perception of
natural expressiveness, then the thesis that natural expressiveness is a result of the perception of musical contour dissolves
into emptiness. Or, to put it another way, not the least bit more
flattering, the claim that failure to read the expressiveness is of
itself failure to read the contour makes our thesis true, at the
cost of making it trivial.

◇ 4 ◇ Perhaps, though, neutral territory could be staked
out, not in music but in Nature; for if we all do not perceive a
common music, we all do surely perceive a common world. What
can nonmusical sounds tell us about musical expressiveness?

We might be tempted to argue that if two cultures expressed
their emotions in a similar manner, then they could be expected,
on the contour model, to find the same emotive expressiveness
in the same "natural" sounds: mournfulness in the train whistle
(the *American* train whistle, not the European, which is high-
pitched and jaunty rather than low-pitched and soulful), cheerfulness in bird songs, and so on. And I have no doubt that some
agreement, anyway, would be found along these lines—the correlation between pitch and energy, for one.

Yet an intriguing difficulty in reading cross-cultural data ob-
trudes even here. For it might just be the case that our perceptions of nonmusical sounds are not altogether free of musical

influence. For instance, there is a bird around my house that I have named the "Bach-bird," because its song, as I hear it, gives the first four notes of the subject of one of Bach's eight little fugues for organ.[7]

EXAMPLE 22:
Bach, *Little Organ Fugue in C*

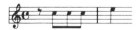

But what does the Indian hear, whose ear has been nourished on microtones? The tones that the bird produces are far from being a perfect, or a well-tempered major third, in common time. However, I have been musically formed to hear the half-step as the smallest possible interval, and whenever possible, I hear natural sounds as constructed of half-steps and whole-steps.[8] On the other hand, the Indian does not hear the half-step as the smallest possible interval, so there is no reason to believe that *he* hears the interval between the Bach-bird's third and fourth tones as a major third. While my musical consciousness is busy fitting the Bach-bird's song into a possible Western notation, based on major and minor seconds, the Indian's musical psyche is just as busy accommodating it to the world of microtones. Does he hear the cheerfulness of the Bach-bird's song? Why should he? He doesn't hear the same "music" in it that I do. I should no more expect him to hear the cheerfulness in the Bach-bird's song than the cheerfulness of Bach's fugue. For he would need *my* musical culture to hear both of them; and that, by hypothesis, he does not have.

To take a similar example, there is a passage in Earl Robinson's *The Lonesome Train* in which the composer imitates the train whistle's mournful sound (see facing page, Example 23). But not only does a train whistle not sound a perfect or well-tempered minor third, it fills up whatever interval it does sound with a glissando. How does the Indian hear our train whistle? And is there any reason to believe, since he does not hear it as the "sighing" motive of Western music, the way Earl Robinson obviously did, that he perceives it as expressive of sadness?

I throw out these questions to suggest that the sounds we hear in "nature" are informed by our musical culture, to some extent yet to be determined. And, therefore, we cannot treat "natural" sounds as a testing ground for theories about musical expres-

EXAMPLE 23:
Earl Robinson, *The Lonesome Train*

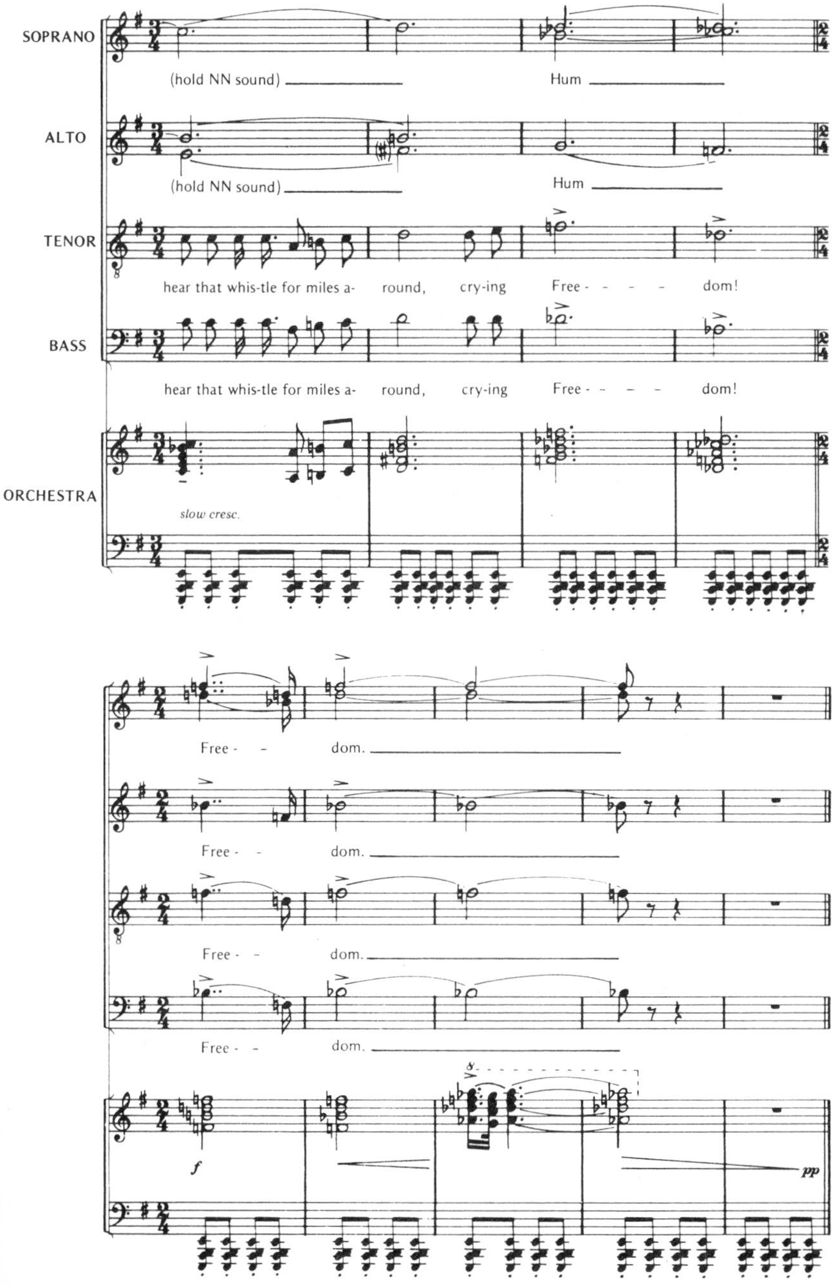

siveness that are entirely free of the influence of musical conventions. If that is the case, we were mistaken in thinking that by appealing to "natural" sounds we can test the contour thesis without the obtrusion of the conventional model. Where there is not music in question, it might be thought, we can be free of the influence of musical culture and conventions; and since "natural" sounds are not music, whatever expressive qualities we hear in them cannot be the result of the expressive musical conventions. But this, clearly, is not the case. If we hear the mournfulness of the train whistle in part as the mournfulness of the minor third which our musical upbringing impels us to hear in it (as *The Lonesome Train* illustrates), then we are hearing the mournfulness of the whistle in part in virtue of the same musical convention that makes us hear the sadness in the minor harmonization of the "Marseillaise."

Thus, comparing the way listeners from disparate cultures report the expressive features they perceive in "natural" sounds is frought, at least to a degree, with the same difficulties that bedevil the attempt to draw conclusions about emotive expressiveness in music from cross-cultural comparisons. For contrary to what one might initially believe, we perceive "natural" sounds under the influence of the way we perceive musical ones. *What* the extent of this influence is I do not pretend to know. But I imagine there might be some ingenious work to be done here which would cast light on a dark and unnoticed corner where music and "reality" intersect.

◇ 5 ◇   The conclusion, then, of this brief excursion into alien musical territory is that drawing conclusions at all is a chancy business. Success in reading the expressiveness of an alien music may reinforce the natural hypothesis. But failure— which I think is by far the more likely result—tells us nothing at all until we can be certain that we have fully mastered the art of listening required of us by the musical tradition in question. Is such mastery even possible? It is not clear. Arguments to the effect that, as humans we are culture-bound—to our own historical period, and to our own cultural place—are all too familiar. And this is not the place to go into the metaphysical niceties of such arguments. It must suffice for our purposes to acknowledge that breaking the culture barrier is at least very difficult, and conclusions relying on such perilous doings, perilous themselves.

CHAPTER X

Tone, Text, and Title

◇ 1 ◇   I return now, as I promised in Chapter VIII, to the relation of music to text; for there is more to be gleaned from it. I began with the assumption that pure instrumental music is susceptible of certain gross distinctions as regards its expressiveness; and I have argued that these distinctions are the result of the affinities such music bears to the expressive behavior of human beings, as well as the result in part of various musical "conventions" of an expressive kind. But I have said nothing so far about the very palpable contribution that extramusical materials—most notably, texts and literary or programmatic titles—make to the expressive character of music. The setting of words has been a pervasive concern of composers since the very beginning of Western polyphony, and music with titles and (at least primitive) programs has been written since at least the seventeenth century, if not before. Both texts and titles have been seen as intimately involved with the expressive powers of music. So it behooves us to examine this involvement with some care. Such an examination will, I think, cast additional light on the expressive hypothesis being advanced and, I believe, will lend support to it. At the same time, the expressive hypothesis will provide a more successful way of looking at the contributions which text and title make to the expressiveness of music than has heretofore been possible. In a way, however, my view will be quite old fashioned since (as in the case of what has gone before), I think one (at least) of the early modern writers has had something valuable to say on this regard; and my aim is not so much to say something new, as to freshen up the old with a new coat of philosophical paint.

Now the "normal" way (if there is one) of looking at the composer's relation to his text, or his title, seems to me to be something like the following. The composer has a text: say, a poem about a violet. Or he has an idea that he wants to write an overture expressive of the dark, stormy moods of the Hebrides. With the text before him, or the idea of the seascape in mind, he contrives music appropriate to his task—music, in other words, expressive of his text or title. And let me establish at the outset that

I shall only be interested here in what we can describe as the emotions or moods associated with texts or titles, since emotive expressiveness is my theme. So what I am saying is that the "normal way" of looking at the composer vis-à-vis the emotional tone of his text, or his title, is this. He first divines the emotion or mood, emotions or moods, of the text or title, and then he invents music that is expressive of the emotion or mood, emotions or moods. In other words, if the composer has done the job properly, the expressiveness of the music will match the expressiveness of the text or title.

I want to suggest here a different view—one that, I think, casts more light on the problem of musical expression. It is not so much that the "normal" view is wrong, as that it is just incomplete. The suggestion I have to make takes its departure from a very little known paper by a slightly better known composer and critic, Johann Adam Hiller, a member of what is called by musicologists today the Berlin School of Song. It flourished in the 1750s and 60s, forming an important artistic and aesthetic link between the Baroque and Classical styles. (Gluck, for one, was influenced by this movement, as his Klopstock odes testify.) The paper of Hiller's to which I refer is titled "Essay Concerning the Imitation of Nature in Music" ("Abhandlung von der Nachahmung der Natur in der Musik"), and was published in 1754, in a musical periodical of the time, Friedrich Wilhelm Marpurg's *Historisch-kritische Beyträge (Historical-critical Contributions)*.[1] It has never, so far as I know, been reprinted, or translated into English.

◇ 2 ◇ Following an Enlightenment tradition, Hiller tries to argue from the supposed origin of music to its aesthetic character. However, the idea that music's origin lies in the imitation of natural sounds—a common one in the seventeenth and eighteenth centuries—is immediately rejected. It is within himself that man finds the origin. "What," asks Hiller, "does music consist of?"

> Of sounds. Where are sounds to be found? Are they not so natural to man that he is distinguished by being able to bring them forth at will without looking for a model to imitate?[2]

Music, then, arises from the vocal utterances of man. But it is the evincing of feelings, not concepts, wherein this primitive source of music lies.

> The understanding occupies itself with images or ideas, the heart with feelings. . . . The understanding has speech as its aid, to make its ideas intelligible to others. [But] the heart is simple: a sound, a sigh is enough for it to express a complete emotion.[3]

Having acquiesced in this commonplace distinction between emotive and cognitive expression, Hiller concludes that "the feelings . . . expressed only through [vocal] sounds, are the basis of music,"[4] hence plumping for a version of what has come to be known as the "speech theory" of the origin of music—the theory, held by such disparate figures as Jean Jacques Rousseau, Richard Wagner, and Herbert Spencer, that music has its origin in the passionate tones of primitive speech, or in some protolanguage of the passions, more akin to music than to articulate speech, which gives rise to them both.[5] Because the origin of music lies in language, in human utterance, and because it is the passionate rather than the cognitive part of human utterance that is its source, the obvious conclusion to be drawn by someone like Hiller, absolutely determined to commit the genetic fallacy, is that music proper, music in its most characteristic and exemplary manifestations, must be vocal music devoted to the "expression" of the passions. This, indeed, is the conclusion Hiller draws.

How, then, is this union of music and text to be accomplished? (Hiller is thinking, here, primarily of the musical setting of poetry.) How does the composer of vocal music go about his business? Primarily, by a musical realization of the natural melody inherent in the words. For in the recitation of poetry there is, according to Hiller, "a kind of melody, the true foundation on which music should be built. . . ."[6] In the imitation of this natural melody, music conforms to the notion of art as imitation; and as this natural melody is the natural language of the passions, in imitating it, music, at the same time, fulfills its destiny as the expressive art par excellence. The notion that there is a "natural melody" in poetic recitation which it is the office of music to capture is not, of course, an invention of Hiller's, but goes back, as we saw in the opening chapters, to the beginning of the seventeenth century and the speculations of the Florentine composers who were in the process of contriving the first operas. Whether Hiller knew these composers, their music, or their aesthetic manifestos, I do not know. But ideas like these had wide currency throughout the seventeenth century, and the first half of the eighteenth, examples having been previously adduced in abundance; and there would have been no dearth of possible sources for Hiller to have consulted. In any event, it is in what Hiller went on to say that his originality lies.

Hiller, like some at least of the early propounders of the speech theory of musical expressiveness, thought that through the imitation of the natural melody of speech, music could arouse emotion in the listener, thus demonstrating that he was in thrall to the arousal paradigm of expressiveness. Where he parted company with the early speech theorists is in the *kind* of emotion thought to be aroused. It is no accident that I used the singular, "emotion," in describing Hiller's theory. For whereas many of the seventeenth- and eighteenth-century speech theorists we have examined thought that music, through the imitation of speech, aroused the individual emotions—love, hate, sadness, fear, and so on—Hiller, on the contrary, believed that one undifferentiated musical emotion was the result. "The feeling aroused by [musical] sounds is unknown [i.e. unnamed] by us, but it excites pleasure in us, and that suffices."[7]

It is, of course, a harmless truism that music "arouses" pleasure, since to say this is to say nothing more surprising or controversial than that we—some of us, anyway—enjoy music. But that music arouses in us some unique musical emotion—a special case of the well-known theory that art arouses unique "aesthetic emotions"—is, it appears to me, an untenable view, long since given up by most philosophers of art for reasons I think it would be pointless and boring to rehash here yet again. (It will suffice, I think, to put it to the reader whether, in his or her experience, the same emotion or feeling is always felt in hearing music, or in hearing the same music at different times, or even throughout the entire hearing of one piece of music at one given time.) I should like, therefore, to amend Hiller, in this regard, to be saying rather that music is *expressive* in a nonspecific sense: perhaps emotive without an emotion, or expressive without being expressive of anything in particular.

How, then, can music attain emotive explicitness? How can it, for Hiller, go from being expressive *merely*, to being expressive of fear, or joy, or sadness, or whatever? Hiller's answer, as I imagine you have guessed, is: by making common cause with the conceptual capacities of language. For, Hiller points out, poetry can convey the cognitive, recognizable aspect of the emotions, so that we can say: "that is love, that is sadness! Or, so speaks love, so speaks sadness!"[8] Whereas music, capable only of being expressive of a generalized feeling, must particularize itself through the offices of speech. So, Hiller concludes, "if music desires to be intelligible . . . it can avail itself of no better helpmate than speech"; they are, as he puts it, "as brother and sister."[9]

Whether Hiller was widely read (or even known) outside of Germany, in the eighteenth century, is not clear. But views very like his on this regard do crop up some years later in Hume's nemesis, James Beattie—specifically, in his *Essays on Poetry and Music* (1762). Beattie, like Hiller, sees pure instrumental music as a kind of expressive surd—one is tempted to say, after Susanne Langer, an "unconsummated symbol." "For, if I mistake not," Beattie conjectures, "the expression of music without poetry is vague and ambiguous; and hence it is, that the same air may sometimes be repeated to every stanza of a long ode or ballad."[10] Or again, amplifying the point:

> Yet it is in general true, that Poetry is the most immediate and most accurate interpreter of Music. Without this auxiliary, a piece of the best music, heard for the first time, might be said to mean something, but we should not be able to say what. It might incline the heart to sensibility: but poetry, or language, would be necessary to improve that sensibility into a real emotion, by fixing the fancy upon some definite and affecting ideas. A fine instrumental symphony well performed, is like an oration delivered with propriety, but in an unknown tongue; it may affect us a little, but conveys no determinate feeling; we are alarmed, perhaps, or melted, or soothed, but it is very imperfectly, because we know not why:—the singer, by taking up the same air, and applying words to it, immediately translates the oration into our own language; then all uncertainty vanishes, the fancy is filled with determinate ideas, and determinate emotions take possession of the heart.[11]

Now if we contrast Hiller's (or Beattie's) view of the relation of tone to text (or title) with what I characterized at the outset as the "normal" view, we find that a little "Copernican revolution" has been made in the aesthetics of music. On the "normal" view, the music comes to the text repleat with its expressive properties, so devised as to be "appropriate"; whereas on Hiller's view, the music comes as a kind of formless, protean expressive clay, its specific expressive properties to be imprinted upon it by contact with the text.

I am sure Hiller's "revolution" has gone too far. For it is difficult to see how, on Hiller's view, music could ever be *inappropriate* expressively, since whatever expressive properties it might have it would have, by hypothesis, from the text it accompanied. Yet we know well enough that there *are* cases—well-known ones—in which we find a disparity between the expressive properties of the music and the mood of the words. It is a longstanding criticism of Haydn's masses that the cheerfulness of the music is often at odds with the somber seriousness of the religious sentiments. *Pace* Hiller, none of the anguish of "Kyrie eleison" has ever rubbed off on the music of the *Missa in Tempore Belli.*

EXAMPLE 24:
Haydn, *Missa in Tempore Belli* (*Paukenmesse*)

Haydn, when asked why his church music was often so light-hearted, is supposed to have replied: "Because whenever I think of my God I laugh with joy." And all the beauty of Haydn's response does not detract from the aesthetic fact that the music of the *Missa in Tempore Belli* is not appropriate to the emotional content of "Kyrie eleison" whereas the music of the *Lord Nelson Mass* (for example) is. So much, I think, for Hiller's notion that music is expressively formless putty that can accommodate itself to the expression of *any* text—which is not to say there is nothing in Hiller's view at all. To the contrary, there is something to his "revolution," for all of that. For we cannot think of the relation of musical expressiveness to text and title as a one-way street, the way the "normal" view has it. Hiller and Beattie are right, I believe, in seeing that the text of a musical setting contributes to the expressiveness of the music; and right, too, in seeing language as, in some sense or other, the "particularizing" ingredient. They simply have the proportions wrong. And I want to go on from here to see if we can get a better "mix" than Hiller and Beattie, while still preserving Hiller's "revolutionary" insight.

◇ 3 ◇   Let me return, now, to the expressive hypothesis I have been trying to peddle in this study. I have suggested that we hear music as expressive (say) of sadness, in many instances—and I am thinking here of "pure" instrumental music—in virtue of its bearing some affinity with the expressive contour of the human voice or body, or in virtue of what I have been calling "conventional" expressive associations. But how "nice" are such distinctions as we can make among the various expressive characters that instrumental compositions can wear? Certainly not so narrow as the distinctions we can make regarding human expression; but certainly not so completely capricious and "subjective" as skeptics like Hanslick and Gurney have tried to make out. The opening bars of Mozart's G-minor Symphony are surely melancholy, or sad, or serious, and certainly not sprightly or gay or exuberant or joyous. The distinctions are rough—but certainly not nonexistent. Thus Hiller and Beattie were quite overstating the case when they represented pure instrumental music as bearing no identifiable expression at all; but they were, on the other hand, correct in perceiving some kind of expressive vacuum, and correct, also, in seeing one of the ways it could be filled.

Alan Tormey speaks of the "expressive ambiguity" of works of art.[12] Pure instrumental music is, to a certain degree, "expressively ambiguous"—that is what Hiller essentially discovered, merely overstating the degree of the ambiguity. Such ambiguity must inevitably result where the expressive cues are limited, as in the case of art works. For the complexity of human expression—the extent of the repertoire, the richness of the circumstances—provides obviously for a more detailed display of expressive features than is possible even in an elaborate work of art. More particularly, Tormey calls attention to the "intentional" context of human expression, which is in sharp contrast to the "intentionless" character of artistic expressiveness. I would like to pursue this point for a moment.

Tormey argues that expression is "intentional," by which he means that "intentionality is characteristic of those states of a person that are expressable and absent from those that are not."[13] Emotions have intentional objects, either real or imagined. I am afraid *of* ghosts, sad *about* the death of my neighbor's dog, depressed *over* my failure to win the Nobel Prize, and so on. And it is the intentional objects of those emotional states—the ghosts, the death of the dog, the failure to win the Prize—that go a long way toward individuating them precisely. It is often what you are angry *about* that tells me what the exact nature of your emotion is; what you are depressed *over* that distinguishes depression as melancholy rather than neurotic morbidity, and so on. But, Tormey argues, art is without intentional objects that make it possible to distinguish these finer shades of expressiveness:

> The expressive "gestures" of art often occur in an aesthetic space devoid of explicit context and intentional objects. And it is the absence or the elusiveness of intentional objects that impedes our critical attempts to dissolve the ambiguity and disclose an unequivocal expressive quality in the art work.[14]

There of course are, at times, intentional contexts given in the *representational* arts. And to the extent that such contexts can uniquely determine the kind of emotions in question, it might seem that expressive ambiguity has been circumvented. But Tormey warns us against drawing such a conclusion; for, he argues, it mistakes the expression of the characters represented for the expressiveness of the art works in which they are represented.

> In works of representational art we can, and should, distinguish between the expressive properties *of* the work and contained or represented expressions *in* the work. . . . It has been said, for example, of Bernini's *David* that it expresses a concentrated and intense determination. But this is misleading. The *work* does not express this, David does. The Bernini work *represents* David-expressing-intense-determination.[15]

I am not altogether comfortable with this; for I think it tries to cut too finely the line between the expressiveness of works and the expressions of the characters represented therein. Surely in very many cases what a represented character is represented as expressing directly contributes to what the work is expressive of. Tormey is certainly correct in forcing us to make the distinction, and warning us that if X represents Y as expressing φ, it does not follow that X is expressive of φ. It does not even follow that representing Y as expressing φ has any tendency at all to contribute to X's being expressive of φ. Nevertheless, it is very often the case that the representation of Y in X as expressing φ does contribute directly to X's being expressive of φ. (One can hardly deny, for example, that Laocoön's anguished expression helps make the *Laocoön* expressive of anguish.) And to the extent that characters' expressions of emotions contribute to the expressiveness of the works in which they are represented—to that extent the intentional context of representational works does help circumvent the expressive ambiguity of art.

However, I do not want to press this general point any further here. Rather, I want to argue a more specific one. I am going to assume, for the sake of this argument, that the intentional context of representational art in general in no way helps to limn in the expressiveness of art works, and for the reason given by Tormey—namely, that to assume otherwise is to confuse the expression of the character with the expressiveness of the work. I shall argue here that in the specific case of musical settings of texts such criticism does not apply. In these instances—or at least in a great many of the most well-known ones—the text does indeed provide an intentionality which serves to particularize the expressiveness of the music because *there is no distinction here between character and work: between expression and expressiveness.*

I can illustrate with an example already alluded to, the "Kyrie eleison" of Haydn's *Lord Nelson Mass*. Imagine I played for you the instrumental introduction, without you knowing it was the "Kyrie" of a mass, and then gave you the following critical "gloss": Expressive of the anguished Christian, in great distress, crying out for mercy and salvation.

EXAMPLE 25:
Haydn, *Lord Nelson Mass*

You would, I suspect, go along with me in describing the music as anguished; and certainly you would at least agree to put the music in the category of the darker emotions, anguish, fear, grief; certainly not in that of good humor, lightheartedness, joy, optimism. But when you hear the chorus come in with its cries of "Kyrie eleison," your perception of the musical expressiveness must surely be altered.

EXAMPLE 26:
Haydn, *Lord Nelson Mass*

For now you hear it as a specifically human utterance; and what is uttered is the Christian cry for mercy and salvation. Add the title to the text—the mass is also known as the *Missa in Angustiis*—and the more specific emotive description now ceases to appear fanciful, or beyond the power of music to satisfy. The text, with its intentional context, has given the music the specificity of expressiveness that, as pure instrumental music, it lacks.

Let me adduce one more example. It has often been remarked that Cherubino's aria, "Non so più," from the first act of *Le Nozze di Figaro*, is a perfect evocation of erotic, adolescent love. The thing has a kind of breathless quality, with Cherubino beginning, impetuously, before there is time for any instrumental introduction. And notice, particularly, those absolutely delicious "interjections" by the winds, like little explosive orgasms, that punctuate the vocal line.

EXAMPLE 27:
Mozart, *Le Nozze di Figaro*, Act I

Now if the music had existed only as an instrumental composition, I am sure we all would consider the description of those wind passages as erotic, or orgasmic, to be pure fantasy—Romantic drivel. But married to that text, and sung by that character, in that dramatic situation, we have all we need in the way of an intentional context to make the description apt; and once one has come to know Cherubino, and *Le Nozze di Figaro*, I think one cannot but hear the music of "Non so più" as erotically amorous, even when performed as an instrumental piece (as it often must have been in the wind-band arrangements which always followed an operatic success).

But, it might be objected, you are forgetting the warning not to confuse characters with works: in these instances, what Cherubino or the utterer of "Kyrie eleison" is represented as expressing with what the music is expressive of. Here, however, it seems to me the warning has no relevance. There is no separation between the expressiveness of the work and what the utterer "expresses." Part of the expressiveness of the work just is the utterance of "Kyrie eleison" by the chorus. There is no "representation" here, as in the case of Bernini's *David*. Vocal music is inevitably heard as human utterance, whether we can actually identify the character, as (say) in Schubert's *Erlkönig* and *Death and the Maiden*, or where there is an "implied" speaker or speakers, as in a Haydn Mass. This is reinforced when one sees the music performed, and can observe the performers "throwing themselves into it," and somewhat discouraged, I suppose, in listening to a recording. In any event, there is little temptation, I think, in many cases anyway, to distinguish between the expression of the musical "speaker" (whether an actual or implied one) and the expressiveness of the musical work. I certainly do not want to say there are no cases when it would be appropriate to make the kind of distinction in music that Tormey makes between what David is expressing and what Bernini's *David* is expressive of. But outside of dramatic representations, the distinction is very difficult to draw. When the "boy" in Schubert's *Erlkönig* expresses fear of the supernatural, he expresses it by singing Schubert's music, which is, I would claim, expressive of this fear partly in virtue of the intentional context Goethe's poem provides. Where, though, can we enter the wedge that will separate what the "boy" is expressing from what the work is expressive of? The work is not merely the piano accompaniment; we cannot say: "The singer portrays a boy expressing fear of the supernatural, but fear of the supernatural is not what the work is expressive of—that is something else again." For the work is the piano accompaniment, *and* the vocal line sung expressively by the baritone portraying a boy expressing fear of the supernatural, *and* Goethe's words—*all* of that is Schubert's work. And the work is expressive of fear of the supernatural in one place just because *all* of those things come together there.

At this point the following objection might be made. The

claim that the *work* is expressive of fear of the supernatural is different from the claim that the *music* is expressive of that. For the song is more than music: it is words as well. So hasn't the subject been changed? It was claimed at the outset that what would be shown is how texts contribute to the expressiveness of *music*. But what has really been shown is how texts contribute to the expressiveness of works of art of which music is a part; and in which the *music* maintains whatever expressiveness it may (or may not) have had apart from the text.

I am inclined to go along with that. What I have shown is how the expressive ambiguity of musical works is circumvented by the addition of text or title, in part by superimposition of an intentional context on an otherwise intentionless medium. I mean by "musical works" such things as sonatas, symphonies, tone poems, songs, masses, motets, operas, oratorios, and any other forms that are commonly thought of as "musical" forms. I do not want to offer a "definition" of "musical form" or "musical work" beyond offering such paradigms, and will only add that there will, of course, be borderline cases, like "melodrama" (the musical accompaniment of spoken words), as well as such things as silent movies with piano accompaniment, where music plays a part, but where we would not, on that account, count the works in question "musical works."

◇ 4 ◇ An account of the relationship between the expressiveness of music and the expressive character of the texts or titles with which it may be associated must deal adequately with four critical "facts" of life: (a) Some musical settings are, by common critical consent, badly suited to the expressive character of their texts: a famous case in point being Gluck's "Che farò senza Euridice" in *Orfeo ed Euridice*. (b) Some musical settings are by common critical consent well suited to the "expression" of their texts. (c) Musicological research, particularly into the music of Bach and Handel, has revealed the re-use of music originally devised for one text, in setting another, with no loss of expressive appropriateness, even when the "expression" of the texts is quite obviously different, as where Handel uses the music of an Italian secular chamber duet to set the words "For unto us a child is born . . ." in *Messiah* (which accounts for the poor musical declamation). (d) There are instances in which the emotive descriptions that critics give of a piece of vocal music go far beyond, in detail, what anyone would accept as a description of "pure" instrumental music, and where the descriptions nevertheless seem appropriate in place. I want to conclude now, as a kind of summary, by going over very briefly the way these four critical "facts" are to be handled on the account I am giving. It is my claim that, of the three accounts I have sketched out here, my own, what I have called the "normal" view, and Hiller's extreme indeterminacy view, only my own will handle them all.

(a) On the "normal" view, the inappropriateness of tone to text is quite handily managed. The composer has simply chosen music with one expressive character to set a text of another incompatible expressive mode. Gluck's music is "happy" music, whereas Calzabigi's text is "sad." On Hiller's view, which might be called the "extreme indeterminacy" view of musical expressiveness, such inappropriateness cannot, apparently, be accounted for at all, as the music is supposed to bear whatever expressive character or mood is possessed by its text, by a kind of osmosis. On my own view, which might be called the "moderate indeterminacy" view, or the "moderate determinacy" view, depending on whether you like to describe your glass as half empty or half full, inappropriateness is seen, as in the "normal" view, to be a mismatch of the expressive character of the music with the expressive character of the text, with the understanding that the expressive character of music alone is rough-hewn in comparison with the fineness of distinctions possible in characterizing the expressions of human beings, or the expressive character of linguistic utterance.

(b) On the "normal" view, of course, the appropriateness of music to text is again easily explained. The composer has chosen music with an expressive character matching that of the text. On Hiller's view, the appropriateness is explained by the text providing the expressive character for the music. And on the "moderate indeterminacy" view, the music roughly matches the text, and the text smooths out the fit.

(c) For the "normal" view, the reuse of music must be a sticky point. It is a view which is endemic to the Romantic movement when, for one thing, little was known about the free use seventeenth- and eighteenth-century composers made, not only of their own previously composed music, but even of the music of other composers. In addition, I suspect the Romantic notion would be that such use of previously composed music in setting a text can never result in the appropriateness of expressive character—a notion which is simply false, on any standard I know by which such things can be measured. As a matter of fact, some of the music of the eighteenth century most admired by the nineteenth for its expressive faithfulness to the text— Gluck's, for example—was just such second-hand property. On the "normal" view, one must either give up "exactness of fit," and argue that music can be re-used, appropriately, for different texts, only because the fit is so loose that it can accommodate many different individuals; or else one must argue with the Romantics that the transference of music from one text to another seldom, if indeed ever, works, being a violation of the muse and a deplorable aspect of "early" vocal music, responsible for much of its lack of expressive integrity—a familiar, but, it seems to me, completely discredited view of seventeenth- and eighteenth-century musical style.

Hiller fares much better in this regard. For he would have no more trouble explaining the expressive fit of the same music to any text you like than explaining how a quart of milk fits variously shaped containers. And that is the *reductio ad absurdum* of his extreme view. My own, more moderate view is that music alone makes rough, but palpable expressive distinctions which texts and titles refine. Unlike the "normal" view, it can accommodate the re-use of music in various expressive contexts, provided they are all similar enough; but, unlike such extreme positions as Hiller's, or Beattie's, it is not so overaccommodating as to allow the music of the Verdi *Requiem* to be appropriate accompaniment for the libretto of *The Student Prince*.

(d) Finally, we have the problem of the more fussy characterizations of musical expressiveness that sometimes irritate the musical purist, but which, I am now beginning to think, are not without some foundation. What account of this phenomenon of "emotive specificity" do we have? The musically hard-boiled might (as I used to do) simply reject such descriptions altogether as critical caprice and musical nonsense. That seems to me now to be counter to common aesthetic experience. But the Romantic notion that music unaided is capable of such fine expressive distinctions *is*, I am certain, critical caprice and musical nonsense. What is left is an account along the lines laid out by Hiller and Beattie in the eighteenth century, suitably modified to give some positive role to music in the demarcation of expressive distinctions, while giving the text the role of "fine tuning."[16] This account, dressed up in the language of intentionality, is what I have tried to develop here.

◊ 5 ◊   A concluding point. I may have left the impression that I believe all music bears some definite expressive character, even though it is a rough one in comparison with the expressions of human beings, or the expressiveness of language. To the contrary, I think a great deal of music bears no recognizable expressive character at all. And when such music accompanies a text, whatever expressive character results must be imparted by the text, much in the way Hiller and Beattie thought happened with all music. And it is this that explains, for example, why the same music may accompany many different verses of a poem, as in the strophic song, without there necessarily being any noticeable inappropriateness of tone to text. Indeed, here it would be a measure of the composer's skill not that he is able to contrive music expressively appropriate to each verse of his poem, which may well be impossible, but that he is able to contrive music of no expressive character whatever, and let his poem do the rest. A great deal of folk music is, I think, of this kind, as are many of the Lutheran chorales and Gregorian chants. Needless to say, this is not the Wagnerian ideal, which probably still dominates the composer of art music, in his attitude toward his text. The musical validity of that ideal of expressive congruence has been a bone of contention in the past, as far back as composers and theorists have pondered over the relation of tone to text. And it still remains a point of division, consciously or unconsciously, in the practice of musical composition, and in the exercise of musical taste.

CHAPTER XI

The Beauty of It All

◇ 1 ◇   The purpose of the present chapter is to develop a possible objection to the general theory of musical expressiveness given in the previous ones, and to essay an answer. The objection, in brief, is that even if the theory of expressiveness proposed is for the most part correct, it is completely trivial. For to call a work of art φ, where "φ" names a nontrivial property, the possession of φ must be directly relevant to our evaluation of that work. But it is not directly relevant to our evaluation, at least of "pure," textless, programless, instrumental music that it does or does not have this or that expressive property: it is not the better or the worse for being sad or cheerful, or any other such thing. Therefore, sadness, and happiness, and other expressive properties of music are trivial properties, and the theory that explains them, a trivial theory—of no importance to the philosophy of art.

This is the objection in brief. But it is not yet clear enough to be dealt with convincingly. We must bring it into sharper focus. However, it might be well to note at the outset that the objection we are developing here is not merely an objection to the theory of musical expressiveness sketched in this book. It is at least a potential objection to any account of what we are up to when we call a piece of music sad or cheerful or whatever. The arousal theory, for instance, which tells us that expressive properties of music are dispositional ones, must also tell us how such dispositional properties can be seen as relevant to the goodness or badness of music before we can grant that such properties are nontrivial. It is perhaps more obvious what line the supporter of the arousal theory might take here. For there are certain states of mind—pleasurable ones, for example—that are immediately seen to be intrinsically valuable, while others are clearly instrumental goods; and music which had the dispositional property of being able to arouse them would be, for that reason, an instrumental good. Both Avison and Webb argue that music can arouse only the pleasurable emotions, never the painful ones.

Thus Avison writes, ". . . I think we may venture to assert, that it is the peculiar quality of Music to raise the *sociable and happy passions*, and to *subdue* the *contrary ones*"; while Webb avers that "if there are passions which come not within the reach of musical expression, they must be such as are totally painful."[1] And it is clear, therefore, what the value of having emotive properties would be, on such theories as these. A piece of music would be the better for having *any* expressive property that such theories allowed, because to the extent that it had it, it would have the power to arouse a pleasurable state of mind in the listener. Pleasure being an intrinsic good, the power to raise it is on that account a good itself, though not, of course, an intrinsic one. But if cheerfulness (say) is an "objective" property of music, not a causal property, it is by no means obvious why music should be the better for having it rather than having no expressive properties at all. We know what is good about a person's being cheerful. But what is good about a theme's being cheerful?

In any event, the relation of expressive features to aesthetic worth *is* a problem for the contour-convention theory. And we must try to make the problem more precise.

There are, to start with, at least two ways in which to state our problem. As I have sketched it out above, it is stated in terms of properties of works of art being of two distinct kinds: those relevant to artistic evaluation and those not relevant, the latter being declared "trivial" on account of their nonrelevance. But to those philosophers who, for one reason or another, have wanted to distinguish between some esoteric "object of art" (an imaginative object, or a phenomenal one) and a physical object (the lump of marble or the pigment on plaster), this might not be seen to be the correct way of presenting the difficulty. What in one view is a distinction between art properties that are, or are not, relevant to the evaluations of art works is, on the other view, a distinction between properties of art works and properties not of art works at all. On the first view, something is a nontrivial property of art works if, and only if, it is a property of art works, and is relevant to their evaluation. On the second, it is a property of art works only if it is relevant to their evaluation. The relevance condition is stated as necessary and sufficient, in the first view, because all I mean by a nontrivial property of an art work is a property of an art work that is valuationally relevant. I state it, in the second view, as merely a necessary condition and leave it an open question whether on all or any such views it is a sufficient condition as well. I imagine it would depend on which particular view of that kind one were talking about.

Those who prefer the second way of formulating the problem are free to make the appropriate "translations" as the argument proceeds. I prefer to go under the assumption that not all properties of art works are necessarily relevant to their evaluations, and state the problem accordingly: Are the expressive features of music trivial or nontrivial features; or, in other words, are they relevant to the evaluation of music, or are they not?

◇ 2 ◇   But before the question is tractable, another difficulty must be confronted. For it is not altogether clear what we mean here by "evaluation." Suppose someone were to say: "This little bronze figurine is better than that porcelain one because its greater weight makes it a much better paperweight. Therefore, physical weight is a nontrivial property of art works, since it is relevant to their evaluation." We would doubtless reply that the valuational relevance we are talking about is relevance to the aesthetic valuation of art, or to its artistic valuation, that is, its valuation *qua* art, and not *qua* paperweight, or whatever. But now, clearly, we have raised a very controversial issue. For exactly *what* it is to evaluate something aesthetically, or *qua* art, is contested territory. I am not even sure the example of the paperweight is a completely unproblematic one. Is the beauty of a Shaker chair, for instance, completely divorced from its function as something to sit on? And isn't a paperweight simply a more mundane example of the same kind of thing? Weight, therefore, would seem to be just as much a potential reason for valuing a work of art as unity or balance.

This is not the place to take on these very basic and crucial questions in the philosophy of art. But it is at least the appropriate place to bring them out into the open, in order to formulate the present problem in such a way as not to beg any important questions, or ignore them either.

We are faced with the problem of deciding whether or not the presence of expressive properties in music is relevant to the *aesthetic* or *artistic* evaluation of the music. If it is not, then expressive properties are trivial ones—as foreign to our appreciation of music as its power (say) to remind me of my high-school Latin teacher. (For reasons that are too boring to relate, Handel's *Judas Maccabaeus* does in fact remind me of my high-school Latin teacher.) But, clearly, we will not have an adequate idea of what solving this problem entails until we have some idea of what aesthetic or artistic evaluation might be. And as the operative words here are "artistic" and "aesthetic," we must give them at least a brief look.

Let me suggest, first, that the word "aesthetic," when used in the phrase "aesthetic evaluation," has a wide sense at some times, and a narrow sense at others. And I am thinking, now, only of evaluations of works of art, not of sunsets or sunflowers. In the narrow sense of "aesthetic," aesthetic evaluation tends to mean evaluation of the "sensual" and "structural" properties of art works: the sounds of words, the vividness of colors, the structure of a play, the thematic unity of a symphony, and so on. On that construal, the importance or significance (say) of the theme of *Paradise Lost* is not part of its *aesthetic* value.

Now there are those who tend to use the word "aesthetic" in this narrow sense, and who also conflate it with the term "artistic," so that to evaluate a work of art *qua* work of art *is* to evaluate it aesthetically, to evaluate it only with regard to those features I have called "sensual" and "structural." (This is not to say, of course, that works of art are the only things that can be evaluated aesthetically.) The importance of the theme of *Paradise Lost*, according to this usage, is a question of philosophical evaluation, perhaps, but not artistic evaluation—which is evaluation only of the aesthetic features of the poem narrowly conceived.

A second way of using the "aesthetic"/"artistic" pair is to narrowly construe "aesthetic," but to construe "artistic" more widely, so that the class of properties relevant to the artistic evaluation of art works is larger than the class of aesthetic properties of art works, all aesthetic properties, however, being relevant to artistic evaluation, the evaluation of art *qua* art. On this construal, the importance of the theme of *Paradise Lost* would be acknowledged not to be an aesthetic property of the poem, but would be judged relevant to its evaluation as a work of art.

Finally, there is a tendency, I think, on the part of some critics and commentators, to use "aesthetic" and "artistic" interchangeably (as applied to works of art), and to construe *both* rather widely. Using them in this way, the importance of the theme of *Paradise Lost*, or the fact that Dickens' novels portray accurately some of the deplorable aspects of nineteenth-century English life, will at times be called "aesthetic" aspects of the respective works and will be thought of as quite properly "artistic" aspects as well. Artistic and aesthetic evaluations will, of course, be one and the same thing, as applied to works of art (although works of art will not be the only things to which the predicate "aesthetic" can apply).

Ordinary language, whatever it is worth as a guide in making such distinctions, does not seem to be very much of a guide here.[2] And, it appears to me, the only way to clarify things for our purposes, short of pursuing the aesthetic and the artistic to the bitter end, is simply to stipulate from the start how one is going to use the terms "aesthetic" and "artistic," and the phrases "aesthetic evaluation" and "artistic evaluation." My own intuition (for whatever *that* is worth) is that there *is* a basic distinction, worth preserving, between the aesthetic and the artistic in our talk about art. I shall, therefore, construe "aesthetic" narrowly, "artistic" widely, and hold that all aesthetic properties are relevant to the evaluation of art works *qua* art works, but that they are not the only ones that are. I will reserve the description "aesthetic evaluation" for those evaluations of art works that concern the "sensual" and "structural" properties. I will reserve the description "artistic evaluation" for those evaluations of art works that concern any relevant properties other than the aesthetic. And my blanket description for all relevant evaluations of art, either aesthetic or artistic (as defined above), will be "evaluation of art *qua* art" or "as art."

At this point it is possible to reformulate our original problem with more precision. The question it poses is: Are the expressive properties of music relevant to the evaluation of music *qua* music (i.e. *qua* art)? And this can now be seen to comprise two related questions: First, are the expressive properties of music relevant to its *aesthetic* evaluation? Second, are the expressive properties of music relevant to its *artistic* evaluation?

◇ 3 ◇   Thus stated, the two-part question raises another: Does music have any artistic—that is, nonaesthetic—values at all? It is said that all the other arts aspire to music. This suggests that music is the paradigm of *aesthetic* art—that it possesses only structural and sensual properties and nothing more, no subject matter. It expresses no ideas, argues no points, teaches no lessons, communicates no messages, paints no pictures. To say, then, that the other arts aspire to music is to say that they aspire to achieve just that pure aesthetic character; they wish, in other words, to divest themselves, as much as is possible, of what I have been calling "artistic" properties, retain and develop only the "aesthetic," the sensual and structural. Whether it is true that all the other arts aspire to the art of music is irrelevant to our concerns. But that aspiring to music is, ipso facto, aspiring to the purely aesthetic, is, if true, of the utmost importance to the argument of this chapter. For it implies two things: first, that expressive properties of music cannot be relevant to the artistic evaluation of music (since there are no artistic values associated with it, it being a purely aesthetic art); and, second, that expressive properties are themselves suspect as properties of music because they immediately suggest something beyond the purely aesthetic—beyond, that is, the sensual and the structural.

With regard to the first implication, the reply might be that whether music is a purely aesthetic art is itself debatable. After all, there is program music; and there have in the past been claims, ranging from the trivial to the modest to the extravagant, as to the "meaning" music has and the information it conveys.

But whether music is or is not a purely aesthetic art is a debate I do not wish to enter; for I want the argument of this book to be invariant with its outcome. I shall, therefore, shun any attempt to show that expressive features of music are relevant to artistic evaluations of it. Whether it has nonaesthetic properties I leave an open question. What I do claim is that to describe music in expressive terms is *not* necessarily to bring in extra-aesthetic considerations. To claim otherwise is to misunderstand the aesthetic or to confuse the present theory of musical expressiveness with others in which the nonaesthetic is of necessity brought in.

To begin with, it is frequently the case that the statement "The music is φ," where "φ" is an emotive term, is thought to be identical with, or imply, the statement "The music is *about* φ," or something else of the kind. And once this illicit move is made, we have already taken music out of the realm of the purely aesthetic. Thus, by way of illustration, Albert Schweitzer, having come to the conclusion that Bach associated certain readily identifiable musical figures with certain emotions expressed in his texts, and, finding these same figures in his instrumental music, came to the further conclusion that the emotive life is what the music is *about*; that Bach's sonatas, for instance, "*depict* soul-states and inner experiences [of Bach, presumably], . . ."[3] a conclusion that is certainly unwarranted. Whether or not music can be about *anything* is a question I prefer not to raise here at all. But that sad music must be about sadness is, it seems to me, completely wrong. To claim that music can sometimes be sad is not the same thing as to claim that it can sometimes be *about* sadness; nor does the one imply the other. The subject of a fugue may be sad, but that is not to say that the subject of the fugue is sadness.

Again, it seems that emotive descriptions of music are a temptation to make "meaning" claims for it. The theme is sad; therefore, it *means* "sadness." Whether or not bringing meaning into the musical context is necessarily bringing in the nonaesthetic is another question I will quite happily avoid. For since the present theory of musical expressiveness is not a semantic theory, the question need not arise for us. The Saint Bernard's face does not mean "sadness" but possesses it. A sad theme does not mean "sadness"; it is expressive of it, and the sadness is a "sensual" property of the music. To describe music in emotive terms is to attribute properties to it. Without subscribing to Charles Hartshorne's elaborate metaphysics of qualities, we accept his general characterization of the relation to color and sound of their expressiveness: "the emotional tonality is a part or aspect of the color or sound quality. . . ."[4]

Finally, we might remind ourselves that mistaking the present account for an arousal theory will also bring the emotive out of the realm of the aesthetic. For whatever virtue there might be in music's arousing sadness, it does not appear to be an "aesthetic" virtue. It has nothing to do with the sensual and structural, but rather with a causal property the music has. But, again, our account explicitly disavows the theory of emotive arousal, and is free, therefore, of such unpalatable implications.

◇ 4 ◇   Having cast aside, then, the question of whether the emotive features of music are relevant to its artistic evaluation, we are left with the question of their relevance to the aesthetic. And having seen that emotive features are not, ipso facto, nonaesthetic ones according to our account of them, we can go on to answer the question of evaluative relevance. Are expressive properties of music aesthetic good-making ones? And if so, why?

It is obvious, on first reflection, that expressive properties of music have a direct bearing on its *appropriateness* in opera, oratorio, lieder—in any instance, in fact, in which words are set, dramatic situations represented, or functions performed. Sad words need a sad song; and if I order a funeral march, I will not be satisfied with a quick march, no matter how good the music. And as, just as obviously, appropriateness is a value, it is clear that emotive properties are far from irrelevant to matters of musical evaluation. The question is: What kind of value is at stake here? Is it *musical* value in the sense of aesthetic value of music *qua* music? What I have in mind is the following kind of riposte. "You promised to show us how expressive qualities are relevant to the aesthetic evaluation of music, the evaluation of music *qua* music. But what you have shown us, instead, is their relevance to music *qua* opera, or *qua* oratorio, or *qua* institutional artifact, intended to perform a specific function in our lives. And although these are art forms, certainly, they are not purely musical art forms but mixed ones, in which music, to be sure, plays a prominent role. You have shown us that expressive properties of music are nontrivial properties of textual settings, and music with specific institutional functions, not nontrivial properties of pure music."

I think there is some justice in this objection. It is certainly true that sadness is a good-making feature of a musical setting of "Requiem aeternam" and a bad-making one of "Gloria in excelsis Deo," because, clearly, sadness is appropriate to the first and not the second. But we want more than that, I suspect; we want to know whether sadness, of itself, is a good-making feature of a violin sonata, or a symphony. And if it is not, we are inclined to wonder how sadness then can be an interesting property of music, or why music critics should waste so much time talking about how sad this sonata, or that symphony, is.

There is one point to notice straightaway: critical language, and even our everyday talk about music, seem to assume the relevance of expressive properties to musical value. And that is not, by any means, a thing of no account. When the analyst or critic remarks on the sadness of a theme, it is not in the spirit of a value-free utterance. Quite to the contrary. One calls a theme sad, more often than not, in a manner charged with positive valuational implications, as: "How very sad!," meaning, "How wonderfully sad!," not "Ho hum, it's sad." When H. C. Robbins Landon, in discussing Beethoven's early Viennese compositions, says, "we would point to a strong characteristic of Beethoven's music at this period, and in particular of the slow movements; and that is a yearning quality which fills the music, often nearly to the emotional bursting point,"[5] the remark is far from a neutral one. We cannot understand it as anything but a positive evaluation. Implicit in it is the suggestion that one of the splendid qualities of this music is its "yearning quality"; that it is splendid music, in part, because of what Robbins Landon calls its "great emotional *density*,"[6] to which the "yearning quality" contributes. Emotive descriptions of music are almost invariably offered as praise. To construe the remark, "How intensely sad!" when made of a musical theme, as anything but a positive evaluation, or grounds for one, would be as implausible as construing negatively or neutrally Sir Anthony Absolute's exclamations over Miss Lydia Languish in *The Rivals*: "Nay, but, Jack, such eyes! such eyes! . . ."

Further, it is clear that the closely related predicate "expressive" bears the same evaluative implications. "Too expressive" is, indeed, a perfectly intelligible remark. But it is not a remark that goes trippingly on the tongue. Whereas "How expressive!" is a common enough compliment to rank as an honorific cliché.

There are, it would appear, two ways in which the word "expressive" is used to describe art works *by itself*—that is, not in company with some specific emotive predicate, as in "expressive of sorrow," or "expressive of yearning," or whatever. One way is simply for the purpose of indicating that an art work is expressive of a great many particular emotions. Thus, if a symphony is expressive of sorrow here, yearning there, joy in another place, it is a particularly *expressive* symphony. When Robbins Landon described Beethoven's early Viennese music as of "great emotional density," he was holding it up for praise because it is expressive of "yearning," and other specific emotions; and he might have said the very same thing by remarking that the music is "expressive" to a high degree.

There is, however, a second use of "expressive" by itself which is not quite the same. When we say "Expressive!" in the first sense, we always have ready to hand an answer to the question "Expressive of *what*?" "Expressive of yearning, expressive of sorrow, . . ." and so on; and "expressive" used alone in this sense is simply short for "expressive of this, expressive of that," etc. But sometimes in music, as in life, we want to call attention to a "passion without a name." Sometimes a piece of music strikes us as being emotionally charged to a high degree, yet not expressive *of* anything specific. In such instances, we are going to describe the music as "Expressive!" and not be prepared to answer the question "Expressive of *what*?" Nevertheless, "expressive" in the second use, as well as in the first, is a value-laden term. And that is the important point to notice.

The argument with which we are dealing is to the effect that the mere possession of expressive properties by music of itself cannot plausibly count as value tending (either pro or anti). What can possibly be good (or bad) about a theme's being sad or happy or yearning or not being expressive of anything at all? How can the presence of such features matter *in itself* to musical worth? We can now see that the antiexpressionist is not on such firm ground as we thought. Indeed, it seems more incumbent upon *him* to explain how it is that expressiveness in music *is not* relevant to aesthetic worth than for *us* to explain how it *is*. For the data of musical discourse are quite against him. We all seem to talk about music as if the mere statement "It's expressive of φ," where "φ" names an emotion, were a positive evaluation, or grounds for one, as we do also when we use "expressive" alone in either of the two senses distinguished above. It may well be that our discourse is misleading or misled in this regard. But I would think that it is innocent until proven guilty, rather than the other way around. We have at least prima facie evidence that the expressive properties of music are nontrivial in the fact that musical discourse treats their presence not only as relevant to the aesthetic value of music but, in effect, tantamount to it.

It would appear, then, that what musical discourse suggests is just what we found initially puzzling, and what the antiexpressionist exploited: namely, that the mere presence of expressive properties in music is a good-making feature. This is not to say, of course, that the possession of one or more expressive properties is either a necessary or a sufficient condition for musical success. A musical composition can be expressive and bad, inexpressive and good; a musical composition can be more expressive than some other, but worse music. A Stamitz as well as a Haydn can write a sad tune; and a good deal of Stravinsky's finest works are intentionally written in a dry, expressionless style obviously in rebellion against *fin de siècle* Romanticism. What is being maintained is that the presence of expressive features always seems to be mentioned with intent to praise. And, further, if an expressive property is possessed to an intense enough degree, an overall negative evaluation seems to be precluded. Consider, by way of illustrating the last point (which is an important one), how very odd it would be to say: "How full of joy Haydn's chamber music is! Horrible stuff!" or "What depths of melancholy are plumbed in the second movement of the *Eroica*! Dreadful piece!"

◇ 5 ◇   Now were we to leave the argument here, we, and our opponent, would be at a stand off. Certainly, our position would be no weaker than his. For while he insisted that there is no obvious connection between being φ and being good music, where "φ" names an expressive property of music, we would insist that whether or not there is an obvious connection, whether or not we understand thoroughly what is going on, the learned as well as the vulgar go on their unconcerned way, forever talking about, and criticizing music *as if* the mere possession of φ were prima facie grounds for a positive evaluation; indeed, as if saying "It is φ" were tantamount to praise.

Fortunately for our position, however, we do not have to leave the argument where it is, due to some very ingenious observations by Guy Sircello in his book, *A New Theory of Beauty*, which makes it apparent that expressive properties are not by any means alone in their value-function; and that what we have observed about them can be seen to fit into a very general theory of the beautiful, valid for *all* properties. I should like to conclude the present chapter by sketching out Sircello's views briefly, and showing how they lend further support, if they are correct, to my claim here that expressive properties are not trivial properties of music.

Sircello's "new theory of beauty" (as he describes it) is based on what he calls "properties of qualitative degree": PQDs, for short. There are two necessary conditions for being a PQD. The first is that the property in question be able to be possessed to a greater or lesser degree. Thus *squareness* (in the strict Euclidean sense) cannot be a PQD because there are no degrees of squareness:

something either is a square or it is not. But the *vividness* (say) of a color is a PQD because (in part) it is susceptible of degrees: something can be more or less vivid a green than something else. The second necessary condition is that the degree to which a PQD is possessed must *not* be realizable in a single numerical scale enabling one to say: *A* is more φ than *B* by *x* amount, or some such thing. Thus *heat*, although susceptible of degrees, is not a PQD because it fails to fulfill the second necessary condition.

PQDs themselves can be divided into two categories: those that are properties of deficiency or lack (i.e. blemishes), and those that are not. And those that are properties of deficiency or lack can be further subdivided into those that are universally such, and those that are such only relative to a given context. So *rottenness* is a universal lack or deficiency, but *roughness* is not; for there are no objects or entities in which rottenness is anything but a defect, whereas there are some things in which roughness is a defect (say, the surface of a polished table) and some in which it is not (say, the surface of a fieldstone fireplace).

With these preliminaries out of the way, we can now go straight to Sircello's theory which, succinctly stated, is this: "*A PQD of an 'object' is beautiful if and only if (1) it is not a property of deficiency, lack, or defect, (2) it is not a property of the 'appearance' of deficiency, lack, or defect, and (3) it is present in that 'object' in a very high degree; and any 'object' that is not a PQD is beautiful only if it possesses . . . at least one PQD present in that 'object' to a very high degree.*"[7]

Rather than go into a lengthy account of the arguments and observations whereby Sircello supports his theory, let us try to unpack this rather dense statement of it intuitively, by the use of an example. Suppose I have a piece of petrified wood of a beautiful polished smoothness. In *smoothness*, let us say, for argument's sake, we have a PQD. (Whether this really is a PQD need not concern us here as it is merely for illustrative purposes.) It is beautiful, according to Sircello's formula, solely in virtue of its extreme degree—nothing else. The petrified wood is beautiful in respect of smoothness, because it possesses smoothness to a very high degree. Does it follow that the petrified wood is beautiful? It does not. For although the smoothness of the wood might be beautiful, the color, say, or the pattern on the surface might be inferior. So "we cannot conclude that an 'object' is beautiful (*simpliciter*) from the fact that it is beautiful with respect to something."[8] The petrified wood may be beautiful with respect to smoothness, but not necessarily beautiful petrified wood. So far, then, Sircello's new theory of beauty seems to capture our intuitions about the individual case.

What, now, of a piece of petrified wood that is *porous* to a very high degree? Is it beautiful with respect to *porousness*? Our intuition tells us no; yet, after all, porousness might be a PQD. But here condition (1) of Sircello's formula has not been satisfied, for porousness is a defect in specimens of petrified wood. Nor would it help if we found out that the wood were not really porous but merely appeared so, for then condition (2) would not be satisfied. And, again, our intuition is supported, for we feel that it is absurd to think of the wood as beautiful in respect to porousness; and we feel, too, that its appearing porous is as much a defect as its being so. Our former case, however—beautiful with respect to smoothness—fulfills both conditions, for smoothness in petrified wood is neither a defect nor the appearance of one.

In general, what Sircello has observed, and attempted to formulate analytically, is a kind of regressive process that begins with an observation like "It is beautiful," or "It is beautifully φ" (which is to say "It is beautiful with respect to φ") and eventually concludes with "It is beautiful because it is so ψ"; and when that point is reached, we have a PQD. The *ultimate* justification for an ascription of beauty is simply that something is present to a very high degree. Thus, Cynthia might be beautiful because of her beautiful hair, beautiful eyes, and beautiful skin; her hair might be beautiful because of its beautiful highlights, her eyes because of their beautiful luster, her skin because of its beautiful smoothness; but, finally, the highlights of her hair are beautiful just in virtue of their presence to a very high degree, the luster of her eyes beautiful just in virtue of its presence to a very high degree, the smoothness of her skin beautiful just in virtue of its presence to a very high degree.

◇ 6 ◇   Without further ado we can now face the issue at hand, which is, of course, expressiveness in music. We have observed that the possession of expressive properties is treated, in and of itself, as a merit in musical compositions. Sircello's theory, if it is correct, helps to remove some of the mystery from this. For if expressive properties are PQDs that fulfill conditions (1) and (2), their being treated, when possessed in a very high degree, as musical merits, is just what one would expect. Far from being unique and strange in this respect, and therefore suspect, expressive properties would be seen to be just another group of PQDs, *all* of which function in the same way.

Are expressive properties PQDs? There seems no reason to think otherwise, and Sircello treats them as such. That being the case, they must fall also into one or other of the two categories of PQDs, namely, those that are, and those that are not properties of lack or deficiency. And, of course, only the latter are capable of being beautiful PQDs. Thus Sircello observes:

> We have no trouble imagining a beautiful serenity or calmness come over a person, which is to say, a kind of radiant and all-encompassing serenity or calmness. One can see a beautiful joy come into a person's face, a joy that completely takes over the face, transforming it and banishing every trace of darkness. Beautiful despondency or brutality, however, are impossible. The reason is that they constitute defects in a person; the despondent or brutal person has lost control.[9]

It would appear, then, if Sircello's observation is correct, that expressive properties fall into both groups of PQDs, some being properties of deficiency or lack, and some not: therefore, some potentially beautiful and some not.

But at this juncture a problem seems to arise—not a new one in the history of theories of musical expression, and one which, in a slightly different form, we have already thrown up to the propounders of expression as arousal. Conditions (1) and (2) place very definite limits on what expressive properties can be construed as beautiful—namely, those that are not lacks, defects, or appearances of them. Yet discourse about music seems to place *no* limits at all on what expressive properties can count as aesthetically valuable. For just as "How full of joy Haydn's 'Emperor' Quartet is!" constitutes praise, so also, it would seem, does the far from unlikely remark, "How splendidly brutal the *Grosse Fuge!*" Yet brutality, as Sircello remarks, is a defect, and, hence, cannot be a beautiful PQD of a person. How, then, can it be one in a string quartet? And has not Sircello's theory therefore failed to do justice to the variety of our discourse about the expressive properties of music?

A number of possible answers suggest themselves. Sircello, who himself recognizes the problem, observes that in some cases at least, it is not the expressive property itself that is beautiful, but the *way* it is handled by the artist. So, of what he calls "the hysterical anger of Donna Elvira of Act I, Scene ii of *Don Giovanni*," and "the bitter, snarling anger of Elektra in the Strauss opera," Sircello observes: "No doubt there is beauty in the . . . two, yet it is not the portrayed anger that is beautiful, but the penetration and skill with which the composers expressed, respectively, hysterical anger and bitter anger."[10] We may add to this explanation that not only are the portrayals of anger here beautifully carried off, but also beautifully appropriate to the characters and dramatic situations. And as far as it goes, this explanation serves well enough. But it does not really go far enough. For the brutality of the *Grosse Fuge*, unlike the anger of Elvira and Elektra, is not *portrayed*, but *presented: exhibited*. The *Grosse Fuge* does not represent brutality; it is expressive of the emotion in the sense of "expressive" we have carefully laid out in the preceding chapters. Nor, of course, in a pure instrumental composition like the *Grosse Fuge* can there be any question of appropriateness, as there is no text, no character, no dramatic situation, no "program" for the expressiveness to be appropriate to.

A second possibility presents itself in the form of the eighteenth-century distinction between the beautiful and sublime, or something, anyway, along those general lines. For Sircello, of course, has given us a theory of *beauty*. And although such properties as brutality might not be "beautiful" properties, might they not be "sublime" ones? The purpose of the distinction between the sublime and the beautiful was, after all, at least so far as we are able to determine, to accommodate certain kinds of natural and art objects that eighteenth-century connoisseurs were beginning to find "aesthetically" satisfactory, but which did not fit into the Neoclassical canon of beauty and good taste. Sircello does not want to go this route, maintaining that "the sublime is in fact a species of beauty," namely, a very high degree of it, since, as he observes, "while 'beautifully sublime' is redundant, 'sublimely beautiful' is not, because 'beautiful' is the more general and 'sublime' the more specific term."[11]

Sircello's argument here is not altogether persuasive. The fact that "sublimely beautiful" works, and "beautifully sublime" does not, need not drive us to Sircello's conclusion. It might still be the case that "beautiful" and "sublime" describe quite different kinds of properties, yet because of the kinds of properties they describe, "sublime" might be a proper modifier of "beautiful" and not the other way around. Both "beautiful" and "sublime" are, of course, honorific terms: they have strong evaluative components of a positive nature. But what the nature of those components is—and how the respective terms can be used to evaluate—has to do with the kinds of qualities described: the respective evaluative components derive their specific linguistic characters from the descriptive meanings of "beautiful" and "sublime."

The many eighteenth-century attempts to characterize the distinction between the beautiful and the sublime have one thing more or less in common. To put it in the crudest possible way, they tend to connect the beautiful with the small and perfect and harmonious, the sublime with the large, the massive, the powerful, the overwhelming.[12] Here, for instance, is Addison's characterization of the sublime, at the beginning of the eighteenth century:

> Our imagination loves to be filled with an object, or to grasp at any thing that is too big for its capacity. We are flung into a pleasing astonishment at such unbounded views, and feel a delightful stillness and amazement in the soul at the apprehension of them.[13]

And here is Kant's, at the end of the century: "The beautiful in nature is a question of the form of the object, and this consists in limitation, whereas the sublime is to be found in an object even devoid of form, so far as it immediately involves, or else by its presence provokes, a representation of *limitlessness*. . . ."[14] The affinity is obvious.

Now *if* this distinction is more or less correct, it seems clear why we can call something "sublimely beautiful" but not "beautifully sublime." For to call something "sublimely beautiful" is to trade on the fact that sublime things are large, powerful, overwhelming, limitless, and so forth. When we say that something is sublimely beautiful, we are saying that it possesses beauty to a very great degree—to the degree that makes the quantity of beauty comparable to the size or extent of something truly sublime. The value component of "sublime" is parasitic on the fact that the sublime is the great, the massive, the powerful, etc. We cannot reverse the procedure because the value component of "beautiful" derives from a descriptive meaning which makes it, as an evaluative, incompatible with the meaning of "sublime." That is why "beautifully sublime" has something of the quality of an oxymoron, like "pretty ugly," whereas "sublimely beautiful" does not. To call something "sublimely beautiful" is to say that its beauty is as great as an object would be if it were sublime. But to call something "beautifully sublime" would be to say that its sublimity is as minutely perfect or harmonious as an object would be were it beautiful (or some such thing, depending upon exactly how one construed the distinction between the sublime and the beautiful). This would not be a contradictory thing to say, any more than it is a contradiction to call someone "pretty ugly." It is merely "odd"—linguistically inappropriate. A beautiful object, on these eighteenth-century views, cannot be sublime, any more than a sublime object can be beautiful. But we can call an object *very* beautiful by calling it sublimely beautiful, because we can trade on the notion of magnitude inherent in sublimity. However, there is no reciprocal trade that can be made to praise the sublime in terms of the beautiful.

Finally, it would be well to remind ourselves of the difference between expressing an emotion and being expressive of one, for there is a logical disanalogy here that might have some bearing on the problem at hand. Despondency is a defect in people, and my expressing despondency is logically dependent upon my being despondent. But music expressive of despondency is not despondent music, in the sense in which a person can be said to be despondent. It is being despondent the way a person is that is a defect of whatever is capable of being despondent in that way. But it is another question whether being despondent in the way that music is, is a defect in whatever is capable of being that. Nor should we confuse being expressive of despondency with appearing despondent, thus making despondent music fail of being beautiful in respect to despondency by failing to fulfill condition (2) above. Expressing despondency implies being despondent, but being expressive of despondency does not; and when music is called "despondent," therefore, it is only in a short-hand sense. The conclusion that φ is a defect is not to be misunderstood as the conclusion that being expressive of φ is also. And thus the possibility is left open that music can be beautifully φ, where φ is *any* emotion whatever, since for music to be beautifully φ is not for it to be φ but only for it to be expressive of φ—"φ" only in that sense.

But perhaps this may seem merely a logical subterfuge. And perhaps Sircello is correct in thinking that the sublime is not a separate category but merely an extreme case of the beautiful. So let us assume the worst, which is that there are limits on what expressive properties can be good-making features of pure music; and that the limits correspond to Sircello's distinction between PQDs that are not, and those that are, lacks or blemishes; further, that the class of emotions that are defects when possessed by people are also defects when possessed as expressive features by music. Even so, our theory of musical expressiveness is in far better shape than (say) the arousal theory, which was forced, in the eighteenth century, to deny that any but the "pleasant" emotions could be "expressed" by music (in spite of clear evidence to the contrary), and more recently has been obliged to employ all sorts of doubtful psychological expedients to show how painful emotions can really be pleasant too, while, at the same time, remaining the same emotions—a parlor trick that invariable breaks the egg in the hat. Nor is it difficult to see why the present theory comes off better. For the number of emotions that are painful or unpleasant is far larger than the number of emotions that are defects. It is unpleasant to experience sadness, but by no means a defect in character to experience it in the proper circumstances; quite to the contrary. And a face beautifully transfigured by sadness is an uncommon occurrence neither in life nor in art. So while the arousal theory, for example, is committed to excluding from music *all* of the "dark," unpleasant emotions, or else declaring them bad-making features, because it can provide no plausible explanation of why we should seek out and value music which "expresses"—i.e. arouses—them, the present theory would be obliged to exclude only those that are PQDs of deficiency or lack.

Perhaps, then, we *are* misled *somewhat* by musical discourse, if it suggests that every expressive property is a good-making feature, a "beauty." Perhaps the *Grosse Fuge* is the worse for its brutality. (It certainly always has been a problematic and controversial work, far from popular—it even troubled Beethoven.) Or, perhaps, what we take for its brutality might better be described as "vitality" or "energy" (if that does not suggest a kind of special pleading). In any case, even if we must acknowledge a limit to what music can be expressive of "beautifully," the repertoire of expressiveness remains a large one, large enough, I think, to present a fairly convincing, and far from poverty-stricken, picture of musical expressiveness in the West.

◇ 7 ◇   The argument of the present chapter has been to show that expressive properties of music are nontrivial ones—that is, properties that are directly relevant to its evaluation *qua* music. Further, it has been argued that the relation between possessing an expressive property and musical value is direct, the value increasing as the degree of the expressive property (all other things being equal). Where φ is an expressive property, the greater the degree of φ-ness in a musical entity X, the greater the musical value or beauty of X; and the more beautifully φX is. This should not, however, be misunderstood to mean that music cannot be beautiful if it is not expressive of some emotion or other, or that it must be beautiful if it is, or that a piece X that is more expressive of φ than a piece Y is more beautiful than Y, it being merely more beautifully φ than Y. Expressiveness is just one of the beauties of music, and the ability to make music that is intensely expressive just one musical ability among others. No one in the eighteenth century could surpass Gluck for sheer expressiveness; yet as great a composer as Gluck was, no one would rank him as the equal of Haydn or Mozart.

◇ 8 ◇   Now it may seem, at this point, that the whole argument of the present chapter is pinned on a rather speculative, and far from firmly established, theory; and that if that theory should fall, the nontriviality of expressive properties of music would fall with it. I do not think this is the case. For even if Sircello's new theory of beauty should prove false or inadequate, it will nevertheless have drawn attention to the fact that in many cases, at least, we do ascribe beauty to objects in virtue alone of their possessing some property or other to a very high degree. That is to say, even if Sircello's account is not a successful account of beauty *tout court*, it does reveal that a wide variety of judgments to the effect that something is beautiful are supported by judgments to the effect that something has some property—the one it is beautiful in respect to—to a very high degree. Given, then, that the expressive properties of music are, in fact, treated in the way of Sircello's theory would predict, and given that they are far from being the only qualities treated in this way, there is no reason to think of them as in any way unique in this regard. It may not be clear *why* having expressive qualities to a very high degree is a good-making (or beauty-making) feature of music, just as, if Sircello's theory turns out to be wrong, it may not be clear why having a great many other qualities to a very high degree should make objects beautiful. But it *is* clear that we do not claim for expressive properties any more than aesthetic discourse apparently claims for many properties in virtue of which objects are said to be beautiful. Were expressive properties singular in this respect, it might be cause to question their nontriviality, and to be suspicious of critical discourse that assumed it. (After all, it could well be argued, there is plenty of nonsense in criticism, and we need not take *everything* the critic says seriously.) However, that they are behaving very like other properties should lead us to suspect that even if we do not have an adequate account of the significance of this behavior, our theory of musical expressiveness is supported by the fact that in demanding such behavior of expressive properties, it is not demanding something of them out of the ordinary or foreign to aesthetic intuition.

CHAPTER XII

How to Emote over Music (Without Losing Your Respectability)

◇ 1 ◇ We began with a "paradox"; not a formal one, of course, but rather a problem about our descriptions of music: that they seem to be intelligible at the cost of being inaccessible to all but the musically expert; or accessible to the layman, at the cost, at least according to the expert, of being either nonsense, or subjective reverie. I claimed that a humanistic musical analysis could be reconstituted and made respectable once again in the form of the familiar emotive characterization of music— but only if two things were established: first, how it makes sense to apply expressive predicates to music (which answers the charge of unintelligibility); and, second, what the public, inter-subjective criteria of application are (which answers the charge of subjectivity).

The general argument of the book so far has directly answered the charge of unintelligibility. But what of the charge of subjectivity? Is it merely a matter of personal quirk whether a portion of music is characterized by one emotive epithet rather than another? I have suggested in the foregoing that there are intersubjective criteria for the application of emotive terms to music, parasitic on the criteria involved in human expression— the criteria, that is, that warrant our conclusions about the emotions expressed by human beings. I have suggested, too, that musical expressiveness is in part a "conventional" matter. However, both of these claims require spelling out before we can consider the answer to the charge of subjectivity complete. This will be the task of the concluding chapter. I begin, for convenience sake, with the second claim.

◇ 2 ◇ In what sense does expressiveness "by convention" deserve to be called "objective"? To answer that question we must add a word or two to what has already been said about it. What *is* expressiveness by convention *exactly*? What sense (or use) of "convention" is involved? The word, after all, covers a variety of cases.

I would like to distinguish here what seem to me to be two senses (or uses) of the term "convention," which I shall call the "rule-governed" and the "association-governed." (Obviously, I am far from advancing this as an exhaustive set of distinctions.) It is a "convention" that we drive on the left; and it is a matter of "convention" that we use the bread-and-butter plate to our left, and the drinking glasses to our right. Both are conventions I would like to call "rule-governed," differing in that in the former case the rule is written down and officially promulgated, whereas in the latter the rule is informally held, and passed on by word of mouth and social example. There is, however, a sense (or use) of "convention" in which something is thus-and-so "by convention," through traditional associations of one kind or another, as, for example, where the perceptual impressions that certain costumes or items of clothing make are due to the circumstances in which they are worn: the top hat and mourning coat, the straw boater, etc. It is not that dress clothes and straw hats "mean" anything; nor is it completely (or in many cases even primarily) intrinsic to the materials and shapes that they are (so to speak) "naturally" thus-and-so. Where they are customarily worn, and under what circumstances—these associations have given such things a palpable quality which is a major part of our perception of them—the emotive aura, or quality of mood that surrounds them. Perhaps it is a misnomer to call this kind of thing having some perceptual quality "by convention." If so, then "convention," as I have used it here, is a term of art. In any event, it is in this sense of "convention" and not in the rule-governed sense that I have claimed music can be expressive "by convention."

These expressive musical "conventions" are more pervasive than one might initially think; and if I have lavished more attention on "contour" than on "convention," it is not because I think the contribution of the latter to musical expressiveness is any the less. There are association-governed conventions that, for example, deeply influence our perception of orchestration: the romantically "outdoor" quality of the horn and "horn-fifths," imparted by the association with the hunt; the "peasant" quality of the oboe, when accompanied (as Haydn likes to do) with a drone, by virtue of its resemblance to the bagpipe; the "martial" quality of the trumpet (so ominously exploited by Beethoven in the "Agnus Dei" of the *Missa Solemnis*, and by Mahler in the *Knaben Wunderhorn*) for reasons of association too obvious to need pointing out; the religious quality of the organ, again for readily apparent reasons of association; the solemn, funereal quality of the measured beat of the kettle drum (as in the Dead March from *Saul*, or the second movement of the Brahms *Requiem*).

Again, few listeners in our musical culture will fail to perceive as expressive of religious moods the "plagal" cadence, because of its centuries-old association with sacred music, from the high musical art of the Renaissance to the "lowest" Protestant hymnbook. Whatever the cause of the original joining together of these musical elements with the emotional contexts in question—and many, as I have argued previously, are due to an expressive appropriateness in contour, for one reason or another no longer perceived—they exist now as purely conventional emotive tags, but not any the less expressive for their "conventional" nature. And these musical "conventions" are so deeply embedded in our musical culture, are acquired so early, that one can find children accompanying themselves at play with the expressively appropriate musical "sound track"—a kind of universal children's melodrama. (I have heard kids, for example, hum buglelike fanfares, obviously in imitation of the Hollywood cavalry charge, while playing "cowboys and Indians.")

Nor should we omit, while trying to limn in the notion of the expressive convention in music, the association of music with words. For the setting of texts, which, I have previously pointed out, has been one, if not *the* central, concern of the composer since the beginning of art music in the West, has undoubtedly played a vital role in the establishing of expressive associations. The joining together of musical figures with texts of a particular "expression," whatever the original reason for the marriage, has without doubt contributed to the expressive associations such figures now possess. We can see how such associations might have been formed in the "big world" of Western music, by recalling the "little world" of the Lutheran chorale, and its role in seventeenth- and eighteenth-century German sacred music. Because the musical audiences of Buxtehude, or Pachelbel, or J. S. Bach connected particular chorale melodies with particular texts—not just consciously but internally, in their blood and bones—the composers could rely on the introduction of these melodies into their music, even without the words, to produce an expressive effect beyond merely what the musical contour and nontextual conventions might provide. The melody of "Aus Tiefer Not schrei ich zu dir" (for example) carried with it to the congregation not just the wonderfully expressive character of the phrygian mode, but, by deeply felt associations, the "expression" of Psalm 130 as well. Now I am not, of course, maintaining that the expressiveness by association with text which the materials of our musical culture at large possess is as neat, tidy, and self-contained, or as easy to pin down, as this example from a small musical subculture might suggest. I am saying that this can be seen as a simplified model of what has taken place in Western music.

◇ 3 ◇   Given, now, these various kinds of association-governed "conventions" of musical expressiveness, we want to ask: Are the qualities such associations impart to music "objectively" there "in" the music, so that responsible description can take them into account? Is the music critic's judgment that music is expressive of such-and-such defensible by reason of the existence of expressive "conventions"? Are emotive descriptions that rely upon expressiveness "by convention" respectable?

The answer is, I think, that within certain limits of a given musical culture, like that of the West, emotive descriptions founded on expressive musical "conventions" are as "objective" as the conventions themselves, as defensible as any statements can be whose truth relies upon the truth of a psychological generalization; and as respectable. But let us be sure we understand just what the emotive describer of music is saying, when he or she describes those aspects of music that are expressive in virtue of conventional associations. When I say "X is φ," where X is some musical entity and φ some expressive property, I am not making a disguised psychological generalization. I am saying simply that X is φ; that X has that property. *What* property? A property that I can rely on others to hear in X because they, as I, have formed associations by virtue of their membership in the same musical culture. It is a fact of human psychology that such associations are formed, and that they have the "psychological" effect they do in our musical perceptions. Does that make φ an "objective" property? Well all one can say, short of giving a dreary philosophical sermon on "objective" and "subjective," is that it is no less "objective" (say) than the property of "cheerfulness" that the color yellow has, or the property of "spaciousness" that light colors will impart to a room and dark colors will subvert, or the "summery" quality of a straw boater and white trousers. No interior decorator would be charged with "subjectivity" or "caprice" if he or she remarked that yellow was too gay for a funeral parlor, or that white will make a small room look larger. No more, then, should the critic be thought of as lapsing into "subjective" or "unscientific" criticism if he or she describes a chromatic passage as "melancholy," simply because it is a complex fact of psychology and musical culture that chromaticism imparts melancholy. Nor need the critic be aware of this fact, any more than the decorator need have a theory of human perception and psychology to work with gay and spacious colors.

The conclusion I want to press, then, is this. To "emote" over music is, in part, to hear what, by association, one's musical culture conditions one to hear; and this emotive color is as much a part of the aesthetic surface of sound, for better or worse, as any of its other properties. To be fixated on this emotive part is, indeed, to "emote" excessively. But to deny the existence of such emotive character as music possesses in virtue of expressive conventions, or to declare it "subjective" in some pejorative sense of the term, is to exhibit an excess of zeal in the opposite direction—to deny the existence of a very palpable quality in music, fit subject for the musically learned to analyze, and the musically vulgar to enjoy.

◇ 4 ◇ Let me revert, now, to the first source of musical expressiveness; what I have called expressiveness "by contour"—that expressiveness parasitic on human expression. There is a question of long standing in the history of modern philosophy over how, or if, I can truly be said to know that someone other than myself is angry, or in pain, or in any other mental state. One traditional stand has been that I know these sorts of things inductively: I know by introspection when I am in pain (say); and I know by observation how I behave when I am in pain. So when I see someone else behave like that, I have a right to assume he or she is feeling as I do when I so behave.[1]

Against the inductive model another has been advanced in recent years, associated primarily with the name of Wittgenstein,
although as a hardened doctrine it exists in the works of the dis-
ciples rather more than in the works of the master. Wittgenstein
wanted to distinguish sharply between what he called "criteria"
and what he called "symptoms." Symptoms are signs of things
that we discover inductively: a rash is a symptom of measles, a
falling barometer a sign of dirty weather to come. But criteria
are something else again: they constitute in part the very meaning of that of which they are the criteria; a criterion is always, in
Wittgenstein's use of the term, a "defining criterion."[2] And pain
behavior, on this view, is not, as the inductive theory would have
it, a symptom of pain, but a criterion (or a set of criteria) of it:
fever or contusion may be a sign that someone is in pain, but
writhing, groaning, rubbing a spot tenderly, are not merely the
signs; they are the defining criteria of pain. It is by and through
them that (in part) we know what "pain" means, and decide with
something *like* logical certainty that someone is in pain.

The criteria for being in pain, or being in any state φ, where
"φ" names an emotion, form, on this view, what Michael Scriven
baptized "cluster concepts," and for which he chose, as illustrative, the criteria for being a lemon.

> A sour taste, a yellow or green skin with a waxy texture,
> being the fruit of a particular tree, an ovoid shape, a certain
> range of sizes, of hardness and so on, are all familiar prop-
> erties of lemons. Which of them is definitive? Clearly no
> single one. . . .

It is, in other words, possible to be a lemon and not be yellow, or
not be of a waxy texture, or not be firm, and so on. Nevertheless,
we cannot do without them all: "The concept of being a lemon
is, after all, not something altogether separate from these properties."[3] Thus, although something might possess *all* these
criteria and *not* be a lemon, it would not, on the criteriological
view, make any sense to ask for further evidence that something
was a lemon if it were richly enough endowed with the criteria of
"lemonhood."

We have, then, in the inductive and the criteriological models,
two ways of viewing the relation of *expressive* features to *expression*. On the inductive model, the relation between expressive
features and the emotions they are expressive of is contingent—

that is to say, they are related in the way that any effect might be related to its cause. On this view, then, if I see someone with a face expressive of sadness, and exhibiting behavior expressive of the same emotion, I can be said to "know" to some high degree of probability that that person is sad. But, of course, I might be mistaken, just as, no matter how many symptoms of typhoid a patient might display, it just might be the case that he does not have typhoid at all but a typhoidlike disease, or some other anomalous condition. On the criteriological view, in contrast, the relation of expressive features to the emotions they are expressive of is noncontingent—that is to say, more like (but not exactly like) the relation between being unmarried and being a bachelor than like the relation between having the symptoms of typhoid and having the disease. And I can be said to "know," on this view, that someone is sad, if he or she displays an abundance of features and behavior expressive of sadness, in a sense of "know" stronger than the sense in which I can "know" that someone's symptoms are caused by typhoid, but weaker than the sense in which I can "know" that an unmarried man is a bachelor.

◇ 5 ◇   Now at this point two kinds of skeptic are likely to come forward: the first "moderate" and the second "extreme." The moderate skeptic will argue as follows: There is no such thing as knowledge "in between" inductive and definitional. What are called by the Wittgensteinian "criteria" are nothing but effects the causes of which are determined by induction, more or less well grounded, depending upon circumstances. And in the case of the psychological states of others, the inductive base is so unsatisfactory as to not constitute knowledge at all. For in trying inductively to gain knowledge of other minds, I have generalized from but one instance, myself, to all other instances of human beings. I might just as well try to reach a "scientific" conclusion about the cause of typhoid by examining only one patient.

The extreme skeptic, like the moderate one, will deny that criteria are anything but symptoms. However, his grounds for claiming that I cannot know if someone else is sad, or in pain, or whatever, are not that my inductive grounds in this kind of case are congenitally weak, but that inductive grounds simply are not rational grounds at all. He is a skeptic, in other words, with regard to induction, and denies that inductive arguments are rational.

But since what I have been calling "expressive contour" in music is parasitic on features of expression, it would seem that unless both the moderate and the extreme skeptic are answered, we cannot be permitted to claim that it is possible to know that the music is sad, or cheerful, or the like. For how could we know that something is a feature expressive of sadness unless we were also sometimes in a position to know that people who display that feature are generally experiencing that emotion? And both the moderate as well as the extreme skeptic deny that we are ever in a position to know this.

This objection, however, is not potent in the case of the moderate skeptic. For what we can take the moderate skeptic to be saying is this: We are never in a position to know that *expressive* features and behavior are *expression* features and behavior. Given that someone's face is expressive of sadness, we are never in a position to know whether or not it is expressing sadness because we are never in a position to know whether or not its possessor is really sad; and we cannot know if the face is *expressing* (as opposed to merely *expressive of*) sadness unless we can know this. But all we are required to know, if we are to know that music is expressive of sadness, is to know that certain human features and behavior are expressive of sadness, not that they are expressions of sadness. And that we are in a position to know that features and behavior are expressive of emotions the moderate skeptic does not deny. (Whether he can give an intelligible account of how we have come to call certain features and behavior expressive of sadness in the absence of knowledge that people are sad is another question.) I know, according to the moderate skeptic, that I frown when I am sad, and, thus, that other people's frowns are expressive of sadness. What I cannot know is whether they are expressing sadness, since I cannot know whether the people involved are sad.

Extreme skepticism, however, is another matter. For since the extreme skeptic denies me the use of inductive inference, it is very doubtful whether on his view I can know anything at all about the external world, and am, therefore, in no position to know whether there are expressive features at all, let alone what they are expressive of.

But it should be recalled that *aesthetic* skepticism is a kind of second-order variety. When skeptical doubts are raised about the "objectivity" of aesthetic judgments, whether descriptive or evaluative, they are invariably measured against paradigms of "objectivity" which are the very ones that the extreme skeptic is calling into question. And it is in comparison to *those* that the aesthetic cases are found wanting. So answering extreme skepticism will not of itself answer aesthetic skepticism; and answering aesthetic skepticism need not await the answering of extreme skepticism. Although if extreme skepticism is right, we cannot, clearly, have anything truly called "aesthetic knowledge." We will have done enough, then, for a theory of musical expressiveness, if we show that judgments about the expressiveness of music are not defective in any special way, as aesthetic judgments are frequently thought to be, on the understanding that if extreme skepticism turns out to be right, claims about musical expressiveness fail ever to attain the status of knowledge, as do claims about human expression across the board.

What now of the question of whether expressive features and behavior are to be considered "symptoms" or "criteria"? Is it relevant to our theory of musical expressiveness? Need we plump for one view or the other? Again, this is an issue that can for our purposes be laid aside. All we need do to make good our case against aesthetic skepticism concerning the expressiveness of music is to show that expressive features of music are enough like those of human beings to share *whatever* claim the human ones may have to "objectivity." And we can leave it an open question whether that "objectivity" is the kind we ascribe to inductive inference, or the kind, if there is such a kind, the Wittgensteinian ascribes to "criteria."

Suppose, then, I know by inductive inference when expressiveness is expression—in other words, the relation between expressive features and the emotions of people that they sometimes (but not always) express are as symptoms to conditions, effects to their causes. If this is the case, I know that a face (say) is expressive of sadness in the same way that I know rash is a symptom of measles or a falling barometer a sign of rain, even though the rash might be caused by an allergy to shaving soap, the falling barometer by a malfunction in the mechanism, and the sadness of the face by a desire to dissemble. I learn by introspection, and by observing my own features, what facial expressions are associated with sadness, as I learn by the appropriate experiences what conditions of the body are associated with measles, and what the glass does before a storm. So features are called *expressive of* sadness by virtue of their frequent association with the emotions. And, of course, if there were no such contingent relation between them, I would never have come to see the features as expressive of the particular emotion.

What, then, is "objective" about the determination that a face is expressive of (but not necessarily expressing) sadness? Simply this: "expressive of sadness," on the inductive model, would mean (very roughly) "frequently associated with sadness," or perhaps "frequently the outward manifestation of sadness" (or something of the kind). And whether or not something were frequently the manifestation of sadness would be an objective matter, depending upon the usual standards of good inductive reasoning. Thus, someone who construed a frown as expressive of joy would be mistaken, as would a doctor who took rash to be a symptom of flu. (It is, by the way, a very different mistake to conclude from a person's frown that they are sad, when in fact they are not, to conclude from a person's rash that they have measles, when in fact they are allergic to shaving soap. We are asking here how someone knows a face is *expressive of* φ, not how they know it is *expressing* φ, although, as we have seen, the two are very closely related.)

On the criteriological view, the connection between expressiveness and expression is, as we have seen, noncontingent. And that means, according to the "criteriologist," that expressive features are, in some sense or other, part of the "meaning" of emotive predicates like "sad," "happy," and the like—part of their "logical grammar," as the Wittgensteinian would say. In brief, then, the difference between "getting things wrong" on the inductive model, and on the criteriological model, is the difference between bad induction and linguistic incompetence. What makes something a "criterion" of sadness rather than a "symptom" of it, is not merely that it has frequently been associated with sadness but that it has, through the process of learning the concept, become part of the meaning. And, thus, on the criteriological model, no less, and perhaps a bit more, than on the inductive, the question of expressiveness is an "objective" one.

Having seen what is "objective" about determining whether or not a face is expressive of sadness, on both the inductive and the criteriological models, let us now ask what is "objective" about determining whether a piece of music is. To perceive the expressiveness of a piece of music, on the contour model, is to perceive some similarity or other between its musical qualities and the *characteristic* features or behavior of human "expressors." That there *are* such characteristic features of expression is a necessary premise of our argument, and, one might think, a fairly safe, unexceptionable one. But every sacred cow has its gadfly. So before we can consider this premise secure, we will have to answer an objection.

◇ 6 ◇　Guy Sircello writes in *Mind and Art*: "The notion that the expressions of *F* are such in virtue of the regularity with which they accompany *F* is, for all its attractiveness, either uninterestingly true or clearly false."[4] He supports this claim, in part, by trying to show that there are no identifiable features regularly accompanying acts of expression (or constituting such acts); that is to say, he denies that there are the kinds of characteristic features of expression which I have insisted are necessary to my account of musical expressiveness. Sircello's claim, that expression cannot be accounted for, or successfully explicated by means of such characteristic features as I have been alluding to throughout this work, is not my concern here. For it need not be false in order for the premise I require to be true. It may well be true that something is not an expression of *F* merely in virtue of constant conjunction of behavioral features with *F*. Such features may be neither necessary nor sufficient for *F*'s being expressed. But it does not follow from this that there are no such features—i.e. features that are readily identifiable as being characteristic of the expression of *F*. What *is* damaging to my account of musical expressiveness is the supporting claim—if it is true—that there are no such features. To that claim we must direct our attention.

Sircello thinks that there are no "common features" in the total range of possible ways anything can be expressed. He does not think that this can be proved, but he does think it can be illustrated, and thus made convincing. Consider, he proposes, the repertoire of expressions of anger:

> First there are verbal expressions ranging from practically inarticulate sounds through all sorts of expletives and curses to eloquent formal speeches and even poetry, like

Coleridge's 'The Dungeon.' Then there is a range of behavior including merely walking fast and firmly, waving arms and clenching fists, hitting, kicking, biting, scratching, throwing, and smashing. Third, there are facial expressions like turning red and the stiffening of jaw muscles. There are scowling brows, blazing eyes, clenched teeth, and any combination of these. Finally, there are more esoteric ways of expressing anger, such as by producing a scathing political cartoon. We can even imagine that writing music of a certain kind might, in certain circumstances, count as an expression of anger.[5]

From considerations of this kind, Sircello concludes "that any hope of finding common features of all the expressions of a given F is futile."[6] Thus, we are not to think that all bodily expressions of anger are rapid, or jerky, or loud, or anything like that. And, for our purposes, it must follow that loud music, or jerky music, or rapid music cannot be expressive of anger *simply* in virtue of its resemblance to the common features of angry behavior, for there are no such common features.

This provides the occasion for an important refinement. The view being put forth here is *not* that music is expressive of anger (say) by having features that various expressions of anger have in common. Rather, it is expressive of anger in that it resembles those sorts of attitudes of face and body and voice that characteristically express that emotion. But, of course, it resembles those attitudes in virtue of those features of sound and movement which those attitudes have.

The question then arises: Are there such sorts of expression? Sircello thinks not.

Is there, then, a regular conjunction between F and each of the *sorts* of expressions of F, given any reasonable way of determining sorts? Here too the answer must be negative. One has only to pose the question: Which of the many sorts of expressions of anger regularly accompanies anger? One has no idea what to answer. Do *scowls* regularly accompany anger? Anger in whom? Doesn't that make a difference? What sort of anger? In what circumstances? Don't these factors make a difference to our answer? How regular must regular be? Must it be more than half the time? Can we honestly say, from our own experience, that scowls do accompany anger more than half of the time? Yet scowls are among the commonest forms of expressions of anger.[7]

What is Sircello up to here? As far as I can make out, he seems to be thinking somewhat along the following lines. In order for us to be justified in claiming that some emotion is regularly conjoined with some item of behavior, we must be able to answer certain crucial questions about the emotion, the behavior, and their conjunction. We are not in a position to do this. Therefore, we are never justified in making such claims, from which we must conclude that we are not justified in believing in the existence of such regular conjunctions.

But, it seems to me, we *are* in a position to answer some of Sircello's questions; and those that we are not in a position to answer are the kinds of questions we cannot answer in all sorts of other cases as well—cases in which we feel perfectly justified in our conclusions about constant conjunction. To show this we will have to go through Sircello's questions one by one, following through with his example of anger and scowling. The argument is meant to apply, of course, *pari passu*, to any other comparable example of constant conjunction.

Question (i): What kinds of people evince anger by scowling?

Answer: The kinds of people who are calm rather than violent, repressed rather than outspoken. Are these the only kinds of people? Of course not. Is this a complete answer? No. But my point is that the question is not so devastatingly intractable as Sircello wants to make out. Any reasonably intelligent person can at least *begin* to answer it; and a sensitive novelist or psychologist can answer it further.

Question (ii): What sort of anger is customarily expressed by scowls?

Answer: Brooding anger, subdued anger, anger tempered with affection (as when one scowls disapprovingly at one's child) rather than anger born of hate or powerful moral sentiments. Again, is this a complete answer? Of course not. But, again, it is the beginning of an answer which can certainly be fleshed out more fully. The question is not, after all, the riddle of the Sphinx—and even that one was answered at last.

Question (iii): Under what circumstances does scowling express anger?

Answer: Enough has been said already, I think, to make the answering of this question unnecessary. The point is that none of us can answer these questions *completely*; but it does not follow from that that we can give no satisfactory answers at all. What, for that matter, would a *complete* answer be like? The present question is no more intractable, for example, than the question: Under what circumstances will a match light when struck? And no one claims we can't answer *that* question, simply because we can't answer it completely (since the defeating conditions would constitute an endless list)—unless, of course, one is raising skeptical doubts about cause, induction, and so forth. Sircello is guilty here, I suspect, of philosophical scare tactics in lieu of a real argument to show that these questions are really unanswerable.

Question (iv): How regular must the conjunction of scowling and anger be? Must it be more than half of the time? Can we honestly say, from our own experience, that scowls do accompany anger more than half of the time?

Answer: I have not considered these questions one by one, since they interlock. They are *all*, however, questions of the same kind: questions for which we have no answers, but which need not trouble us on that account. As to how regular conjunction must be, I think it clear this is a question that can seldom be answered in any of the ordinary, nonscientific cases in which ordinary people make the inductive inferences necessary to the conduct of their lives. And unless we mean to raise by this observation some kind of skeptical Humean argument against inductive inference, it should trouble us no more in reaching conclusions about the constant conjunction of scowling and anger than in reaching conclusions about any other of the trivial events that fill our days.

The question, Must it be more than half of the time?, suggests something else, however. Here, I suspect, the objection is as follows. Surely, of the numberless ways in which anger has and can be expressed, the cases in which scowling has, can, and will express it must be impossibly small in comparison. So what sense can it make to call scowling a constant, frequent, or regular concomitant of anger? Not only is it not present in over fifty percent of the cases, it may not even be present in five percent, or one.

But consider the following analogy. A rash, it is fair to say, is a frequent or regular concomitant of illness. Think, however, of the numberless illnesses that afflict us, and the kinds of illnesses there are, and how few, in comparison with that large number, are the diseases that produce rash. Surely rash does not accompany illness fifty percent of the time. Five percent? Does this suggest we are mistaken in saying that rash is a frequent or regular symptom of disease? I would think not; and if not, analogous considerations need hardly make us repent of the assertion that scowling is a frequent or regular expression of anger.

Finally, what are the implications of Sircello's belief (which I think must be true) that in cases like scowling we cannot honestly say, on the basis of our own experience, anything about the frequency with which the behavior accompanies the emotion? Surely it is not, as Sircello seems to suggest, that we cannot therefore be acting on such inductively based principles of constant conjunction. The failure to be able to produce, from one's own experience, a table of statistical frequencies, or even an informal account, must not be taken to imply that one has not internalized some principle "inductively." How many of our perfectly reliable hypothetical imperatives could stand up to such a test? What *would* be damaging, I think, to such a claim about constant conjunction would be the failure to pass a rigorous test, should one be given; or unwillingness to accept such a test as relevant to the claim. But I cannot see that such generalizations as "Scowling regularly accompanies anger" are less capable of test and confirmation (or refutation) than "Rash frequently accompanies illness." Indeed, in recent years, there have been interesting studies of the bodily manifestations of emotions, and their muscular substructure, even to the extent of working backward from the bodily expressions for the purpose of "educating" people with social disorders caused by the inability to express certain socially appropriate emotions.[8] One would be as surprised to find that scowling is not a characteristic, and frequent concomitant, of anger as to find that rash is not a frequent manifestation of illness.

◇ 7 ◇   We can now return to the question at hand. On the contour model, we perceive expressiveness in music in that we perceive some similarity between the features of music and the features of human behavior that characteristically accompany human emotions as their "expressions." We must ask ourselves, then, in what sense it is an objective matter at all whether

or not we perceive such similarities? After all, isn't it much the
same as being "struck" by the similarity between a cloud and a
weasle? I see it, you don't—it's a "purely subjective matter." How
could either of us be wrong?[9]

But let us ask ourselves what a reasonable reaction would be
(say) to someone's insisting that a "blues" is not sad at all but really rather cheerful and spritely? (I am thinking now of an instrumental rendition, without a text to give a nonmusical hint.) I
can't imagine that the reply, "Oh well, it's purely a matter of
taste, some think it's sad, some don't," is a plausible or likely one.
The *first* response, I imagine, would be a purely musical one: to
question the speaker's musical competence. I don't mean by that
technical competence; you don't have to be a musician to ap-
preciate the expressiveness in the blues. However, you do have
to be a member of the musical culture in which the blues
flourishes, or have learned in some other way to hear it. You
have to be a competent listener, adequately prepared, one way
or another, to hear music and not just sound. It would be as
foolish to expect Ali Akbar Khan to recognize the expressiveness
of the *Saint James Infirmary Blues* as it would be to expect Josh
White to hear *ab initio* the expressiveness of the *Shri rāg*.

Thus any attempt to understand how we hear expressiveness
in music must assume that the listener we are trying to understand is the musically competent listener. Musical competence
must be granted from the start. This is not to say there are no
philosophical problems surrounding this concept. To the contrary, musical competence in particular, and artistic competence
in general, raise all sorts of sticky aesthetic issues, including issues of "objectivity." But, after all, if we want to know what *special* issues are raised by expressiveness in music, it will do us little
good to get bogged down in the question of musical competence.
It will be assumed, then, that we do have some general criteria
by which, at least in the central cases, we can reasonably decide
between the qualified and the unqualified.

What, now, is left to say to the person who finds the blues
cheerful and spritely, after his or her musical competence has
been established? One thing I am convinced of: musical expressiveness is such an integral part of our musical culture and
experience that it is almost impossible to imagine full musical
competence in the absence of the ability to make the basic emotive distinctions in music. (Even the musical purist, who has put

such "trivia" behind him, and listens only to unadulterated, emotion-free sounds, knows when and where he must guard against the expressive heresy.) If you haven't come to hear the sadness of the blues, it is hard to imagine that you have really become a competent listener. But it will do no good for our case to make the ability to apply expressive predicates to music analytic to the notion of musical competence. That would simply change the question of whether expressiveness is "objective" to the question of whether musical competence is, and no progress would have been made. Let us, therefore, try to imagine the unlikely, but nonetheless possible, situation in which the musically competent listener fails to hear the sadness of the blues. We try to help him out by showing him the expressive features of the music, and showing him their resemblance to the expressive features and behavior of human beings. Still no luck! Are we not now in a position to begin to suspect that somehow or other we are up against someone who is seriously deficient in a basic human accomplishment? This is not just a matter of Hamlet and Polonius being in disagreement about whether a cloud looks like a weasel or not. That may be an isolated case which does not cut very deep—"merely a subjective matter." They may both agree, on another occasion, that the cloud looks like a whale. But someone who is musically competent, yet fails to perceive the expressive analogy, is, I would strongly suspect, someone who must fail to see expressiveness *tout court*—someone who is deprived in some very basic way, either not having performed the proper inductive inferences (if the inductive model is correct) or not having learned what emotive terms really mean (if the criteriologist is right). In other words, I am saying that expressiveness is a seamless web. One cannot, given the relevant musical abilities, fail there, and succeed elsewhere. To fail to "read" musical expressiveness is to fail to "read" expressiveness in general, given that one is not musically incompetent.[10]

Is this saying that it is an "objective" matter whether or not the blues is sad? Well, enough has been written about the concept of "objectivity" to show that it is a concept covering a wide variety of cases. Let me conclude simply by saying that the question of whether the blues is sad has as objective an answer as the question of whether the Saint Bernard's face is sad, or whether a certain set of human features and human behavior is expressive of sadness. If you want to call the latter two "objective," then I think you must call the former "objective" as well. If you don't, I would not want to cavil over the word. For I think a great deal will have been done to answer the aesthetic skeptic just by conflating musical expressiveness with expressiveness in human beings, without deciding if *either* is "objective."

We can, at this point, finally give the rest of our answer to the paradox of music criticism with which we began. Music criticism need not be "inhuman" to be respectable. For the traditional emotive depictions of music, which the musically "learned" reject as irretrievably subjective, or wholly nonsensical, are really no more defective than our emotive depictions of each other and the world around us, on which, according to the contour model, they are parasitic. Excesses aside (and what is free of them?), there are intellectually respectable ways of determining whether or not an emotive description "fits" its musical object. The theme of the second movement of the *Eroica*, which Tovey describes as "utterly broken with grief," *is* utterly broken with grief. Tovey's music criticism, on the whole, far from being mere subjective maundering, is "scientific" without ceasing to be "humanistic," and remains, as a previous generation saw it, a model of its kind. And neither the musician nor the layman need be embarrassed either by its intelligibility or its openly emotive vocabulary. If the argument of this book is correct, and the criteria of musical expressiveness can be identified with those of human expression, then it provides a rational foundation for the emotive criticism of music. That should be welcome to the "vulgar," and at least tolerable to the "learned."

Part Two

Paying the Piper
Further Reflections on Musical Expression

The musician can close his eyes to the
material world; but, no matter what he
does, he cannot suppress the analogy of
the sounds he employs with those of the
instinctive language.

JULES COMBARIEU
(Trans. Jennifer Day)

CHAPTER XIII

And Nevertheless It's Sad

◇ 1 ◇   It seems both an unaccountable, and yet, to date, irrefutable fact that one of the correct and most pervasive ways to describe pure music—that is, music without text, title, or program—is in terms of what I shall henceforth call the "garden-variety" emotions: anger, hope, sadness, happiness, and others of that general kind. I say it is *one* of the correct ways to pass notice immediately that I in no way wish to suggest the emotive description of music is the only correct and illuminating way of describing it (although it is the most common). And I am certainly not suggesting that music has some sort of special mission with regard to the emotions over and above the other arts (which has frequently been claimed). What I am saying is that, in spite of centuries of unconvincing speculative effort to explain how music alone (as I shall call it) can be happy, or hopeful, or sad, and in spite of recent attempts, starting with Eduard Hanslick in 1854, to discredit entirely by powerful skeptical arguments the description of music alone in emotive terms, lay people and experts alike remain obstinate in error (if error it be) and go right on calling the music sad.

Now an appeal to common sense or the *vox populi* as a philosophical strategy has little appeal to me; for on many issues in the philosophy of music I am at odds, I suspect, with both. But the persistence of emotive descriptions even among those who claim to know better—Hanslick, for one, relies on them quite heavily in his own musical criticism [1]—suggests something more than merely obstinate error or the persistence of illusion. It suggests, indeed, that kind of Humean necessity for believing outside of the philosopher's closet what one finds skeptical arguments for doubting within. And it is at least a minor scandal for philosophy that we still don't seem to have a consensus even on whether it is sometimes correct to describe music emotively, not to say how music comes to possess the emotive properties we ascribe to it.

In the modern era (say from 1600), there have been two standard positions on what the purported emotive properties of music might be: the one that these are dispositional properties of the music to arouse the garden-variety emotions in listeners (so the music merits the epithet "sad" because it makes you sad), the other that music embodies emotions as perceived phenomenal properties of itself. Each of these two positions has, in turn, generated various subtheses as to exactly *how* music either arouses emotions or embodies them. The dispositional theorists have been more prolific in this regard, going with an explanation of how music arouses emotions, suggested by whatever scientific or philosophical theory of the emotions may have been current at the time. Those who have favored the embodiment theory have had, until recently, only one real option: to see music as "representing" the emotions in some way or other. But since the 1930s, another avenue has opened, through the work mainly (as I see it) of three distinguished thinkers: the psychologist Carrol C. Pratt and the philosophers Charles Hartshorne and Susanne K. Langer.

Which direction to go? Skepticism is always tempting; and there are those, particularly in professional musical circles, who do, indeed, deny that emotive description of music is a respectable enterprise. But the musical experts themselves are by no means unanimous in this; and appearances are certainly against it. I know of no skeptical arguments that hold water, certainly not those of Hanslick; and the emotive description of music goes on unabated. To be sure, it is a healthy outcome of emotive skepticism that we now are sensitive to the danger of talking emotive nonsense: perhaps it is a case of having to aim at an extreme to hit the mean. It is enough to attribute melancholy to a passage of music, without pretending that one can read into it the melancholy of Hamlet. What the constraints are on emotive descriptions of music I will have occasion to discuss later on. But, needless to say, we need not revert to the excesses of the Romantic imagination in putting forth the modest proposition that calling music sad or yearning sometimes fits the facts.

Skepticism aside, then, two alternatives seem available: the view that music is sad in virtue of arousing sadness in listeners (what I call musical emotivism), or the view that music is sad in virtue of possessing sadness as a quality that we can hear in the music, not that we feel in ourselves (what I call musical cognitivism). In the past, I have elaborated and defended, in various places, a version of the latter: that is to say, musical cognitivism.[2] Much work has been done by others since I first expounded my views in 1980 in *The Corded Shell*. My own views have been roundly (and for the most part fairly) criticized in the literature. I myself have not been idle, but have been rethinking, reworking musical cognitivism in light of the new material. I have not seen reason, so far, to give up the cognitivist position. But there is no denying that recent work, both my own and others', has revealed problems and lacunae in my earlier version. The time is ripe, therefore, for a re-examination in which I hope to consider some objections, revise where necessary, and, all in all, present a stronger, clearer, more complete, and more consistent musical cognitivism than my previous attempt, although, in spirit, compatible with it. That, in effect, is the enterprise that I wish to contribute to—but, I must emphasize, only contribute to, not complete—in the following pages: to amplify, defend, and clarify my previous statements of the cognitivist position in *The Corded Shell* and elsewhere, but not, on the whole, to reject them.

◇ 2 ◇   The first matter for consideration, it seems obvious to me, should be the grounds for rejecting musical emotivism. Now in one sense, the grounds have preceded, and are to follow, for they simply are, I have come to believe, the superiority of cognitivism over emotivism in making sense of the musical experience as a whole and in various particulars. But I have, in the past, found the following four considerations together persuasive.

(i) If music is expressive of emotions in virtue of arousing them, then it would seem that listeners would shun, for example, music expressive of anguish, or melancholy, or any other of the unpleasant ones. For why should anyone voluntarily submit to being made melancholy or anguished—in short, unhappy? Yet, clearly, listeners do not shun music expressive of the unpleasant emotions. Therefore, it seems highly implausible to think music is expressive of these emotions in virtue of arousing them.

(ii) Normally, emotions are associated with modes of behavior: they are not merely psychological episodes with no behavioral implications whatever. When I am angry, I strike out; when I am melancholy, my head droops and my appetite wanes. But no such consistent behavioral manifestations of the emotions are observed in the concert hall or (as far as I have been able to determine) in front of the hi-fi. Granted, a person might monitor his or her behavior in public, to the extent of suppressing some of the more overt and violent emotional reactions. But that we should observe no behavioral signs at all of anger in people listening to the angry contortions of the *Grosse fuge*, or of anguish in people listening to the anguished passages in the symphonies of Schumann and Brahms, to instance a few obvious cases in point, seems powerful, if not decisive, evidence that those emotions are not really felt in the presence of that music. Yet these people still persist in recognizing this music as angry and anguished. Surely this would seem to suggest that musical cognitivism, not emotivism, is the more plausible alternative. Of course, ad hoc explanations can always be manufactured to order to explain why, in the case of music, we get the emotions but never the behavior. However, they seem to me to be merely attempts to defend a bankrupt theory in the face of some simple and recalcitrant facts.

This is not, I hasten to add, to deny that we are emotionally moved by music. Of course we are; and we do show overt behavioral signs of that both during and after a performance, in our expressions of excitement and approval. (Joy in the presence of a *Marcia funebre*.) I shall have occasion to discuss this very important matter in a subsequent chapter. Suffice it to say, at this point, that we are not to confuse the power of the *Grosse fuge* to move us emotionally by its awesome angry beauty with its supposed power (which I am denying) to move us to anger.

(iii) Modern philosophical analysis has reinforced the obvious point that such garden-variety emotions as anger and fear, love and hope, anguish and joy are dependent for their existence not only upon human physiology but upon beliefs and upon intentional objects at which they are directed. In the standard case, I come to believe something, and my belief functions in some understandable way to arouse me emotively about or over or toward something that we say is the "object" of my emotion. The belief that I am threatened arouses fear of my perceived attacker; the belief that I am rescued arouses joy at my escape and love of my rescuer. But music—the organized and expressive structure of beautiful sounds—provides no opportunities, except in bizarre and idiosyncratic ways to be discussed momentarily, for the formation of such beliefs or the provision of the objects of such emotions. This is why musical emotivism has always had to rely on exotic theories of emotion to make it plausible somehow to think that music can do what it manifestly cannot: give us beliefs, if it is melancholy music, that will make us melancholy and objects for our melancholy to take. This very impossibility seems to me now to be the very strongest reason to think that musical emotivism cannot be right.

(iv) Furthermore, where we can, on something like the standard model, construct plausible scenarios for how music might arouse the garden-variety emotions, the emotions are irrelevant to the real expressive character of the music and are the result of personal associations: what I called above the bizarre and idiosyncratic. Of course, the *Grosse fuge* might arouse the anger of some listener or other by reminding him of an angry encounter with his boss; so too, however, might the tranquil strains of the *Spring Sonata* (if his boss happens to be a Beethoven lover). This is a familiar enough phenomenon; but it has nothing whatever to do with the expressiveness of music except by accident (angry music reminding me of angry words with my boss). Thus the only really plausible account (consistent with the known facts of what emotions are and how they are aroused and sustained) of how music sometimes may arouse the garden-variety emotions provides no aid and comfort to musical emotivism; for the emotions that it arouses may or may not be the ones it is expressive of. And so the account fails, clearly, to tell us what it is in virtue of which angry music is angry, even when angry music manages, by association of ideas, to make someone angry (since tranquil music might have done so as well).

These, then, are what might be called the *prima facie* reasons for rejecting musical emotivism. And it is here that my reexamination must begin. For in a recent and impressively acute defense of the emotivist position against my own, Colin Radford has cast doubt in one way or another on them all. I shall deal with some of Radford's points in a succeeding chapter, where they are more relevant. Others it is appropriate to consider here.

◇ 3 ◇   Let us begin at the beginning, with the first (and most commonly cited) reason for rejecting emotivism: that if music aroused the unpleasant emotions that it is (correctly) said to be expressive of—like anger, and anguish, and the like—people would shun such music, which they manifestly do not. To this Radford replies: "If it *is* paradoxical that people should knowingly choose to be moved to sadness by listening to sad music, it is also paradoxical that they should choose to be moved to sadness by going to see tragedies, and moved to fear by going to see horror films, ghost films, or reading horror stories and ghost stories."[3]

I should say at the outset that Radford has muddied the waters sufficiently with his response to render this first objection to musical emotivism rather less impressive to me than heretofore; and I am inclined now to place less weight on it. But it is also fair to say that he has by no means dislodged it, as we shall now see.

Radford accepts it as obvious that people do feel fear and anger and sadness when reading or otherwise experiencing fictional works: I am afraid that the hitchhiker will murder the driver, angry that Othello is lied to by Iago, sad about Violetta's death. Yet the experiencing of these unpleasant emotions doesn't keep us from going back again and again to such works as arouse them. Why, then, should we not go back again and again to the sad music that makes us sad? That is the argument.

But Radford knows, only too well, that the arousal of emotions by fiction is philosophically puzzling. (He has written on the subject himself with considerable insight.)[4] The puzzle is this: it seems as if I cannot feel sorry for Violetta. For in order to, I must genuinely believe that something bad is really happening to her: that she really is dying of tuberculosis even as her lover and his father are being reconciled to her and to each other. Yet I believe no such thing. What I do believe is that I am watching a fictional work in which singers are portraying roles: no one is really dying, no one is really being reconciled with anyone. There are no rational grounds whatever, therefore, for my feeling sad. And, indeed, were I really feeling sad about Violetta's plight, I oughtn't sit there like an idiot but rouse myself, stand up, and ask if there is a doctor in the house, or at least offer her some chicken soup.

These considerations alone have led some philosophers to deny outright that people really do feel toward fictional characters and their vicissitudes emotions of the kind they would feel toward their real counterparts in real situations.[5] Thus, there is substantial justification for denying the premise on which Radford's argument is based: there is substantial reason to deny that we do feel sad over the fate of Violetta. So the defender of cognitivism might quite reasonably deny that our obvious and insatiable appetite for ghost stories and tearjerkers is any evidence at all that we willingly choose to be frightened and saddened by works of art, since the emotions we are supposed to be feeling are completely inconsistent with the beliefs we incontestably have. And if our appetite for fiction is no evidence of our appetite for unpleasant emotions, it still seems sound, in the face of this appetite, to argue that music cannot be expressive of the emotions in virtue of arousing them; because if it were, people would not choose to listen to, as they undeniably do, sad music, and anguished music, and angry music.

As I say, the musical cognitivist could argue this way—but *this* musical cognitivist will not. For, to be perfectly candid about it, I have not thought the case of emotion in fiction through to a firm conclusion; and the point of the present enquiry, as in all respectable research, is to get at the truth, not score points. I find the paradox of feeling sad over the fate of a character I know to be make-believe altogether perplexing; and yet my gut feeling is that we do feel sorry for Anna Karenina. So here I shall have to pronounce the Scotch verdict of "not proven." And because, at this time, I am loath to deny categorically that sad fiction makes me sad—even though there is, as we have seen, a fairly persuasive argument for doing so—I am reluctant, as well, to place much weight, in rejecting musical emotivism, on the unintelligibility of someone's willingly choosing to listen to music that will arouse the unpleasant emotions. To that extent, Radford's point is well taken. However, that does not overly concern me; for, I think, the case against the musical emotivist is overdetermined.

◇ 4 ◇   Another response of Radford's, this one essentially to the cognitivist's second argument against musical emotivism, is, to my mind, somewhat less than convincing, but nevertheless troublesome enough to deserve notice. The cognitivist argues that listeners show none of the behavioral responses to expressive music that would suggest sad music makes them sad, and so forth. But, after all, linguistic utterances are behavioral responses. And, as a matter of fact, some listeners do report that sad music makes them sad. Well, it might be argued, there is *one* kind of behavioral response that is symptomatic of being made sad by sad music. As Radford puts the point, "Listening to sad music does make people sad. To deny this . . . involves the cognitivist maintaining that when people say that this is what has happened, they are mistaken."[6]

Of course, the quick, obvious, and, it seems to me, altogether satisfactory answer to this response is simply to point out that people also say that sad music doesn't make them sad. Or, to put it more precisely, some people say that sad music does not make them sad. To instance two cases in point, Colin Radford sincerely believes and sincerely reports that sad music makes him sad, while Peter Kivy sincerely believes and sincerely reports that sad music does not make him sad. (Indeed, were this not true of Peter Kivy, he surely would not be a musical cognitivist.) So, as between the musical cognitivist and the musical emotivist, the evidence of personal reports, at least at this primitive level of analysis, favors neither one side nor the other, and Radford's response comes to nothing.

Surely, though, we cannot just leave it at that. The cognitivist owes us a reasoned response to the reports of some that sad music saddens them. Of course, the emotivist owes us a reasoned response to the reports of some that sad music does *not* sadden them. So neither has the advantage on that regard. But being a cognitivist, I am obliged to set my own house in order. And I will leave the emotivist to tend to his or hers, with this observation. There is just the hint, in what Radford says, that he believes that the reports of people who claim they are saddened by sad music are such hard, incontrovertible evidence as to be incorrigible. That is to say, there is the suggestion that people cannot be mistaken about whether they are feeling sad, or angry, or whatever. Now that avenue, it seems to me, is open neither to the cognitivist nor the emotivist (and everything twentieth-century psychology and philosophy have revealed about the human psyche supports that conclusion). Somewhere along the line, the cognitivist is going to have to insist that some people, anyway, are genuinely mistaken when they report that sad music has saddened them, are genuinely mistaken, sometimes, in thinking they are really sad in its presence. However, this can give no comfort to the emotivist who wants to insist that emotive reports are incorrigible. For somewhere along the line the emotivist too will have to claim that some people are genuinely mistaken about the emotions they are feeling (or not feeling), namely, cognitivists like me who deny that sad music makes them sad. Again, in this regard, it is a standoff.

Radford writes that "people say" sad music makes them sad. He surely cannot mean to suggest—although the quoted phrase can easily be taken that way by the unwary—that *all* people say it. I don't say it nor do other people of the cognitivist persuasion; and, in my experience, lots of people of no persuasion at all with regard to these matters don't say it either. Some people say it and some people don't; and I suppose the knee-jerk reaction of the modern reader is to ask, "Well, how many do and how many don't? Let's take a survey, like the kind showing that seven out of ten doctors questioned would prefer aspirin to Tylenol on a desert island."

Whatever the philosophical payoff of such a "scientific" survey might be, anyone who has ever tried to frame the proper questions for listeners quickly discovers how hard it is not to give the game away by putting one response or the other into the listener's mind. What one does find—at least what I have found in doing informal classroom experiments—is that there is remarkable agreement ("remarkable" only to the skeptics) about how musical examples are to be characterized, where the characterizations are appropriately general, and that when pressed (not bludgeoned into submission by an authority figure), students sometimes claim they are describing the music and sometimes claim they are describing how the music makes them feel. Nothing very surprising or controversial here.

Again, based merely on my limited, personal, and unscientific experience, I can frequently get someone to back down who claims that he or she called the music sad or angry or whatever in virtue of its making him or her feel that way. (It is, of course, crucial here not to *make* the listener say what you *want* said.) One does this simply by getting the emotivist to see plainly what the real implications are of saying that the music made you sad, *really sad.* Was it anything like the way you felt when your canary died or when you lost your favorite pair of earrings? Did you really have that feeling of palpable distress? Notice I have avoided loading the dice by asking questions like, "Did you feel the way you felt when your mother died of cancer?" The emotivist of Radford's eminent good sense will surely insist that he or she is committed to no such foolish belief as the asking of a question like that would suggest. Of course the emotivist need not be claiming that sad music puts us into deep states of mental depression, as would the loss of a loved one. But he or she must, after all, be making some substantial claim to the effect that real

sadness—the kind that feels bad and really has an effect on us—
has been aroused by the music, or else the claim seems contentless. And it is my own experience that when people have their
noses rubbed in it, when it is vigorously put to them that if they
mean what they say when they say the music makes them sad,
they must be feeling that same kind of feeling as when Tweety
died or when they lost their favorite baubles, many of them realize that that is not what happened at all. I am claiming, then,
that the members of one substantial group of people who initially
report being saddened by sad music are just mistaken about it:
mistaken about what they are really feeling; and they realize it
when they are brought to see what the true implications of their
reports, if true, would be.

But why, you may ask, do these people mistake their emotions?
It is a fair question, and I am not really sure I have a firm answer.
Many of them, I suspect, though, are, one way or another, on the
basis of little if any reflection, in thrall to some vague version of
musical emotivism. Now, add to this the fact that the emotions
in their milder forms do not exert the kind of influence over us
that takes full possession of our being, and we have, I think, a
reasonable idea of why such people as are at some level unreflec-
tive devotees of emotivism report themselves as being saddened
by sad music. Take the case of Miss Jones. She is listening to the
opening measures of the slow movement of Beethoven's Seventh
Symphony. She recognizes a quality of funereal melancholy here
and is not possessed by any strong emotion that would domi-
nate her consciousness and make itself unmistakably at variance
with that emotion. She has not thought much about these matters but holds, if pressed, the vague belief that music arouses
emotions. Because she is not in any emotional state to a very
high degree, as she would be if she had just heard that she had
won the Irish Sweepstakes, it is fairly easy for her to report that
she is sad without noticing any great psychological incongruity
between her possibly being sad and whatever rather innocuous
emotional state she is now in. Given, then, that she is not over-
powered by any obvious contrary emotion, given, as well, that she
believes in some vague form of musical emotivism, she naturally
reports that, since the music is experienced by her as something
like funereally melancholy, she must have been melancholy while
listening to it, without noticing any striking incongruity between
the reported sadness and the rather nondescript state she actu-

ally was in. When, however, we force her to reexamine the situation, to think seriously about what emotional state she really was in while listening to the music and what it would mean if music really made her sad, she sees her mistake and recants. Such is my hypothesis.

Thus I am claiming that the members of one substantial group of listeners who report that sad music makes them sad are simply (and understandably) mistaken in their appriasals of how they really feel. Further, since I do not believe that personal emotion reports are incorrigible and have some kind of reasonable explanation for why such listeners give mistaken reports of the emotional states they are in, I am not much troubled by the phenomenon.

◇ 5 ◇   A second group of listeners who report being saddened by sad music troubles me even less. This is the group of listeners who really are saddened by sad music but provide, when interrogated, a perfectly acceptable explanation of why that is altogether compatible with musical cognitivism. Consider in this regard the cases of Mr. and Mrs. Dugan. Mr. Dugan is saddened by the opening bars of the slow movement of Beethoven's Seventh because it always reminds him of his nephew's funeral, at which it was played. Naturally, thinking about the untimely death of his nephew saddens Mr. Dugan, and it is listening to the Beethoven slow movement that initiates the causal chain. Mrs. Dugan, on the other hand, is what I call a "visual" listener. She tends to let the aesthetic properties of music raise images, even stories, in her mind, and the slow movement of the Seventh, because it is sad, tends to raise sad images and stories, the contemplation of which makes her sad, the way reading *Anna Karenina* might do.

There is, of course, an important difference between the Dugans. Mr. Dugan's emotive arousal is due to accidental association. It is simply a fact of his personal history that the slow movement of the Seventh reminds him of his nephew's funeral and makes him sad. If it had reminded him of the happiest day of his life, because he happened to have heard it that day, it would, though a sad piece of music, make him happy. So Mr. Dugan's sadness bears no direct relation to the sadness of the music. But Mrs. Dugan, on the other hand, lets her visual imagery be stimulated by the expressive properties of the music, and these, of course, tend to stimulate images appropriate to them: sad music stimulates sad images, happy music, happy ones. And since the contemplation of sad images naturally makes Mrs. Dugan sad, happy ones happy, there is a direct and regular connection between the expressive properties of music and the emotions aroused in Mrs. Dugan's case: sad music evokes sad images, which arouse sadness, happy music evokes happy images, which arouse happiness, and so forth. But in neither the case of Mr. nor of Mrs. Dugan do we find evidence for the emotivist contention that music is expressive of the emotions in virtue of arousing them. The case of Mr. Dugan hardly requires further comment. For in cases like his, where personal association is at work, a sad piece of music might just as well arouse happiness as sadness, depending upon the personal history of the listener—clearly indicating that the two things are independent, even when, accidently, the emotion of the music and the emotion aroused are the same. "Visual hearing," of the kind Mrs. Dugan and many others indulge in, might seem to offer a firmer foundation for emotivism in music. For here we have a regular, predictable relation between the emotions in the music and the emotions aroused by it. Since sad music tends to stimulate sad images, and the contemplation of sad images tends to make one sad, sad music will, in fact, generally be the music that, for this group of listeners, arouses sadness, and likewise, of course, for the other emotions. But even here there will be enough incongruities to make the connection far from infallible. Thus, for example, a sad piece of music might well raise the image of a villain's funeral in Mrs. Dugan's imagination, the contemplation of which makes her happy. However, she surely would not, on that account, call the music happy rather than sad, showing quite convincingly, I think, that she (and we) cannot be calling the music "sad" in virtue of its arousing sadness, even when it does it on a fairly regular basis. (Why one might still want to insist that even though sad music is not sad in virtue of arousing sadness, it does arouse sadness on a regular basis, we will consider in a succeeding chapter.)

But there is another powerful objection besides the foregoing, and that is that the musical cognitivist simply will not allow "visual listening" to be, shall we say, a proper, bona fide way of attending to pure music. And the cognitivist is surely not alone in this, but shares the assumption with all respectable authorities. Or, to put it another way, to be emotively aroused by the mental images music excites is not to be emotively aroused by the music. It is not, therefore, a counterexample, strictly speaking, to the assertion that music is powerless to arouse the garden-variety emotions.

Now I am not for a moment suggesting that anyone can ever completely realize the ideal of pure musical concentration that fully image-free musical listening requires. The fact is, of course, that we are not in total control of the associative train. And each of us experiences, in listening to music, the eliciting of un-willed, unexpected, and unpredictable images, which, in turn, may arouse fleeting emotions. These images and emotions, how-ever, have no more musical significance than the desire for a corned beef sandwich that I usually experience toward the end of *Die Meistersinger*. The pure listening experience is an ideal that is to be pursued but, alas, never fully attained unless you are a Mozart. But it is the pure listening experience, and that alone, that merits philosophical analysis here. The rest is dross.

◇ 6 ◇   I have, then, discussed two substantial groups of musical listeners who report that sad music makes them sad: those who are mistaken, and those who are correct but whose emotions are aroused in musically irrelevant ways that the cogni-tivist is fully aware of. Neither group, I have argued, represents a counterexample to the cognitivist position. But a third group remains: the "hard cases," like Professor Radford, who report (truthfully, I must assume) that sad music makes them sad and who do not admit to being either "visual listeners" or victims of personal associations. This group I would like to postpone talk-ing about until later. For the case Radford is making for such listeners as he sees himself to be is best seen in the context of the cognitivist's views on what emotions music does legitimately raise, inasmuch as the cognitivist need not—indeed should not —deny that music is emotively arousing, merely that it arouses the garden-variety emotions.

◇ 7 ◇   I am satisfied, at this juncture, that I have suffi-ciently defended my four initial reasons for preferring musical cognitivism to musical emotivism against recent criticism; and I will now go on to pursue the consequences of this choice. Indeed,

I rather think the best defense of the doctrine is really to be found in understanding it in some detail, and thereby in perceiving how well it accommodates the plain facts of musical listening. But one stumbling block to acceptance of musical cognitivism must certainly be the *prima facie* absurdity of saying that the *music*, not the listener, is literally sad. For how, it might be (and has been) wondered, can any nonsentient entity be in an emotional state? And isn't it an emotional state we ascribe to something when we call it (literally) sad or happy? So how can music be sad or happy? Clearly, the cognitivist owes us an explanation.

It was the main purpose of *The Corded Shell* to give such an explanation of how music can possess, as phenomenal properties, the garden-variety emotions. The nuts and bolts of this explanation will of course be known to the reader of the preceding pages; and there is no need to rehearse it in any detail here. But various difficulties in my account have emerged in my own mind as well as in the minds of others since *The Corded Shell* was first published. And these need to be addressed. I cannot possibly cover them all here, but some considerations seem particularly pressing. To these I will now turn my attention.

◇ 8 ◇   The general argument of *The Corded Shell*—outlining what I called the "contour model" of musical expressiveness—went something like this. The sadness is to the music as the sadness is to the Saint Bernard's face: both the music and the face are expressive of sadness, not expressions of sadness; for neither the Saint Bernard nor (*a fortiori*) the music is sad, in the sense of being in the conscious state that word describes. The sadness, I want to say, is a perceived quality of the face and the music.

But what exactly does it mean to say that the sadness is perceived as a quality of the music and the face? Here philosophical argumentation seems to fail, at least for me, at this time and this place. I want to say I perceive the sadness in *much the way* I perceive the redness of the apple, or *as if* it were a color of an object. Yet I know it is not literally a secondary quality of objects, whatever one's analysis of secondary qualities might be. All I can do here is describe my own experience, as accurately and circumspectly as I can, hoping it will coincide with the experiences of others, hoping I am neither singular nor self-deluded. Here is the way it seems to me.

Begin not with a Saint Bernard's face but with a human one. Surely we all recognize *immediately* the "hang dog" expression of Buster Keaton's well-known countenance. And if we are asked in virtue of what we find it so, we have no trouble tracing the lineaments of melancholy therein. Nor, needless to say, do we first toll up the features that contribute to the melancholy quality and then infer melancholy. We perceive melancholy as a quality of a face but can, after the fact, *sometimes* explain what it is about that face that makes it melancholy. Furthermore, it must be emphasized, we are certainly not dealing here with necessary conditions for the mournfulness of a face, and probably not sufficient conditions either. And, finally, there is no mystery about how (or whether) we recognize sadness in a face, although there certainly are problems and disagreements about how we are to interpret what we do vis-à-vis philosophical psychology and the philosophy of mind.

Now it seems to me, and that was what I was trying to make out in *The Corded Shell*, that we can move effortlessly, without any real question of substance arising, from the face of the man to the "face" of the dog. So if you find it unproblematic that Buster Keaton's face possesses melancholy as a perceived quality—which is to say, is expressive of melancholy—and unproblematic that you can, after the fact, recover the features of the face that (at least in part) impart it, then I believe you will find the same things unproblematic about the face of the Saint Bernard, with of course the crucial difference that whereas Buster Keaton's face is a human face, the Saint Bernard's "face" is not and is seen as expressive of melancholy only in virtue of some perceived analogy to the human face in a melancholy configuration.

The passage from the face of the man to the face of the dog seems to me to be as crucial as it is effortless. For if we can go from the face to the "face" (which is *not* a face), we can, it seems to me, go to all of those nonhuman, even nonsentient perceptual objects that present expressive properties in the same logical stance, and with the same psychological ease. I do not say that we truly understand everything that is perceptually and psychologically going on when I perceive the mournfulness of a weeping willow or the anger of the *Grosse fuge*. But I find it hard to believe that we are not encountering the same phenomenon as the melancholy of the Saint Bernard.

Three things are, it seems to me, obviously the same in all of these cases. There is general, ballpark agreement about what the perceptual object is expressive of. The expressiveness is perceived immediately as a quality of the perceptual object, as is its color or shape. And there is general, ball-park agreement about what other features one points to, after the fact, to explain or justify (I think both are going on) the expressiveness or judgment that. . . . We point to the lines of the face, the sad eyes, the sagging mouth, the drooping limbs and leaves, the angular and thrusting melodic line, with its wide, jagged leaps, the profusion of dissonance almost beyond the syntactic limits of the style, and so on.

Where, of course, agreement ends is in the account one gives of the musical cases beyond the mere pointing to the explanatory or justificatory features of the music. No one, I suppose, is much disposed to disagree with the assertion that the mournful quality of the Saint Bernard's face is the result of some perceived affinity between it and the mournful faces of people. But when, as in *The Corded Shell*, it is suggested that the mournful or angry quality of a musical passage is the result of some perceived affinity between it and the mournful or angry features of people—features of their appearance, of their behavior, or of the expressive sounds they utter—such suggestions are, as is only to be expected, the occasion of vigorous dispute.

It would be pointless, not to say intellectually dishonest, for me to claim that *The Corded Shell* gave a trouble-free, entirely satisfying account of how music is perceived to possess expressive properties. Certainly it has not entirely satisfied its author. And if not him, then whom? But it still does seem to me that in general outline, anyway, it must be the way things go. For the alternatives seem limited, and there is a strong argument from parsimony, I would think, for seeing the expressiveness of the Saint Bernard and the expressiveness of music as instances of the same phenomenon. They appear to me to have "logic" and "phenomenology" in common; and the respective justificatory procedures appear to be of a piece (although to assert that categorically would simply be to beg the question from the start). A different accounting for the music would introduce a glaring discontinuity in what appear to be two examples of the same perceptual phenomenon.

◇ 9 ◇ What are the alternatives? What other single explanation might there be for the sadness of the Saint Bernard and the sadness of the music? I am sure that there are many with which I am not acquainted, and many ingenious ones to come, perhaps. Nor, needless to say, am I fool enough to launch some transcendental argument to the effect that mine is the only possible account. But of the two alternative accounts that immediately come to mind, one, although it may hold out possibilities for the other arts, is not, for a reason that will soon become apparent, promising for music; and the other is so metaphysically audacious as to be, for all of its elegance, unpalatable, I would think, to the contemporary philosophical consciousness, as it amounts essentially to a form of panpsychism.

The former, sometimes called the "fusion" or "empathy" theory, and somewhat akin to Ruskin's "pathetic fallacy," has it that in perceiving the Saint Bernard, or the music, I feel the sadness, which I then project psychologically onto the perceptual object and perceive it as if it were an "objective" quality. It will suffice to point out that if this theory is correct, then the whole project of which *The Corded Shell* is a part must be totally misguided, since it is an attempt to defend the view that the music is sad, *without* succumbing to the view that the music makes us sad. That is why I maintain that although there may be some merit in the fusion view elsewhere, in the discussion of musical expression it is useless.[7] The fusion of an emotion with an object requires, it must not be forgotten, that a genuine emotion be aroused in the first place. Or, to put it negatively, to commit a pathetic fallacy I must really have an emotion, which I then project onto the world and perceive as if it were there. Now fictional works and representational paintings, because they possess recognizable objects and emotion-producing situations as part of their content, may indeed (although that is not altogether clear, as we have seen) be capable of arousing garden-variety emotions that can be fused with, or confused with, objective properties. But absolute music, music alone, possesses no such content and, therefore, no such arousal capabilities. It therefore provides no possible foothold for the fusion theory. Fusion requires just what I have argued in *The Corded Shell*, and elsewhere, that music cannot provide: the arousal of the garden-variety emotions. The number of fallacies committed in the name of music surpasses the imagination to encompass. It ought to come as something of a relief, therefore, to find out that there is *one* fallacy, anyway, namely the pathetic one, that *cannot* be committed on its behalf.

The second view of which I have spoken has it that when I describe a nonsentient entity in expressive terms, I am doing *exactly* what I am doing when I so describe a sentient, conscious one. In other words, the weeping willow is "sad" in just the same sense in which I am. And that is because the weeping willow is *not* a nonsentient entity. There is an unbroken continuity from human minds to electrons, and hence no problem about how things other than sentient, conscious beings can be described in emotive terms. Asks Charles Hartshorne, "What can there be in common between physical and psychic energy?" Further embellishing the question: "And then there are the other qualitative variables. Surely they at least have no physical analogues!"[8] His answer is extreme:

> The only answer I am able to suggest falls under the general head of "panpsychism." If nerve cells are living and sentient, then the "warmth," "pleasantness," etc., of human sensation may not be without parallel in the sentience of these cells. . . . Lack of explicit organ does not spell lack of function, but primitive form of the function. If anyone could show that sentience as such involves more complexity than a microbe possesses structurally, we should have to admit that the microbe cannot feel. But I do not see that the idea of feeling posits any greater complexity than even an electron exhibits.[9]

Elsewhere Hartshorne refers to nerve cells as "fellow-animals";[10] and as sociability is for him a necessary condition of sentient experience, he is not above ascribing a social life to stones, albeit perhaps a somewhat pallid one. "From the standpoint of continuity, what one must say is that the perception of the stone may be one in kind but very different in degree as compared with experiences generally recognized as social."[11]

Now the last thing in my mind is to hold Charles Hartshorne

up to ridicule. On the contrary, he is a true philosopher, in the very best senses of the word; and even the most skeptical, metaphysically wary empiricist can read *The Philosophy and Psychology of Sensation* with profit, .as regards the question of expressive properties. But if one is seeking a single explanation for the sadness of the Saint Bernard and the sadness of the music, while lacking Hartshorne's metaphysical courage, what is offered in *The Corded Shell*, for all of its difficulties and lacunae, may yet seem an attractive alternative to a world full of souls.

◇ 10 ◇   Well, what are the difficulties that have emerged? It seems obvious to me both from my own ruminations and the ruminations of those who have reviewed or discussed *The Corded Shell* in print that, as Malcolm Budd put it, the book "does not *make clear* the nature of either the experience, or the characterization of music as expressive of emotion."[12] And by that I take him to mean not that I have somehow failed to describe adequately the subjective "feel" of the experience of musical expressiveness (which I never meant to do) but that I failed really to explain adequately and in enough convincing detail—that is to say, *make clear*—the underlying mechanisms, logical, psychological, epistemological, of musical expressiveness: how the sentiment really gets into the sound. And with this I wholeheartedly agree, at least to the following extent.

The notion that the expressiveness of music (in *some* sense or other of "expressiveness") is due to a relation of "resemblance," "analogy," "representation," "mimesis" (or what have you) to human expressive behavior and expression is, I believe, as old as Plato and as perennial as Platonism. "It has been found very difficult," Davies and Vaughan say in their translation of the *Republic*, when they reach the subject of music, "to interpret the terms of ancient music in those of the modern science."[13] Even with that caveat taken to heart, however, it is still hard not to interpret Socrates as laying the emotive effect of music to the imitating of human expression, where he refers, for example, in Book III, to "that particular harmony which will suitably represent the tones and accents of a brave man in a feat of arms. . . ."[14] And I am willing to bet my last kopeck that whenever, in the Western tradition, anything like expressiveness in music is discussed, the same explanation for it, or one of its many incarnations, will be found among the contenders.[15] From the sixteenth century onward, it was, of course, ubiquitous.

Now this is not meant to be the first premise of a *vox populi* argument. What I do want to suggest is that any philosopher who rejects the "analogy" explanation of musical expressiveness owes us some account of the persistence of the illusion. But, needless to say, any philosopher who embraces it equally owes us an account of how it really works, beyond the familiar platitudes and vague generalities.

◇ 11 ◇   In *The Corded Shell* I relied on what now appears to me to be the rather pallid, not to say problematic, notion of "resemblance." The problem I now see with the notion, and the account based on it, is this.

I argued, in *The Corded Shell*, that hearing music as "animate" is the same phenomenon as seeing things in ambiguous figures such as clouds: what we have called, following Wittgenstein, "seeing as," and what Richard Wollheim now calls "seeing in."[16] Now, of course, there is nothing in the nature of the case that would prevent someone from seeing nonanimate things in clouds or hearing them in music. If I can see the Matterhorn in a cloud, I can hear a stream in a passage of music. But such an admission would seem to be disastrous for my project; for it would leave unexplained the fact that, although music can be and has been described in terms of nonanimate as well as animate phenomenological predicates, it preeminently has been and continues to be described in animate and, particularly, expressive ones. Why so, if we can hear equally in it nonanimate as well as animate phenomena?

The answer I gave in *The Corded Shell* was, essentially, that we do *not* hear equally the nonanimate and the animate; and my explanation for that was through-and-through psychological and biological. I claimed that we are evolutionarily hard-wired to perceive things as animate, when they do not otherwise prevent that reading; that we are so hard-wired by natural selection, because this tendency has survival value. An example I used was seeing a stick as a snake. If the visual cues are consistent with either stick or snake, better I "see" snake rather than stick. For I will be startled and run, in the former case but not the latter; and if it *is* snake, I will be safe, whereas if it is stick, there will be no harm done in the mistake. But were I to "see" stick, or be indifferent in the matter, then if it turns out snake, I am for it. So I have inherited a tendency, by natural selection, to "see" snake: to perceptually, as it were, shoot first and ask questions afterward.

The example, however, is not a completely happy one for me; and it reveals a problem. In the case of seeing the snake in the stick—a clear case of Wollheim's "seeing in"—and other cases like it, I am fully conscious, fully aware of what I am "seeing." That indeed is what makes me run and what gives the "seeing in" survival value. Were I not to take the stick for a snake, I would not run; I would not protect myself.

But this cannot be exactly what is happening when I hear "life" in the music. I was at pains, in *The Corded Shell*, to avoid the suggestion that absolute music is a *representation* of human expressive behavior, and achieves its expressiveness by way of representation. And one of my principal reasons for insisting on this was just that, in listening to absolute music, we need not be, and often are not, conscious of the "life" in the music, when, by means of it, we hear the expressiveness in the music. If there is something analogous to Wollheim's "seeing in" here, it is our hearing the expressive properties in the music: that is what we are fully conscious of in our listening experience. The perception of that analogy of music to human expressive behavior must lie at some deeper, nonconscious and pervasive level, although we can, of course, bring it to consciousness by analysis and scrutiny if we wish; and the snake in the stick, being an example of the fully conscious "seeing in" phenomenon, is ill suited to illustrate it.

For all of that, I am convinced that some such deep-level perception is at work in the hearing of musical expressiveness, and that it is a vestige of the same process of natural selection that left us hard-wired to see the snake in the stick rather than the other way around.

But my conviction cannot do duty for an argument; and being in the form of a psychological and biological conjecture, as it were, what it really awaits is not so much an argument—at least a "philosophical" one—as some hard data and theorizing by the psychologist and evolutionary biologist. Nevertheless, I can perhaps advance my conjecture just a little further before I drop it in the laps of the experts.

I have advanced the hypothesis that the same evolutionary

process of natural selection has produced two similar but, in one important respect, dissimilar perceptual mechanisms in us—one in the sense of sight, the other in the sense of hearing. It is what might be called a built-in "startle mechanism." In the sense of sight it takes the form of a tendency to see things, when in doubt, as animate and, hence, dangerous: things to be feared and fled. It is a fully conscious startle mechanism that enables us to flee what we immediately take to be dangerous without waiting to ask questions and, in the process, suffer the fate of Hamlet or Archimedes. In the sense of hearing, it seems, at least in the musical cases, to take the form of a subliminal "animation" process— a kind of "living background noise" that, in turn, causes us to hear (among other things) expressive properties in music and, no doubt, other sounds. The mechanism manifests itself consciously in one sense modality, unconsciously in the other.

But *why* should the mechanism manifest itself as fully conscious in the sense of sight but as subliminal in the sense of hearing? The skeptic may, with some apparent justification, object that it is a purely ad hoc subterfuge hurried in to bolster a sagging theory. It is conscious in one sense, unconscious in the other because Kivy needs it that way to save *The Corded Shell.*

Well, things are really not as shabby as all that. There are, I think, reasonable grounds, independent of the truth of the theory they are supposed to support, for suggesting that what I have called the "startle mechanism" could be expected to manifest itself in a fully conscious manner in seeing, but subliminally in audition. And, clearly, the place to start is with the obvious fact that the two contrasting manifestations of the mechanism are in two *different* sense modalities. Surely, it is plausible to suppose that there is a relation: that the difference in startle mechanisms devolves from the different roles these two sense modalities presently play, and have done in the lives of human beings.

I begin with the assumption, both of biology and of common sense, that vision is our most important sense modality, which is to say, the one upon which our survival has most firmly rested. For other creatures—dogs, to instance a case in point —it is rather the senses of smell and hearing that are most relied upon, sight not being as well developed. Imagine, then, the following possible evolutionary scenario. As the senses of our ancestors, both human and prehuman, evolved, we gained, among other aids to survival, the startle mechanism. Let us suppose that at one stage in our ancestors' evolution, sight had not gained predominance, but they relied more upon hearing. At that stage, the startle mechanism would have manifested itself in a fully conscious way in the sense of hearing. Instead of seeing snakes in sticks, our ancestors would have (very consciously) heard snarls in sounds. But gradually, because of advantages as an information gatherer, the sense of sight evolved in us as the survival sense par excellence; and in the same process, the sense of hearing, although by no means becoming negligible, began to play a lesser role. It is only to be expected, then, that as the sense of hearing slipped from prominence as a survival sense, its startle mechanism should gradually fade into the background, leaving us what we now have: a subliminal vestige of a startle mechanism that once was as vivid and conscious as its visual counterpart is at present.

Pure conjecture, no doubt. But it is a conjecture that meshes prettily with another I have made elsewhere about why sounds, rather than visual images, developed into so extensive a nonrepresentational art: that is, the art of pure instrumental music.[17] My conjecture there is that sound does not so strongly demand interpretation as do visual patterns, just because of the ear's more lowly place vis-à-vis survival value, in the human being's perceptual system. Being the survival sense par excellence, vision is a compulsive interpreter, whereas hearing, which serves a lesser function in that regard, does not possess that compulsion, or at least, not to the same degree. It does, I think, have another compulsion: the linguistic compulsion to make sounds meaningful and well formed. But far from being inimical to the theory being presented here, this particular propensity plays directly into my hands, because the propensity to hear linguistically is, to begin with, the propensity to hear sound as human utterance—which is, of course, exactly what I was claiming in *The Corded Shell*. The ear, to be sure, fails in this on the semantic side, since pure music has no semantic component. It succeeds to an extent on the syntactic side, since music does have a quasi-syntactic component. And finally, this propensity to hear linguistically but not "representationally" is borne out, I would suggest, by the preponderance of meaning-ascriptions over representation-ascriptions throughout the long history of misguided attempts to give "content" to pure, contentless instrumental music.

Thus, to conclude, the strong compulsion to interpret is at

cross purposes, in vision, with the goal of nonrepresentational visual art, which is to defeat representational interpretation. Whereas the auditory sense, with its lower survival priority and its (therefore) far weaker propensity to interpret, accepts more readily, and without resistance, the abstract patterns of sound of which absolute music is the embodiment. So the same perceptual function—or lack thereof—that pushes the aural propensity to "animate" sound under the surface into the subliminal but nonetheless present background dulls the propensity to "interpret," and makes pure music possible.

Such, then, are my two intermeshing conjectures. Do two pure conjectures weigh more than one in the evidential balance? Or would that be like trying to get duration from instants or lines from points? Farther than this, I cannot go here. The evidence isn't yet in. I will push on, therefore, to other matters.

CHAPTER XIV

Newcomb's Problems

◇ 1 ◇ The most careful, thorough, and perceptive critique of *The Corded Shell* by a musical scholar that has come my way since the book's publication is that of Anthony Newcomb. Newcomb's essay is both a critical analysis of recent work in musical "expression," including my own, and a positive contribution to the subject in its own right. I shall have a great deal (naturally) to say about the former aspect and at least something on the latter. However, the amount that I have to say as well as the quality and range of Newcomb's essay, which seems to me as well as to others to be one of the best short pieces on the subject to have appeared in recent years, necessitate a separate treatment, rather than an attempt to work Newcomb's somewhat heterogeneous points, and my responses to them, into any other of these supplementary essays.

◇ 2 ◇ Newcomb has problems, to begin with, with the notion that, as I put it in *The Corded Shell*, we are "hard-wired" to perceive music as "animate" utterance and gesture. As has already become apparent, I have problems with it as well. But my problems are not Newcomb's problems; and his problems I do not really see as problems at all.

Here is what Newcomb says with regard to what he describes as "the concept of animation, according to which the human being instinctively endows everything he encounters with the qualities of animate life. . . ." "It is this instinct," he explains, that, according to me, "causes us to hear music as utterance or gesture and to judge its expressive content according to our own expressive behavior." He continues:

> There are two difficulties with this concept. . . . First, it seems to place creation of expressive meaning strictly in the mind of the perceiver, leaving no room for intended expression on the part of the creator. . . . Second, some of the expressive qualities we ascribe to it are not animate ones: for example, references we commonly hear in it to water, glass, fire.[1]

Let me deal with Newcomb's first problem by introducing an oversimplified *reductio*, which I will refine in a moment. We are hard-wired—we have an "instinct," if you prefer—to perceive reflective bodies of a certain kind, under certain conditions, as "blue." This leaves no room for intended blueness on the part of the creator. Or, in other words, it is no part of Reynolds' artistic intention that I see the *Blue Boy* as blue. The *Blue Boy* can be seen only as blue, no matter how strongly Reynolds may have intended us to see it as yellow.

Well, of course, Reynolds chose paint with a certain reflective surface—that is, blue paint—just because it was part of his artistic intention that the *Blue Boy* be blue. *We* are hard-wired to perceive the kind of paint Reynolds chose as blue; but *he* was not hard-wired to choose that kind of paint.

Let's get back now to the problem of expression that Newcomb raises. The problem has a problem; and it stems, to begin with, from an overstatement of my thesis. Newcomb has me saying that "the human being instinctively endows everything he encounters with the qualities of animate life. . . ." But that is far too strong; that is not what I said. I said that we are hard-wired with a tendency, a proclivity to perceive patterns as animate where they are ambiguous, or lend themselves to it. We have a tendency, hard-wired, to eat when we are hungry. That does not mean either that we always eat when we are hungry or that we eat everything. The tendency to perceive animately is defeasible and can be encouraged. Walking frightened and alone in the half-light of a strange and threatening jungle, there is a strong likelihood that I will see a snake in every stick, and a set of jaws in every shadow. Show me a black square on a white background in broad daylight while I sit in the comfort and security of my own back yard and I am unlikely to see it as a face.

Now when this is understood, it will be seen to be plainly false that my thesis places "the creation of expressive meaning strictly in the mind of the perceiver, leaving no room for intended expressive meaning on the part of the creator. . . ." In a moment I will make clear why I find such phrases as "expressive meaning" misleading as characterizing my position. But leaving that aside for the time being, it is clear that my view allows both creative freedom as to what a musical composition is to be expressive of (within the limits of music's expressive power) and as to whether it is to be expressive at all; and the former, by the way, is a freedom allowed to the creator even if one interprets my thesis in Newcomb's (mistakenly) strong way.

Clearly, just as it was open to Reynolds to make a blue boy or a yellow one, it was open to Mozart to write a triumphant conclusion to his last symphony or a subdued, contemplative one. Reynolds painted a blue boy by choosing materials we are hardwired to perceive as blue, Mozart chose materials, some of which we are hard-wired to perceive as triumphant (given, always, that we perceive music, or any other art, in a network of conventions). All artists make use of what they know about how people perceive in order to get their desired effects; and some of those ways people perceive are hard-wired. There is no more reason to think that, on my account of musical expressiveness, the composer's freedom to make music expressive of what *he or she* intends is curtailed than to think that (as I believe) some aspects of representational seeing are hard-wired implies undue constraints on the painter's freedom to represent what he or she wills. But, obviously, *all* artists are limited in what they can do by the genetic endowments of human beings: what we can or cannot hear, or see, or comprehend.

Newcomb's second problem with the "animation" thesis is that "some of the expressive qualities we ascribe to it [music] are not animate ones: for example, references we may commonly hear in it to water, glass, fire." Now what must strike one straight away as very strange in this objection are the "expressive" properties that Newcomb suggests are "not animate"; for what is perfectly obvious, to begin with, is that they are not "expressive." Music may possess a fiery quality—that is, be fiery—but it hardly makes sense to say that music is "expressive of" fire or fieriness. Not all of the qualities music can possess are expressive ones, nor was any such thing suggested in *The Corded Shell*. Furthermore, this is no mere verbal quibble. Words that name expressive properties are, *eo ipso,* words that name those mood- and emotion-states of human beings that can be expressed. That, of course, is why the "animation" thesis is supposed to explain them. Expressing is animate—that is to say, it is a human action. That is why music can be expressive (say) of melancholy, but not of fire (or fieriness). It can *represent* fire; but that of course is another story.[2]

But why, it may be asked, place so much emphasis on the *expressive* properties of music, when there are all these others as well? Perhaps that is part of what motivates Newcomb's second problem. Music can be watery and glassy and fiery, and half-a-hundred other things besides mournful and triumphant and angry. So why all the fuss and feathers over the latter? Why write a book just on *those*? More important, perhaps, if the hard-wiring, "animation" thesis explains *only* expressive, animate musical properties, is it not a rather strange anomaly that, "by nature," as it were, we are predisposed to perceive just these features? And are we not in danger of multiplying hard-wired "instincts" beyond what rational theory-making can allow? To invoke a natural propensity, bequeathed by evolution, to explain the perception of expressive features in music is to take a rather serious—some might say desperate—step. And if it does not, at a stroke, account for all those other features as well, it would seem a highly questionable explanatory procedure. The heavy ordnance should settle all of the questions, once and for all, or not be brought up in the first place, at such prohibitive expense.

But this is to forget two very important things. First, it was not *The Corded Shell*, and the particular eccentricities of its author, that somehow brought the expressive properties of music out of the chorus and into the footlights. They have been stage front since antiquity, always peculiarly and importantly ascribed to music above all other "phenomenological" properties (as I propose to call them). They have been the properties the consideration of which has motivated musical revolutions; and they have been the properties, above all others, that "humanistic" criticism has talked about or talked about not talking about. And, second, *they* are the phenomenological properties that present the special "metaphysical" difficulty (if I may so call it) of how a certain kind of object, musical sound, can possess a certain kind of property, the garden-variety emotion, that can belong only to a very different kind of object, namely, a sentient, thinking being. It is this extreme difficulty, coupled with the critical and historical importance of the properties that justify an extreme remedy— mine or some other. But it hardly requires such drastic hypotheses, I would think, to understand how both the sea and a passage of music can both be fiery. Thus there is every reason in the world to expect that an account of how music possesses expressive properties properly so-called—which is to say, properties of emotion and mood—will not be an account applicable to the other phenomenological properties of music that Newcomb mistakenly calls "expressive." And if the basis of expressiveness in music *is* biological, as I hypothesize, it cannot be surprising that expressive properties have exceeded in importance all others that music might possess.

◇ 3 ◇   I concluded, in *The Corded Shell*, that pure instrumental music can support only what I called "gross distinctions" in expressive characterizations. "No doubt," Newcomb observes, "musicians will find this to be the most serious fault of the book."[3] Why so?

At the start, this objection presents itself in a philosophically naive way; and before we get to its deeper implications we had best divest it of its trivial ones. The language of philosophy is easily seen as equally through-and-through profound by the credulous and just plain silly by various kinds of "outsiders." It is, I think, in the vein of the skeptical and somewhat grumpy "outsider" that Newcomb remarks: "Kivy's opinion of the power of music seems to have been indelibly marked by the tendency of aestheticians to discuss the expressivity of music only in simple, very general expressive predicates, like 'sad' or 'joyous.'"[4] And again:

> Nearly every aesthetician who writes on musical expression seems to see as the goal of the discussion the question whether or not the second movement of the *Eroica* Symphony is "sad." What virtue could such a one-word description possibly have as an interpretation of that piece, or of any other of similar richness? To struggle to give shape to a theory that permits no more than such a statement is like struggling to articulate a theory that permits us to do no more than call *Paradise Lost* sublime.[5]

Now the philosopher's first reaction to this must be one of extreme impatience. Surely it is obvious that, in the present context, "sad" and "joyous" are placeholders, and "The second movement of the *Eroica* is sad" is merely a dummy sentence. And to criticize the philosopher of art for the triviality of these would be like dismissing Tarski's theory of truth out of hand because all the great logician talks about is "Snow is white." Who cares? Of course snow is white. It needs no Tarski to tell us this. I suppose I could have used "∅" instead of "sad." Would that have been better? Perhaps it would have made it completely unmistakable that you can fill that in with whatever the traffic will bear. But over the years I have tried to liberate myself from "ø," because it suggests a rigor that my subject does not possess, and makes philosophical prose even more unreadable than it has to be.

Further, the felony is compounded by the suggestion that the "aesthetician," of which I am a case in point, not only believes that "sad" and "joyful" are just about the only expressive predicates music will support, but that, by use of the dummy sentence, "The second movement of the *Eroica* is sad," he or she (or Kivy) means to imply that the second movement of the *Eroica* is sad *tout court*, from beginning to end, and so much for its emotive characterization.

But surely that is an unjust caricature of my view. As a matter of fact, I do not characterize the opening of the *Eroica*'s slow movement as "sad," except in the perfectly proper sense that its expressive character is a particular species of sadness, namely, it is "funereal" (which any sophisticated listener would know, by the way, from the pure musical parameters, independent of the title). And *of course* it is not funereal throughout. At measure 12, the brief sojourn in E flat introduces a more "happy" mood; and a prolonged change of mood occurs in the section for oboe solo in C at measure 69. Nor do I think "happy" is as specific as I can get here. For because the opening is not merely sad, but obviously funereal, it seems entirely appropriate to suggest that the brief suggestion of E flat, and the longer section in C, are not merely happy but "consoling." And so on. Expressive detail at this level of specificity is perfectly consistent with the theory sketched in *The Corded Shell*. Of course there are, on my view, limits to how specific one can get. And I shall talk about that at length in a moment.

◇ 4 ◇   But there is an additional error here in the direction of philosophical "naivete" (if I may so put it) that must be gotten out of the way before I go on to what I take to be the deeper implications of Newcomb's criticism in this regard. Combined with the mistaken notion that all the argument in *The Corded Shell* can allow for as expressive properties of music are such as "happiness" and "sadness" is the equally mistaken notion that vouchsafing such properties for music, if it were my only goal, is a trivial accomplishment: as "trivial" as assuring "sublimity" to *Paradise Lost*. I gather the idea here is that the mountains are in labor. . . .

What has been forgotten, however, is that *The Corded Shell* is an answer to philosophical skepticism with regard to the expressive properties of music: a skepticism that denies to music *any* expressive properties whatsoever. And were *The Corded Shell* to have succeeded only in establishing that the second movement of the *Eroica* can *really* be sad, it would have accomplished a very great deal, from the philosopher's point of view. Indeed, it would have accomplished a similar philosophical task to the one struggled with by some of the giants of Enlightenment aesthetics, including Kant, of establishing that something, *Paradise Lost*, for example, can *really* be sublime. It is hard for me to see either of those tasks as philosophically trivial. And if we cannot make out a case for music's being happy and sad, then we certainly cannot make out a case for its being any of the more subtle expressive things that Newcomb and others think it is. But let me now get on to these subtleties, and to the more profound implications of Newcomb's criticism.

◇ 5 ◇   There is another argument lurking here. Let me try to bring it out.

I shall call the expressive properties that Newcomb thinks are the only ones *The Corded Shell* can countenance "gross expressive properties" (or "geps" for short); and those more interesting ones that Newcomb thinks music can possess "subtle expressive properties" (or "seps"). Here is the argument I think Newcomb is making. It is very simple; it is valid; and it goes like this:

> Music possesses seps.
> On Kivy's theory, music cannot possess seps.
> Therefore, Kivy's theory is false.

It is valid. But is it good?

Well, the first place to look for an answer ought to be the second premise. Is it the case that, on the view propounded in *The Corded Shell*, music cannot possess seps? Clearly, that all depends on how "s" the "eps" are.

Newcomb apparently thinks that the only expressive properties *The Corded Shell* can countenance are ones at the level of generality of "sad" and "happy." Perhaps there are passages in the book that suggest that; but it is not the position I hold, as I have said previously. Thus, I certainly believe that in pure instrumental music we can distinguish (say) between triumphant joy, or exuberant good spirits, and calm or contemplative joy; between funereal melancholy and anguished melancholy; between violent anger and a less violent kind; and so on. So let us say that, along with geps, *The Corded Shell* also countenances properties more subtle than they, but not so subtle as seps: I will call them "meps" (for "moderate expressive properties").

We must now turn to the first premise and inquire whether in fact music possesses seps; for if it does, then the theory expounded in *The Corded Shell* must be false, since, although it countenances geps and meps, it does not countenance seps.

This question is not an altogether straightforward one. The reason is that the answer has a kind of dual role: it is both the beginning *and* the end of theorizing. It is the beginning, because before one can make a theory of musical expressiveness, one must first decide what data the theory is to account for: that is to say, what expressive properties of music it has to explain. But, on the other hand, once one has the theory, and is convinced of its truth, it is only to be expected that what the theory does and does not countenance as an expressive property will, at least in part, determine what expressive properties one wants to say music does or does not, can or cannot possess. We find a similarly complex interrelation between theory and data in ethics, where the task may be seen, if one is an Aristotelian, of fashioning a theory that will accommodate existing moral intuitions, subsequently finding, when one's theory is in place, that it will not accommodate all, and inevitably using the theory to declare some of these purported intuitions ungenuine.

The theory put forth in *The Corded Shell* was fashioned under the assumption that music possesses what I am now calling geps and meps, but not seps: it was fashioned, in other words, to explain, given that music does possess geps and meps, how this is possible.

But why assume from the start that music possesses geps and meps but not seps? What rational grounds have I for doing so?

I will say nothing here about why we should assume music to possess expressive properties of any kind in the first place, as Newcomb and I are agreed on that point. But as regards which ones to countenance, I suppose the most openly empirical approach, completely free of question-begging scruples, would simply be to assume as a methodological principle that any successful theory of musical expression must accommodate *all* the expressive properties ascribed to music in the music-critical literature since (let us say) the beginning of the seventeenth century or (if one wanted to be even more liberal than that) since the beginning of polyphony in the West. This would leave no room for complaints that the philosopher's theorizing has in any way unjustly constrained or been unfaithful to established critical practice.

But who could hope to satisfy such an oceanic requirement? And who would want to? Surely it is not the duty of philosophy to find a theoretical foundation for every piece of emotive extravagance that has been visited upon the great instrumental compositions of the last two and one-half centuries. The answer to Hanslick's critique is not to reinstate, across the board, the whole apparatus of Romantic criticism, including the excessive emotivism that that critique was so insightful in crying down. No one wants that: so select we must; and some rational method of selection can justifiably be expected of anyone endeavoring to give a philosophical account of the expressive in music.

Now to a certain extent the selection must be based on such imponderables as instinct, musical taste, and aesthetic judgment. What I hear in music—what *I* hear in music—must be the basic data for my theory. And what *I* hear in pure instrumental music are geps and meps, but not seps. My musical instinct, my musical perception, my aesthetic judgment all conspire in this. Of course they are not infallible—nor are anyone else's. But what they all conspire in, in my case, is the conclusion that geps and meps are believable, seps an extravagance.

But that is not the end of it. For we must recall the dual role of expressive properties: both the beginning and the end of theorizing. It is not merely my aesthetic judgment and the rest that I rely upon in selecting out geps and meps while rejecting seps. It is also a consequence of my theory that geps and meps are *echt*. Now this may sound like a vicious circle. It is not. It is, rather, a case of benign boot-strapping, in which theory-making and the selection of what properties the theory must accommodate reciprocally interact. I may start off with aesthetic and musical intuitions about what expressive properties music can possess. I *also* start off with some informed philosophical opinions about what the possibilities for theory-making are: what kind of theory is feasible, given my philosophical commitments and predilections; what reasonable hopes for the range of expressive properties a philosophically plausible theory might allow; and so on. It is this reciprocal process that legitimizes both the expressive properties of music and the theory that explains their presence. Others, with different musical sensibilities from mine, may, like Newcomb, begin by countenancing seps. But they who do will face the inevitable and unenviable task of finding a theory to accommodate them. But there is more to it than this; and before I go on to other matters, it would be well to look a little more deeply into the matter of seps and the gulf that separates Newcomb's way of looking at music from mine that this look reveals.

◇ 6 ◇   The phrases that Newcomb uses most frequently to refer to the expressive properties of music are tell-tale ones: "emotive content" or "meaning." These, and phrases very much like them, occur far too frequently for us not to take them seriously; and if we do, it explains convincingly why Newcomb must reject my theory and why I must reject the argument of his, outlined above, to the effect that since my theory cannot accommodate his expressive properties, it cannot be right.

Clearly, the word "content" suggests subject matter, which, in turn, suggests propositional structure, information, "aboutness." In other words, it suggests semantic significance. If I say that *Crime and Punishment* possesses psychological content, or *Paradise Lost* political content, I am saying that, in part, *Crime and Punishment* is about psychology and *Paradise Lost* is about political matters; that they convey psychological and political views, respectively. Small wonder, then, that in seeing the expressive part of music as "content" or "meaning" or "significance," Newcomb finds my theory hopelessly inadequate as an account of musical expressiveness. And small wonder, too, that he sees music as possessing seps; because it is only through something like semantic content that, I believe, an artwork could ever come to possess expressive properties so specific and fine tuned.

But we can now easily see the wide gulf that separates my view from Newcomb's; for I was determined in *The Corded Shell*— and that determination is even firmer now, as my views have developed and their implications become clear to me—to avoid any suggestion that my theory of musical expressiveness is a theory of expressive "meaning" in music, or anything else of that kind. I have, whenever possible, avoided the phrases "emotive" or "expressive content"; and when I have used such phrases, it has been in a way (I hope) innocent of its literal implications. Indeed, I have come to see myself as a formalist of Hanslick's stripe, with regard to pure instrumental music, the only difference being that I believe expressive properties are some of the *musical* properties that musical structure can possess, and Hanslick (as I read him) believed that music cannot possess expressive properties. (I shall return to this point in my final chapter.)

Pure instrumental music, then, on my view, possesses expressive properties but not expressive "content." And if, as I suspect, expressive "content" and the possession of seps come as one package for Newcomb, it should be altogether obvious why I reject the syllogism I have extracted (I hope not unfairly) from Newcomb's essay. For we can now, perhaps, rephrase it in the following way:

Music possesses expressive "content."
On Kivy's theory, music cannot possess expressive "content."
Therefore, Kivy's theory is false.

We can, in this form, make quick work of it. The argument is valid but unsound. The first premise is false. On to other matters.

◇ 7 ◇   I am both justly and unjustly chastened by Newcomb for failing, in *The Corded Shell*, to discuss the expressive character and role of the larger musical structures and forms, concentrating exclusively on motives, themes, short harmonic progressions, and chords. Justly, because it is quite true that I neglected to enter into such a discussion, and should certainly have done so, given its obvious importance. Unjustly, however, because Newcomb leaves the impression, perhaps, that the expressiveness of large-scale structure and form would be difficult or impossible for the theory propounded in *The Corded Shell* to accommodate. But just the opposite is true. And nothing I said in *The Corded Shell* does anything but encourage me to wholeheartedly endorse Edward T. Cone's assertion, in a recent essay, that "musical form is itself expressive."[6]

The reason I say that it is easy rather than difficult for the theory I am propounding to accommodate the larger musical structures and forms is that that theory ascribes expressiveness to *structure*: it says that music is expressive of this or that to the extent that its structure bears analogy to the appropriate aspect of human expressive behavior. The more structure the better for this theory. Where it has trouble is with the minimal parts of music that do not exhibit enough structure to allow the analogy to the structure of expressive behavior to go through. Here, as in the case (say) of the melancholy quality of the minor triad, some appeal must be made to the larger structure of music in which this musical unit may perform a syntactic function. But where the structure is big, and palpable, the theory is in its element. And far from thinking that the larger musical structures do not exhibit expressive properties, I have made use of the fact that two of them do—namely da capo aria form and sonata allegro form—in my recent book on the opera.[7]

But this is not all Newcomb has to say on the subject; and to get the rest we had better now take a look at his own words. Newcomb begins by noting what he takes to be a basic difference in approach among the aestheticians who theorize about musical expression. "The fundamental division is between those who look for musical meaning (expressive or otherwise) in what we might call the individual musical image—the small-scale musical detail, be it interval, motive, theme, or phrase—and those who look for it in process or overall form." I myself am included, of course, in the former category, to my discredit. "For most musicians, a major failing of Kivy's book will be his almost exclusive reliance on detail, usually melodic detail, as the seat of musical meaning."[8]

Now I myself do not feel at all committed, as I have suggested above, to the "microcosm" over the "macrocosm" view of musical expressiveness, although I do freely admit that my failure to discuss the latter in my book gave Newcomb ample grounds, no doubt, for believing that I was. Indeed, I think it quite clear that local expressive qualities contribute to large-scale ones and, it also needs to be emphasized, vice versa. Nothing in *The Corded Shell* precludes either. And I hope Newcomb is wrong in thinking that there is a face-off between those who maintain music is locally expressive and those who think it is expressive in the large. That would be about as silly as thinking one was forced to take a stand either for the meaning of words or the meaning of sentences. Can one have one without the other?

What does Newcomb believe? Well, for one thing, he is completely out front, and talking freely here about expressive "meaning." For another, he thinks that my failure to consider the expressive potential of large-scale musical structure has led to my restriction of expressive properties to geps and meps. "This restriction to detail is the main reason for the limitation to 'gross distinctions' that [Kivy] must place on musical expression."[9]

But *how* is large-scale structure supposed to impart the subtle expressive properties, where "detail" cannot? Newcomb refers us for an answer to another article of his in which, I take it, the revealing of what I have called "seps" is supposed to be exemplified in the interpretations offered there of musical form. However, I find nothing in these interpretations—which, by the way, I both admire and find convincing—to support such a claim. And indeed, the reason why becomes apparent even before one gets to Newcomb's interpretations. Newcomb tells us that his "concern in this paper is with large forms and procedures—with those forms and procedures that give shape to the music drama; to the large, symphonically conceived sacred work; *to the symphony, sonata, concerto, and the constellation of related genres of absolute music*—that is to say, the most imposing genres of 19th-century music." His thesis is "that formal processes themselves create expressive meaning." He then adds, in a somewhat offhand manner, considering the crucial importance of the remark, "Although this kind of formal criticism will work equally well for music that has no verbal component whatever . . . I shall practice it here on music with words, since this gives us some exemplification of the kind of expressive content intended in the passage, against which we can check our interpretations."[10]

Now the author of *The Corded Shell* need read no further than this in Newcomb's paper to be reasonably certain that nothing that follows can produce a convincing illustration of how seps can be revealed in "the symphony, sonata, concerto, and the constellation of related genres of absolute music" through Newcomb's interpretive strategy. For as soon as one learns that it is to be worked solely on "music with words"—indeed, Wagnerian music drama, plot, characters, mis-en-scène, and the rest—one can expect, from long experience, that anything in the way of getting beyond geps and meps to seps will be through the good offices of the words and other theatrical paraphernalia. And that, to be sure, is what we find in reading on.

Here is but one example. Newcomb writes, of the question-and-answer scene between Wotan and Mime, in *Siegfried*, act I, scene 2:

> Wagner uses gradual acceleration of tempo to embody and express his formal process. In one abstract sense, then, the acceleration is a purely musical embodiment of the centrifugal, disintegrating formal thrust of this part of the scene. In another more dramatic metaphorical sense it is, throughout most of the process, an expression of Mime's mounting pleasure, confidence, and finally joy at his success in answering the Wanderer's questions. It is then a crushing reversal of formal and dramatic meaning when, at the third question, the climax of the tempo process becomes a *sehr schnell* not of joy but of pain. The full import of this reversal comes to us in musical as well as dramatic terms when Mime's increasingly fast tempo and his increasingly cocky characteristic motive of this second section of the scene is transformed before our ears into the moderate tempo and the cry of despair that had directly preceded the entire scene. . . . Thus the *sehr schnell* of joy first becomes a pain striken one (a reversal of dramatic meaning) then, by means of this shift of the level on which one hears the beat, the *moderato* of the opening cry of despair (a dramatic and a musical reversal).[11]

In terms of expressive properties, then, Newcomb sees the formal structure of the passage in question as a progression from mounting pleasure, to confidence, to joy and then, through musical reversal, to an emotive reversal, where joy becomes panic and finally despair. Now in reading the passage this way, Newcomb is, doubtless, cutting things finer than *The Corded Shell* can (or its author wants to) countenance in regard to *pure instrumental music*—which is quite beside the point, however, as it is very apparent that those things beyond what *The Corded Shell* can countenance in pure instrumental music in the way of more subtle expressive properties are accomplished here not by some magic worked in large musical structure. Rather, the subtleties are due entirely to the words and dramatic situation, which is no more than was allowed for in *The Corded Shell*, where it was urged that texts can supply the "fine tuning" that pure musical materials cannot. And without the text and dramatic situation to aid him, I see no evidence in Newcomb's paper to suggest that the analysis of large musical structure he practices can give anything beyond what *The Corded Shell* will allow, namely geps and meps. I confess, indeed, that this strategy of appealing to large-scale form and structure as somehow being able to impart subtle expressive properties to music, where detail cannot, seems to me as so much whistling past the graveyard. *Of course* large-scale musical structure can be expressive; and Newcomb is right in pointing this out. But as yet, I see no evidence that the expressive properties it does possess go in subtlety beyond the ones my own theory allows for.

◇ 8 ◇   What is altogether perplexing about Newcomb's position on this regard is the way he justifies his concentration on music with words, to the exclusion of pure instrumental music, in the essay under discussion. I have in mind here, particularly, the passage quoted above, where Newcomb says: "I shall practice [formal criticism] here on music with words, since this gives us some exemplification of the kind of expressive content intended in the passage, against which we can check our interpretations." Now the logical model suggested here is, in my estimation, quite bizarre. If I read this passage correctly, it suggests, first of all, that, independent of the words, I can make an expressive interpretation of a musical structure like *Siegfried*, act I, scene 2, and *then* verify or disconfirm my interpretation by comparing it with the expressive intention of the composer, as evidenced by the words. Does it require argument to convince anyone that this could not happen? Surely it is only through knowing the words and the music and their reciprocal relations that an expressive interpretation such as Newcomb gives can be arrived at.

Furthermore, a second thing that this passage suggests, as I read it, even more logically bizarre, is that a musical structure without words can really possess equally subtle expressive properties, it being a mere contingency that, because words are lacking, we cannot verify our interpretation. This would, of course, license the most detailed expressive interpretations of pure musical structures. For when the interpreter is called to account, all he or she need reply is that, because of the lack of a text, the interpretation is "unverifiable"—but possibly true for all of that. But I think we want a stronger judgment here than "unverifiable." We want to say, "Out of bounds: pure instrumental music *cannot* possess such properties." We want, in other words, to be able to separate interpretation from fantasy, no matter how interesting and inventive that fantasy might be.

Another way of putting it is this. A text does not merely provide the means of verifying the expressive properties that are in the music. It plays a vital part in *imparting* such properties as the musical work has to it: to, that is, the musical work of which the words are an integral part. If it is true that Berlioz, in later years, expressed the wish that the *Symphonie fantastique* be performed as a piece of pure instrumental music, sans program, then he was, essentially, willing into existence a new work; and one of the crucial ways the new work differs from the original is in respect of its expressive properties. In my (unfortunate) terminology it possesses only geps and meps, whereas the earlier version, with program and movement titles, possesses seps as well. And one can imagine a kind of example, dear to the heart of Arthur Danto, and close to the heart of his theory, in which an auditor listens to the later version of the *Symphonie fantastique*, under the mistaken impression that he is listening to the earlier.[12] What does he *hear*? Well, in one sense of "hear," he hears exactly the same "sounds" that he would if his assumption were correct. In another obvious sense of "hear" he hears something very different: he hears seps; yet they are no more "in" the work he is listening to than the fanciful story that A. B. Marx (we would say) "imagines" is "in" Beethoven's *Farewell Sonata*.

Thus the whole picture Newcomb seems to be giving of the word-tone expression complex in the essay under discussion is logically askew. Pure musical structure does not possess seps that words reveal there; words do not provide the means by which the presence of pre-existing seps are verified. Words transform geps and meps into seps. They *make;* they do not *discover*. And this is both consistent with and explicitly formulated in Chapter X of *The Corded Shell*, albeit in a logically more primitive way.

◇ 9 ◇   It would be unfair to Newcomb, I must add, in concluding this discussion of the expressive structure and expressive interpretation of music that might be based on it, to suggest that he has put all his eggs in one basket. The analysis of music with words is not the only kind that Newcomb has attempted; and he refers us also to the work of others of which he approves, in which pure instrumental music is given expressive interpretations.

Every such interpretation deserves a separate hearing. There is no deciding, a priori, that no structural interpretation can possibly succeed in making a convincing argument for seps in a piece of absolute music. There are, as I have tried to make clear, general considerations of musical sensibility and philosophical theory that, a priori, dispose *me* to be skeptical of such a possibility. But, as I say, nothing short of a critical examination of each and every claimant can clinch the matter; and that, clearly, would be beyond the purview of this chapter or this book. What is, however, both possible and desirable, I think, in forwarding the argument here is the examination of one example; and it would seem altogether appropriate that that example be taken from Newcomb's own efforts in this regard. I have chosen, rather, to examine instead an analysis by Edward T. Cone, cited with approval by Newcomb, of Schubert's *Moment musical* in A flat, opus 94, no. 6, because it presents the issues in wonderfully concise form, whereas Newcomb's rather longer and more involved analysis of Schumann's Second Symphony, also cited, goes into issues of musical allusion and reference beyond those that are relevant in the present context.[13] But what I have to say about Cone's analysis, concerning musical expressiveness, applies, *pari passu*, to Newcomb's analysis as well.

Cone presents, in the essay under discussion, a technical and formal analysis of the Schubert piece in familiar music-theoretical terms.[14] The expressive description he gives us of this formal structure, which is what concerns us here, is as follows:

> What, then, is the expressive potential of *Moment musical* No. 6? What kinds of human situations present themselves as congruous with its structure? . . . As I apprehend the work, it dramatizes the injection of a strange, unsettling element into an otherwise peaceful situation. At first ignored or suppressed, that element persistently returns. . . . When the normal state of affairs returns, the originally foreign element seems to have been completely assimilated. But that appearance is deceptive. The element has not been tamed; it bursts out with even greater force, revealing itself as basically inimical to its surroundings, which it proceeds to demolish.

Cone concludes: "That is an account, in as general terms as possible, of the expressive potential I find in the principal song form of the *Moment musical*."[15]

So far so good; and were Cone to have been content with an expressive interpretation at this level of generality, it would have been entirely consistent with what was countenanced in *The Corded Shell*. And the way Cone sees the emergence of expressiveness—as the result, as he puts it, of expressiveness being "congruous with . . . structure"—is, again, entirely consistent with my contention that musical expressiveness results from the resemblance of musical structure to expressive behavior. But, alas, Cone is after bigger game, in the form of far more expressive specificity than my theory will allow.

But how to get from the general expressive characterization quoted above to a more specific one? Obviously, the musical structure alone has gotten Cone as far as it can, for *it* yields only the expressive interpretation "in as general terms as possible. . . ." Not surprisingly, he goes to that perennial source, the composer's biography. His progress there is by stages of interpretational refinement.

The first refinement takes us from the abstract expressive areas of the first approximation to the experiences of a "protagonist," described in general terms.

> One can imagine the protagonist becoming more and more fascinated by his discoveries, letting them assume control of his life as they reveal hitherto unknown and possibly forbidden sources of pleasure. When he is recalled to duty, he tries to put these experiences behind him and to sublimate the thoughts that led to them. At first he seems successful, but the past cannot remain hidden. What was repressed eventually returns and rises in the end to overwhelm him.[16]

Now this second approximation has already gone beyond what music *alone* can possibly be expressive of, on my view. And Cone must surely see the difficulties on this regard. For he describes this second stage of refinement as "the personal contact I make with the psychic pattern embodied in the musical structure of the *Moment musical*." How, then, can we get from mere private fantasy, as the phrase "personal contact" suggests, to an interpretation that might have some intersubjective validity? Clearly, one answer is contact with the composer. Such considerations, one would suspect, lead to the third approximation:

> I can go further and suggest a more specific interpretation of that context: it can be taken as a model of the effect of vice on a sensitive personality. A vice, as I see it, begins as a novel and fascinating suggestion, not necessarily though often disturbing. It becomes dangerous, however, as its increasing attractiveness encourages investigation and experimentation, leading to possible obsession and eventual addiction. If one now apparently recovers self-control, believing that the vice has been mastered, it is often too late: either the habit returns to exert its domination in some fearful form, or the effects of the early indulgence have left their indelible and painful marks on the personality—and frequently, of course, on the body as well.[17]

On the body as well; and here, as anyone a little familiar with the particulars of Schubert's life will have guessed, we have arrived at the appeal to biography. "It is well established now that Schubert . . . suffered from syphilis. . . . Did Schubert's realization of that fact, and of its implications, induce, or at least intensify, the sense of desolation, even dread, that penetrates much of his music from then on? (Our *Moment musical* dates from 1824.)"[18]

So here, in a sketch, is Cone's interpretive progress. The basic expressive "plan" of op. 94, no. 6 is congruous with its form, which is a song-and-trio, implying (in the most abstract terms possible) "something," "something else" (trio), and the return of the first "something" (da capo, not necessarily literal). In the first approximation, in expressive terms, the composition comprises a "peaceful situation," "the injection of a strange unsettling element," and a return of "the normal state of affairs," but with the presence still of the "strange unsettling element," which "has not been tamed." In the second expressive approximation, we have a "protagonist" who becomes "fascinated by his discoveries," which take control of his life, a recall to duty, but, nevertheless, an inability to put aside his new experiences, which "overwhelm him." And, finally, in the third approximation, we read the *Moment musical* as going from a virtuous to a vicious life, the recovery of moral self-control, but not entirely, as the moral lapse has left "indelible and painful marks on the personality," and perhaps on the body as well; this third, and most detailed reading being supported by evidence of Schubert's having suffered from vene-real disease, the connection being too obvious to require further comment.

Now let me proceed by suggesting three possible ways of look-ing at what Cone has done here. I shall argue that in two of the ways, what Cone has tried to do is entirely consistent with my own theory, and in the third, which is not consistent, I simply deny its plausibility, for reasons that have already been made clear.

◇ 10 ◇   *The first view:* Cone's first approximation of Schu-bert's *Moment musical* is, as I have remarked before, at a level of generality perfectly consistent with theory. Cone refers to it, interestingly enough, as giving the "expressive potential" of the piece. I would suggest, rather, that it is the second and third ap-proximations that do that. The first approximation in fact tells us just what the piece *is* expressive of. The second and third ap-proximations tell us some of the things it could (potentially) be expressive of *if*. . . . If what? If Schubert had provided it with a program or programmatic title, capable of imparting to it the more explicit content of the second and third approximations. But he did not: he simply gave it the title *Moment musical*, op. 94, no. 6, and there's an end on it. The piece could have been ex-pressive of those other things because it is also congruous with their forms; but without the fine tuning of title or program—that is to say, a text—it can be expressive only at the level of the first approximation.

The second view: But, it might be replied, Schubert *did* give op. 94, no. 6 a program: a hidden one that has to be discovered. And that is exactly what Cone has done: he has discovered the hidden program by analysis of the music and, ultimately, appeal to the known facts of Schubert's life.

Now whether the biography of an artist has relevance to the in-terpretation of his or her artworks has been a disputed point for generations of philosophers and critical theorists. And certainly it could be disputed as well whether such facts about Schubert's life as Cone adduces could possibly provide grounds for assign-ing a program to op. 94, no. 6. Happily, however, neither ques-tion needs detain us here. All we need be concerned with is the hypothetical. If what has transpired in Cone's analysis has not established the hidden program in Schubert's *Moment musical*, then it has not established the second and third approximations as anything but potential; and I have no quarrel with that. If, on the other hand, Cone has succeeded in revealing a hidden, unsuspected program underlying Schubert's piece, I have no quarrel with *that* either, at least from the point of view of the theory of expressiveness in music, just so long as it be acknowledged that *that* program, stated in Cone's words, or words like them, is now seen as part of that composition; just as much a part of it as the familiar program and titles are part of Berlioz' *Symphonie fantastique*. For it is the program that imparts the specificity that gets us from the first approximation to the third, and is nothing more than *The Corded Shell* allows, in acknowledging that texts can fine tune the more general expressiveness of music.

The third view: Another alternative might be to see Cone as attempting to show that Schubert *intended* to make a piece of pure, absolute music expressive of the content of the third approximation by appealing to the facts of the composer's life as he does. Let us assume, for the sake of the argument, that Cone has succeeded in revealing Schubert's intentions, as described above. What should we then reply?

The relevance of artistic intention is, of course, another much disputed issue in philosophy and critical theory. Again, happily, it is an issue we need not enter into here. What I have to say is meant to apply only to the particular matter at hand; and it is this. If Cone has shown that Schubert intended to make op. 94, no. 6—a piece, by hypothesis, of pure, absolute music—expressive of the content of the third approximation, then he has shown that Schubert intended to do the impossible; and so we may safely disregard *this particular intention* in interpreting the piece. It is just flat out impossible for a piece of pure instrumental music, sans text or title or program, to be expressive of anything at the level of specificity of the third approximation, or even the second.

Nor need this failure of intention cause undue distress, or seem paradoxical. Many great artworks (I am tempted to say most) are created under the influence of false theories, and in the service, therefore, of intentions impossible of fulfillment. I dare say that many nineteenth-century composers, in the wake of Schopenhauer's metaphysics, intended to reveal in their music the inner workings of the metaphysical will. I leave it to my readers to decide for themselves whether this was a possible intention to carry out, in the light of contemporary thinking on the subject of speculative metaphysics. In a word, one cannot reveal the workings of what does not exist.

But, of course, Schubert had many other artistic intentions besides the one—if he had that one at all—of expressing the content of the third approximation in op. 94, no. 6. Some of these intentions he fulfilled magnificently, which is why, having written these words, I can now sit back and listen to my recording of the *Moments musicaux* in all of their glory.

Which of these views of what Cone has done (or tried to do) is the correct one? I rather imagine he has tried to do the third, and rather hope it was the first; but I will leave it at that, as I think it is time, now, to go on to other matters.

◇ 11 ◇   In *The Corded Shell* I labored long and hard over establishing some sort of intersubjective criteria for the application of expressive predicates to music. What I gather from Newcomb's remarks is that he thinks recent critical theory has made such preoccupations passé. He writes:

> Close intersubjective agreement, then, is not a proper requirement to make of interpretations of the expressive meaning of music, and, in this, music is not alone. Recent criticism has been making the same point about the expressive meaning of language.[19]

Now of course it would require a book, or books, to canvass any such difficult and extensive topic as "recent criticism" *überhaupt*. But, at least with regard to the two recent critical theorists whom Newcomb invokes, Jonathan Culler and Stanley Fish, neither the quotation from the former that Newcomb adduces nor Fish's most influential work to date, *Is There a Text in This Class?* bears out his claim. Indeed both, it seems to me, when the musical issue is put in its proper light, support mine.

Let us begin with some ground rules. It was never my intention in *The Corded Shell* to claim that the degree of agreement aimed at or required in regard to the emotive characterization of music was in the range of mathematics or the hard sciences. It lies somewhere beyond the allowable range of disagreement in our characterizations of the expressive behavior of human beings, on which it is parasitic. I did not take a stand there, nor do I here, about whether there is one and only one correct interpretation of a work of art, expressive or otherwise, or a plurality of correct interpretations. What I would insist on is that if there is a plurality of correct interpretations, there are criteria for distinguishing those that are correct from those that are not.

But this is no more than Jonathan Culler insists on, in the passage quoted by Newcomb where he says:

> What one is attempting to explain—and it is something that deserves detailed explanation—is the fact that for any work there is a range of interpretations which can be defended within the conventions of reading. We have little difficulty setting aside the idiosyncratic response whose causes are personal and anecdotal (simple discussion with other readers can eliminate these). The problem is to make explicit the operations and conventions which will account for a range of readings and exclude any we would agree to place outside the normal procedures of reading.[20]

It seems perfectly clear that, far from eschewing intersubjective agreement, Culler is suggesting that it exists, and that its existence is a datum of literary criticism that critical theory is supposed to explain. Of course Culler is suggesting that agreement covers a range of interpretations, rather than converging on a single one. But that "range of interpretations . . . can be defended within the conventions of reading," and "the problem [of critical theory] is to make explicit the operations and conventions which will account for a range of readings and exclude any *we would agree to place outside the normal procedures of reading.*" I underscore the concluding phrase, obviously, to emphasize that Culler is assuming intersubjective agreement, not rejecting it.

What goes for Culler goes for Fish as well. The quotation from Culler is indeed a gloss of Fish; and it is perfectly clear that the author of *Is There a Text in This Class?* is at pains to defend his critical theory against the charge of implying "anarchy" in interpretation.[21] Anarchy in interpretation means, of course, complete lack of intersubjective agreement; so a defense against it means a commitment to just that thing, which is to say, intersubjective agreement in interpretation (to the extent that that discipline allows) and to the philosophical analysis of the criteria on which such agreement rests. Fish denies neither that there is consensus (at a given time) on the range of possible interpretations of a text nor that there is consensus (at a given time) on the critical methods for reaching correct interpretations. Indeed, without the methods, we could not have the interpretations. Where Fish, and others of his stripe, depart from the older critical theories of such writers as Monroe Beardsley and, more recently, E. D. Hirsch is not in denying intersubjective agreement or intersubjective criteria of interpretation, but in how these interpretive strategies derive their force. For where others might see them as deriving from immutable canons of meaning or authorial intention, Fish sees them as quite mutable artifacts of an evolving institutional practice. It is Fish's view that what intersubjective argument and reason-giving we see in literary criticism—and, on his view, we *do* see these things—are assured by this institutional grounding of critical strategies. He may be mistaken in this.[22] Be that as it may, it is surely mistaken to take him, as Newcomb apparently does, as intending to dismiss intersubjective agreement as "not a proper requirement" of interpretation. He must believe it is a "proper requirement"; for one of the most extensive (and labored) parts of *Is There a Text in This Class?* is his attempt to assure us that his theory allows for it. There are those among the "deconstructionists" who seem to eschew intersubjectivity and who, indeed, delight in tolerating the contradictory. But, so far as I can make out, Culler and Fish are not of that particular company.

◇ 12 ◇   But let us not get hung up on the question of whether the authors adduced do or do not support Newcomb's view. Far more important to us is whether Newcomb is correct: whether intersubjective agreement, within, of course, certain acceptable limits, is or is not some kind of necessary condition for "objectivity."

At one place, significantly, Newcomb invokes the metaphor or model of wine tasting to make his point—significantly, because, whether by intention or serendipitously, this will immediately call to the aesthetician's mind a passage in Hume's masterful essay "Of the Standard of Taste," which has excited a good deal of discussion in recent years. What Newcomb says about wine tasting is this:

Kivy demonstrates that the application of expressive terms to many of the situations which we meet in everyday life is no more and no less strictly rule-governed than the application of such terms to music, but such demonstrations go further than is necessary for the refutation of the strict constructionist. Disagreement on the application of interpretive terms is in principle no reason for rejecting the idea of musical expression. We might just as well say that because a group of wine tasters (whether experts or not is irrelevant) would probably write widely varying descriptions of the taste of a fine wine, that the wine has no taste, or (with Hanslick) that the taste may be there but is not an important component of the wine. The situation is rather that our language is ill equipped to cope with the phenomena of expressive meaning in music. This no more reflects on the existence of expressive meaning in music than it does on that of taste in wine.[23]

Two preliminary points need clearing up before we can get to the meat of this passage. To begin with, the contention that wine tasters "would probably write widely varying descriptions of the taste of a fine wine" is equivocal. On one interpretation it is quite benign. This can be illustrated by example. On my first visit to Scotland, I described the taste of a certain malt whisky as "smokey." My host described it as "peaty." A little discussion revealed that "smokey" and "peaty" were descriptions of the same quality of the Scotch. I take it that this is not what Newcomb means when he talks about "widely varying descriptions," but, rather, that he means widely varying descriptions in the sense of descriptions indicating wide disagreement about what particular feature or features a wine (or whatever) possesses. For, of course, I am not suggesting, nor did I suggest in *The Corded Shell*, that varying descriptions of the former kind are evidence of the absence of the features named. That would be a foolish claim indeed.

The second point is more serious and, I think, must amount to a logical howler. In effect, Newcomb is presenting a purported *reductio* of my claim that wide and endemic disagreement about what expressive properties musical works possess would be evidence (not *conclusive* evidence, by the way) for there not being expressive properties in the music at all. My argument, he claims, is as absurd as arguing that because we disagree about the taste of wines, wines have no taste at all; and I quite agree that to argue the latter would be absurd indeed—mad is more like it.

The problem with Newcomb's supposed *reductio*, however, is that his analogy is completely out. To argue that disagreement about the qualities of wine is evidence for wine's having no taste at all would be like arguing that disagreement about the qualities of music, expressive or otherwise, is evidence for music's having no sound at all—which would, needless to say, be absurd in the extreme. The valid analogy is this. To argue that wide and endemic disagreement over whether wines are "fruity" or not is evidence that fruitiness is not a proper feature of wine at all would be like arguing that wide and endemic disagreement about whether music is sad or not is evidence that sadness is not a proper feature of music at all. That is a proper analogy, but no *reductio;* for both arguments are valid. Newcomb is quite mistaken on this point. Wide and endemic disagreement about features of wine would be evidence (not conclusive) that wine does not have the features in question; and wide and endemic disagreement about expressive features of music would be, if it existed, evidence (not conclusive) that music does not possess expressive properties. As Ronald de Sousa has put the general point recently, "common sense will not be dislodged from the assumption that intersubjective agreement is valued as evidence of truth."[24]

To see that Newcomb is mistaken in thinking that disagreement provides no evidence for absence of qualities disagreed over, let us consider the following case. Mr. and Mrs. Bibulous are members of a wine tasting club. Mrs. B tastes a wine and declares it a bit "corky." Mr. B tastes the same wine and declares it a bit "metallic." (Readers of Hume's essay on taste will recognize a relative of one of Sancho Panza's "kinsmen" here.) No one else of the company finds the wine either metallic or corky. Now at this point in the proceedings the other members of the club might well conclude that the wine is neither metallic nor corky, but that Mr. and Mrs. B have tainted palates and are experiencing purely "subjective" tastes. Another explanation, of course, is also possible, namely, that Mr. and Mrs. B are more sensitive than their fellow tasters, and have experienced qualities in the wine that the others are incapable, at least at present, of detecting. Which is the better explanation? How do the club members go about deciding? What they would do, I suppose, being lovers of wine, is taste the vintage again, with Mr. and Mrs. B's descriptions in mind, and try to see if by further practice, and further concentration of their oenological faculties, they can come to taste what Mr. and Mrs. B do. In other words, they are aiming at consensus.

Now imagine the following outcome. Gradually, most of the club members come to experience the taste of corkiness in this particular vintage, and declare Mrs. B's original judgment correct: the wine really is corky, really has a corky quality to it. But no consensus at all emerges with regard to the metallic quality that Mr. B reports. At one session, one member or another reports tasting it, but reports not tasting it at the next. "Blind trials" produce judgments for or against the wine's having a metallic taste about at the level of chance. In short: there is apparently irresolvable disagreement all around.

What will, what ought the club members conclude about whether or not the wine is metallic? They might conclude that Mr. B has some special faculty for tasting that they do not have, and elect him permanent president of the club. But, I suggest, they would not do this, nor ought they. What they would, and should do, given the evidence they have, is to conclude that the wine is not metallic at all, does not possess that quality, but that Mr. B's reaction is purely "subjective," due perhaps to some temporary or permanent defect in his palate: a mineral deficiency, perhaps, that makes things taste metallic to him; or a congenital abnormality in his taste buds. If, of course, Mr. B did turn out, after physical testing of some kind, to be suffering from such a condition, that would clinch the matter. Even, however, if no defect in Mr. B's perceptual apparatus were ever discovered, the wine club would still be arguing to the best explanation in taking its inability to reach any kind of consensus on the metallic taste of the wine as evidence (not conclusive) of the taste's being a subjective artifact of Mr. B's palate and not a property of the wine.

Surely, too, this is the way things should go in the case of the expressive properties of music. Hanslick was absolutely right in thinking that the argument from total disagreement over the expressive properties of music to the conclusion that music does not possess expressive properties is a valid argument. What he was wrong about was thinking that the argument is good; for there is no such disagreement over the expressive properties of music at what I have been calling the first approximation, or the level of geps and meps. Indeed, in *The Corded Shell*, and in the preceding chapter, it was argued that there is consensus, at least within the limits the subject matter allows.

What we would do, what we *do* do when confronted with an expressive characterization of a piece of music, is to go back to the music itself with that interpretation in mind, to see if we, too, can hear what the interpreter claims to hear. And if no consensus develops, surely we are arguing to the best explanation here, as in the case of the aberrant judgment about wine, when we argue that that characterization is "merely subjective." What else, for example, could we say, or need we say, to Sigmund Spaeth, who wrote the following words to the first four measures of Mozart's 40th Symphony:

> With a laugh and a smile like a sunbeam,
> And a face that is glad like a fun-beam.[25]

Furthermore, if the whole class of expressive properties were subject to endemic and irresolvable dispute—if consensus were absent across the board—we would be equally justified in taking that as strong (not conclusive) evidence that music does not possess expressive properties. And this is why, to conclude, I was obliged, in *The Corded Shell*, to make an argument for the existence of agreement with regard to the expressive properties of music, in what I called there their general form, and what I have been calling here their first approximation, or the level of geps and meps.

◇ 13 ◇   Newcomb believes, quite unaccountably, so it seems to me, that wine tasting exhibits a vast amount of disagreement. My impression is, quite to the contrary, that wine tasting is a discipline with a well-established terminology, well-established parameters, and wide consensus with regard to what wines have what tastes. Indeed, philosophers of art have been known to use, as Hume did, wine tasting as a model for how something can be both "a matter of taste" and intersubjective at the same time. But this factual question about the nature of wine tasting is quite irrelevant to our concerns here. What is relevant is that Newcomb thinks discussion of the expressive properties of music is in the same chaotic state. From this he draws the familiar conclusion "that our language is ill equipped to cope with the phenomena of expressive meaning in music." And then it is but a step to an equally familiar one: ineffability.

> Furthermore, to admit that musical import is finally ineffable is not equivalent to believing that we somehow act improperly toward music in trying to write and talk about it. Hundreds of mystics have written about the ineffable mystic experience, and have treasured and learned from the writings of other mystics about the experience, without either claiming that their words offered a direct equivalent of the mystic experience or refusing to write about the experience because words rendered its significance imperfectly. Should we musicians be holier than they?[26]

I would like to conclude this chapter on Newcomb by giving some thought to these puzzling claims.

I take it to be an argument for the ineffability of an experience-type—mystical experience, or the experience of tasting a wine, or experiencing expressive qualities in music—that one's language is ill suited to describe the experience-type in question. So let us begin by examining Newcomb's claim that "our language is ill equipped to cope with the phenomena of expressive meaning in music." What grounds are there for it?

Let me urge that there are no grounds at all, and, indeed, that there are, on the contrary, grounds for believing our language to be no less well equipped for talking about the expressiveness of music than for talking about anything else we commonly encounter in our everyday lives—the everyday lives our language has, of course, evolved for the express purpose of describing and otherwise coping with. It is fair to ask someone who claims that language is ill equipped for this or that how one goes about deciding *what* language is or is not equipped to describe. What one suspects, in the case of those who claim that language is ill equipped to describe the expressive properties of music, is that the grounds are really not independent of decisions already made about musical expressiveness. The argument seems to be this. Music possesses expressive properties. There is complete disagreement about what, in any given case, those expressive properties are. And this disagreement must be due, therefore, not to the fact that music does not possess expressive properties (since it has already been agreed that it does) but to the fact that language is ill equipped to describe them.

Of course, a lot rides on the first premise; and one cannot accept it without qualification. What level of specificity are we talking about? The level countenanced in *The Corded Shell*? In that case, of course, I deny the second premise: there is general consensus within acceptable limits. The level of Cone's (as I call them) second and third approximations? In that case, I deny the first premise: music does not possess such expressive properties, and the inevitable irresolvable disagreement in the critical literature over expressive properties at these levels of specificity is not evidence that language is ill equipped for the expressive in music, but evidence (not conclusive) that music does not possess these properties at all. Thus, the familiar claim that language is ill equipped to deal with expressive properties in music may very well conceal the begging of the question at issue; namely, whether music is expressive at the level of specificity that requires appeal to the supposed infirmities of language.

Thus it seems to me incumbent upon anyone appealing to the inadequacy of language in support of a theory to give us evidence of the inadequacy of language independent of the mere assumption of the theory's truth. There are, indeed, perfectly good, uncontroversial examples of appeal to the inadequacy of language; and a look at one will, I think, suggest what some of the acceptable criteria might be for such an appeal, and just why they are not present in the case of musical expressiveness.

It is commonly accepted—and a familiar plaint of those who try to give popular, nonmathematical accounts of recent discoveries in physics—that ordinary language is ill equipped to convey the concepts of contemporary physical theory; and we needn't accept this merely on faith, for it is quite obvious why it is so. Ordinary language has gradually evolved for, among other purposes, describing the material world as it is perceived and manipulated by ordinary people at the level of tables and chairs, and rocks and dirt, and eggs and butter, and hands and feet. But the material "objects" of the contemporary physicist and astronomer—the inconceivably large and impossibly small—with their properties, bizarre beyond anything in our experience of our ordinary world, cannot, of course, be adequately described in ordinary language, just because ordinary language has been formed by the experience of our ordinary world. This is all thoroughly understandable.

But now we can see exactly why there is no reason, at least

of this kind, to believe that ordinary language is ill equipped to describe the expressive properties of music. For music is as old as language itself, perhaps older, if the theory of Rousseau and others is to be credited, which places the origin of language in music. And so also must be human expression. If language evolves in tandem with human emotive expression, then there is no reason to think that the capability of describing musical expressiveness is any less developed than the capability of describing expression *tout court*. Language is, indeed, ill equipped to describe the expression of the inhabitants of the planet Mongo, who, as everyone knows, are rational crystals; and it is ill equipped to describe the expressiveness of their "music" too, no doubt, as it is based upon vibrations we cannot hear. For the life of me, though, I cannot see any reason for believing that my language is ill equipped to describe the expression of human beings, or the expressiveness of their music.

For far too long now we have heard that music has "deep meaning" that the initiated would be glad to impart to us were it not for the infirmities of "mere language." I think this is a cover-up for the awful truth that the deep meaning just isn't there. You might just as well convince me that but for the infirmities of language, I might be apprised of the hopes and aspirations of the Continental Shelf. I think the time has come to call this particular bluff.

◇   14   ◇   If the reason, then, for thinking music ineffable, as regards its expressive character, is that language is ill equipped for describing its expressive properties, we can reject that claim, for the reason comes to nothing. But the claim itself merits some attention, for Newcomb seems to take it as no very serious matter that music in general, or musical expressiveness in particular, might be ineffable. Rather, he thinks we will have business as usual: the talk can go on. This, however, is a serious mistake. What is ineffable is *ineffable,* and there is an end on it. About the ineffable we cannot talk or write or whistle or even think. And if that is, God forbid, where our theory leads, then we have no recourse, if we are to shun hypocrisy, than, like the Greek skeptics, to take the vow of silence. I don't care to answer Newcomb's rhetorical question. I don't care if musicians are holier than the mystics or not. I do hope that they will be more rational.

Now it is important, I think, to notice that other notions besides what we might call the pure, unadulterated, ineffable are mixed into the passage on ineffability quoted above. And it is perhaps this confusion of "ineffables" that enables Newcomb to think we can go on describing the indescribable. Let us take a look at two of these pseudo-ineffables. They are contained in the following sentence: "Hundreds of mystics have written about the ineffable mystic experience, and have treasured and learned from the writings of other mystics about the experience, without either claiming that *their words offered a direct equivalent of the mystic experience* or refusing to write about the experience because *words rendered its significance imperfectly*" (my italics).

It would appear from this sentence that one of Newcomb's glosses for "ineffable" is something for which words cannot offer a direct equivalent. This, however, would be an absurdly stringent condition: indeed, it would be, I think, to confuse logical categories. An adequate description of a piece of music need no more be a "direct equivalent" of the music than an adequate description of a thunderstorm need be noisy and wet. A description is not a substitute or replica or clone of what it describes. If being a "direct equivalent" in any of these senses is what we mean by an adequate description, then *everything* is ineffable (except perhaps descriptions themselves?). That, I would think, is sufficient argument against the notion that music is "ineffable" in the sense that words cannot be its "direct equivalent."

A second gloss of "ineffable," equally unacceptable, I would think, that emerges from the sentence quoted, is something imperfectly rendered by words. Now, unless that formula is allowed to collapse into the previous one, and come to mean that words cannot be a "direct equivalent" of music, it is a perfectly benign claim, and scarcely amounts to "ineffability." Of course, descriptions of anything vary in degree of adequacy; and it is a harmless truism that all fall short of perfection. No description of a blade of grass, either the naturalist's or the novelist's, quite captures everything about my experience of it. Nor, *a fortiori,* can any description of Beethoven's F-Minor Quartet capture completely my experience of it. But in both cases, some do better than others; and those who through inspired use of the language capture something we cannot articulate ourselves we call blessed for their gift. This, however, is not ineffability. It is merely the human condition; and it precludes neither intersubjectivity nor consensus. It precludes perfect intersubjectivity and perfect consensus. But who ever thought we could have those? Indeed, if we had the latter, I would have reason to suspect we didn't have the former.

◇ 15 ◇   Criticism, far more than plagiarism, is the most sincere form of flattery. And that is why this chapter has grown so long. So let me make an end by remarking that although there is much in Newcomb's article that I disagree with, there is much also with which I agree, including its *spirit*. This spirit is expressed with eloquence and conviction in more than one place, but no more eloquently or forcefully than where he writes:

> Here lies a challenge and an opportunity for music criticism today. Expressive interpretation that is both historically and analytically informed can bring into a close, actively engaged relationship with fine music a much larger audience than now really attends to it. Conversely, musical awareness might thereby become a less marginal area for the cultured person in our society. Philosophical aesthetics has given us a workable conceptual basis for this enterprise, and we should get on with it.[27]

Perhaps Newcomb has paid philosophical aesthetics a somewhat premature compliment in saying that it has already delivered into the hands of the musicologist and critic a workable conceptual basis for the expressive interpretation of music. But we are trying; and certainly great progress has been made in recent years. It is encouraging to discover that musicians are now making common cause with philosophers in this endeavour. Because we need one another, if the conceptual basis sought is to be both musically and philosophically sound. Speaking for the philosophers, all too often what they have produced in this regard, even the great ones, has been philosophically clever but musically absurd. I do not suggest that philosophers should write books for trombone players. What I do urge is that *if* a trombone player takes the trouble to read and to understand what a philosopher says about music, it should make musical sense.

CHAPTER XV

And Nevertheless It Moves

◇ 1 ◇ Since the publication of *The Corded Shell*, there has been a spate of articles in the philosophical literature purporting to show that music arouses the garden-variety emotions, how it can do this, and what role such arousal might reasonably be thought to play in a person's experience. Whether this is a case merely of *post hoc*, or *propter hoc* as well, is difficult to say. Some of the articles appeared too soon after the publication of my book for it to have had any effect on them. Others refer to it specifically. But all attest to some deeply felt need, apparently, for emotivism to be true. The need is real enough and, when properly understood, fully justified. It is, however, misdescribed as a need for music to arouse the garden-variety emotions. The need, its description, and the means of its fulfillment are the subjects of the present chapter.

It seems to me that it would be counterproductive to examine all of the efforts, since 1980, to construct an arousal theory of musical expressiveness. But there is some real utility, I think, in looking at some, and seeing why they have failed. First, the failures may help to convince the skeptical where positive arguments cannot, that cognitivism is the right way to go. That so many versions of the arousal theory have failed is, of course, no conclusive argument that emotivism is false. There is always the possibility that the next one will succeed. Nevertheless, optimism must stop somewhere. And perhaps I can encourage some of the emotive optimists to stop here, with the latest failures of the doctrine.

Furthermore, I think the critical examination of some of these new attempts to float musical emotivism will give us a notion of just how deep this need for the arousal paradigm to be true does indeed run; for the conclusion of this chapter will be concerned with how that need can be allayed, without resorting to the totally implausible view that music is sad in virtue of making us sad, angry in virtue of making us angry, and so forth.

Source: Sections 4 and 5 of this chapter are a revised version of my note, "Sound Sentiment: A Reply to Donald Callen," *Journal of Aesthetics and Art Criticism*, XLI, no. 3 (Spring 1983). Reprinted with permission.

I shall examine here three versions of the theory that music arouses the garden-variety emotions, but they also represent three different kinds: what I call the *stimulus model*, the *representation model*, and the *property model* of how arousal takes place. This procedure will, I take it, give my refutations more teeth, as they will be not merely refutations of individual theories but refutations of three different theoretical strategies; thus refutations, at the same time, of any other theories that may fall under any of these three theory types, unless drastically revamped.

One further point of clarification before I get on with it. The arousal theory generally takes the form of a theory that music is expressive in virtue of arousing the garden-variety emotions. But it needn't say this. It may say instead that music is expressive of the garden-variety emotions for some other reason, and does, additionally, arouse the emotions it is expressive of. Just why someone might want to claim this will be made explicit later on. For the time being, though, I am interested merely in the supposed mechanisms whereby music is said to arouse the garden-variety emotions. Where the other question—the question of whether music is expressive because of arousal—is relevant, it will be readily apparent from the discussion.

◇ 2 ◇   Let us say that I claim sad music is sad in virtue of arousing sad emotions, happy in virtue of arousing happy ones, and so on; and that someone answers: "This cannot be so, because frequently a listener is not made sad by sad music, may even be joyful in its presence, yet perfectly well recognizes the music he or she is listening to is sad."

In answer to such an exchange, John Nolt has argued that "there is no contradiction in saying that a person feels joy in the presence of sad music. What is proscribed is that joy is the usual reaction to sad music—and that seems right. Sad music does *tend* to make us sad." [1]

Nolt's point is that an arousal theory of musical expressiveness is a dispositional account: that is to say, the expressive properties of music are taken to be *tendencies* of music to arouse emotions; and that being the case, it is no more a refutation of the claim that a piece of music is sad to point to a person who is not being saddened in its presence than it would be a refutation of the claim that a lump of sugar is soluble in water to put it in a glass of water that does not dissolve it. Nor is it a refutation of the claim that musical expressiveness is dispositional to cite instances where arousal fails; for, of course, any disposition can fail if appropriate conditions are not satisfied; witness the case of the lump of sugar failing to dissolve in water, for whatever reason.

That being said, however, it becomes immediately apparent that a dispositional account of musical expressiveness has deep problems. To start with, it seems to beg the question right from the start, at least in Nolt's version. For Nolt simply states, without argument or evidence, that "sad music does *tend* to make us sad." But that is highly debatable, where the statement, for example, that "sugar does *tend* to dissolve in water" is not. In other words, whatever account one might give of how and why sugar dissolves in water, it is agreed on all hands, to start with, that sugar does dissolve in water. Whereas an account of how and why music arouses emotions founders from the start, there being no agreement as to whether it arouses emotions at all or what evidence counts for or against the claim that it does.

Second, no dispositional account of any property whatever can get off the ground without some well-founded set of defeating and enabling conditions. It is no good to say that sugar tends to dissolve in water without stating at the same time under what conditions it does and does not, as it is clear that sometimes it fails to do so. There is general agreement with regard to sugar, about what the conditions are, and what kinds of conditions are relevant. But here again music fails to meet these requirements for a genuinely dispositional account. For no one can really say, on the basis of any agreed upon theory or set of reasonable criteria, what the relevant conditions might be for the arousal of emotions by music, except for trivial and uninteresting ones. Is it a defeating condition, for example, that I am very sad, and (therefore?) that joyful music fails to make me joyful? What is one to say? One cannot simply assume that since the sad music failed to make me sad, there *must* have been some defeating condition, without simply making the arousal theory true by conventionalist sulk.

These problems seem daunting enough. But there is yet another that seems to me, though less obvious, far more instructive; and I would like to pursue it at greater length.

Suppose I am listening to a piece of music for the first time, that is failing to make me sad, but that I recognize as expressive of sadness. Surely any proper account of musical expressiveness in terms of emotive arousal must acknowledge that such cases are possible, and explain to us how they are possible. What explanation is available to the dispositional account?

Well, obviously, if I know that this piece of music *tends* to arouse sadness, then I can know it is expressive of sadness without its making me sad. How might I know, in the absence of the appropriate effect on me, that it tends to have that effect on me and others? One way I might know—and this is the way I want to consider here—is by perceiving in it musical features possessed by other pieces of music known to me to regularly arouse sadness in myself and in others: minor mode, slow tempo, chromatic harmonies, "weeping" melodic lines; things like that. (It would be the same kind of inductive evidence I might have for believing that a lump of white granules is soluble in water even though it is lying in a glass of water before my eyes and stubbornly refusing to dissolve.)

So far, so good for the dispositional account. But consider, now, another case. I am listening to a piece of singularly overblown and inept music that is boring me silly, and, on that account, I pronounce it expressive of boredom. "Foul," cries the proponent of emotive arousal. "We have to distinguish between those emotions music might arouse that it is not expressive of and those it might arouse that are, by virtue of the arousal, part of its expressive character." Perhaps so. But how are we going to do this?[2]

The obvious strategy would seem to be to compare the features of the sad music that make one sad with the features of the boring music that make one bored. For, it might be argued, it must be the nature of the features that, in the one case, licenses us to call the music "expressive of sadness," but does not, in the other case, license us to call the music "expressive of boredom," but, rather, "boring."

Well, we already know the features that sad music tends to have: minor modality, slow tempo, chromatic harmonies, "weeping" melodic lines. What about our example of boring music? I suppose there are unlimited possibilities; but let us say that the piece in question is limited in its harmonic vocabulary, has no particular melodic or contrapuntal interest, and goes on much too long for its extremely modest musical materials to sustain it.

Now what one immediately wants to say is that we perceive sadness in those familiar features of sad music, whereas the features of boring music enumerated above merely *cause* boredom but do not "embody" it. The difference, then, between music that is expressive of an emotion in virtue of arousing it and music that arouses an emotion but is clearly not expressive of it is that the emotion aroused in the first case is aroused by emotively "relevant" features, and in the second case by emotively "irrelevant" ones, an emotively relevant feature being one we can somehow recognize as possessing or embodying the emotion it arouses, an emotively irrelevant feature one that simply arouses but in no way possesses or embodies the emotion aroused.

What is to be noticed straightaway about this strategy is that it appears to be collapsing the arousal theory of musical expressiveness into some form of the cognitive theory, or, at least, buying into the major difficulty of musical cognitivism that emotivism is supposed to circumvent; namely, the puzzle of how music can "embody" emotions. For it now looks as if the emotivist must say one of three things: that music is expressive of emotions in virtue of possessing them as properties, and these emotions are aroused when we recognize them in the music; or that expressiveness is a complex fact of music's possessing emotive properties and arousing them in listeners; or that music is expressive in virtue of arousing emotions, the relevant means of arousal being the recognition of them in the music. But in *all* of these ways of putting the arousal view, the arousal theorist must, like the cognitivist, face the problem of how music can embody emotions. And although there is a reason, as we shall see later on, for wanting to maintain that music *both* arouses emotions *and* embodies them, the view has no attraction for those who hold the arousal view *because* it avoids the problem of emotive embodiment. How can they prevent insidious infiltration of that notion into their view?

◇ 3 ◇   Contrast the case of music with the most obvious case of emotive arousal in the arts: being moved by fictional characters in literature. I read a novel, understand the pitiable situation in which the heroine finds herself, and am, quite understandably, moved to sadness by it, much as I would be if I were to encounter such a happening in "real life." (I am brushing aside, here, the well-known problems of "feeling for fiction" that were discussed previously.) Now if there is an analogue in music to the way fiction is supposed to arouse my emotions, then there must be something in the music that I recognize, that I understand, and that can reasonably be thought to arouse the garden-variety emotions in me. What can that "something" be?

Well it seems to me there are but two plausible alternatives. Either, as in the fictional case, the music represents something —emotions, or emotionally charged situations—the recognition of which can reasonably be thought to arouse my garden-variety emotions. Or, the music embodies emotions as phenomenological properties, the recognition of which causes me to have emotional reactions to them, as I might be made depressed by "dreary" surroundings. These alternatives seem to me to exhaust the possibilities of what might be *recognized, consciously perceived* in music, that could plausibly be thought to arouse the garden-variety emotions in listeners. And it is just these "representation" and "embodiment" mechanisms that the arousal theorist we are talking about here is at pains to avoid. So it looks as if such a proponent of the arousal theory will have to reject altogether the notion that there is *anything* in the music the conscious recognition of which arouses emotions in the listener.

That leaves, of course, the unconscious, subliminal properties that somehow stimulate emotions in the listener by some kind of psychological or physiological mechanism. It is this that I call the *stimulus* model of arousal. It was held by many in the seventeenth and eighteenth centuries, under the influence of the Cartesian and (later) the associationist psychologies, and is still, I think, at least hinted at by those who wish to maintain the arousal version of musical expressiveness while avoiding what they take to be the undesirable characteristics of representation and embodiment mechanisms.

Here is an example of what I have in mind; or, at least, it gives the appearance of being one in many places. "The arousal theorist" a recent proponent writes, looks in the direction of "the immediate effects of sound itself." He continues:

> The remarkable power of sound to arouse feelings is well documented, most graphically in the extreme "startle" effects produced by sudden loud noises. . . . The strategy of the arousal theorist is to find more subtle correlations between musical forms and emotive reactions. In this re-

gard, there seems to be a marked correlation between felt tensions and the frequency and intensity of a stimulus. In general, increasing the intensity or frequency of a stimulus within fairly wide limiting conditions will produce a felt rise in tension, other things being equal. Conversely, decreasing the intensity or frequency will produce a release of tension. Obviously, a summation effect will occur when the tension producing or relieving variables act concurrently. If these effects (which can be physically correlated with measured galvanic skin response and micro-tension in the muscula-ture of the body) are clearly apparent when the stimulus is intense, then it seems reasonable to extrapolate that more subtle effects of a similar nature are produced across the entire dynamic range.[3]

And again: "the feeling aroused by the musical contour is caus-ally dependent upon the immediate stimulus, a function of mo-mentary stimulation."[4]

Perhaps a more charitable choice of quotations might absolve the author (if he wishes to be absolved) of presenting what I call the stimulus model. But assuming that it is the stimulus model that we have here—and at least the quotations I have adduced support that assumption—then what should one say about it? The stimulus model of emotive arousal in music is a special case of the general theory that our enjoyment of music is a process of being pleasantly stimulated by sound. I have argued elsewhere, at some length, that this is a completely untenable view of the musical experience.[5] All I think I can do here is to state, rather than to argue, that position, and to hope that the unconvinced reader will seek out my more extended exposition of these views in the source cited.

Music is an object for the mind, at no matter what level it is appreciated. When it ceases to be that, as when soft, soothing sounds calm a babe in arms, it ceases to be music.

If emotions are any part of the bona fide musical experience, then they, too, must be objects for the mind, or, if experienced by the listener, then the understandable result of the listener's perceiving something in the music, as the understandable re-sult of my perceiving the pitiable condition of the heroine in a novel is the arousal in me of pity and sadness, or whatever the appropriate emotion might be.

There is no need, by the way, to deny that sounds might have the power to stimulate directly feelings of some kind or other in us. What one does want to deny is that these feelings are either interesting or relevant to the musical experience. An unexpected loud noise will, no doubt, startle me, whether it comes from the depths of the jungle or the depths of a symphony orchestra. And I dare say a listener might be mildly alarmed upon hearing for the first time the "surprise" chord in Haydn's 94th Symphony (whether or not the absurd story of its origins is true). Would one honestly want to say that alarm is an aesthetic feature of this work? Or that the feeling of alarm is an aesthetically appropriate response to it? There is no need to deny that musical sounds may stimulate transient feeling states in listeners. Perhaps every physical stimulus does. But it is difficult to see how these effects can do duty for a theory of musical expressiveness. Indeed, the author all but admits this; for we find, stowed away in a footnote, the caveat that "obviously sad music does not make us sad. The feeling engendered by music is but a faint recall of the convulsive real life feeling."[6]

One meets such admissions again and again in the writings of the arousal theorists, just because it is so wildly implausible, when one thinks about it, to maintain that pure instrumental music has the wherewithal to arouse the garden-variety emotions in us, or because, when we really make introspective examination of our emotional states while listening to it, we cannot honestly say that we are in the emotional states that we ascribe to the music. But the admission has special significance for the proponents of the stimulus model because, of all the models available, it is the least able to give even an initially plausible explanation for how music might raise the garden-variety emotions and (therefore) least able to give a plausible explanation for how music might come to be correctly described in terms of the garden-variety emotions at all.

Suppose we grant, for the sake of argument, that musical sound, simply as a subliminal stimulus, and not a perceptually cognized intentional object, has the power to raise "feelings" or "emotions" in us. As I have already admitted, I suppose that it does. Now consider a straightforward example. The *Grosse fuge* is "angry": expressive of anger. Put aside, for a moment, the question of whether the *Grosse fuge* really can, in the normal cases, arouse anger in listeners. Just ask yourself whether it is even the least bit plausible to believe that the musical sounds comprising it can directly stimulate anger in us, independent of our recognizing something in it the recognition of which might raise anger the way things in our ordinary lives do.

When I read *Uncle Tom's Cabin*, I become angry at the cruelty of Simon Legree. When I look at *Guernica*, I become angry at the Nazis who perpetrated this outrage. Whether this is *really* so with regard to *Uncle Tom's Cabin* and *Guernica*, at least it has some initial credibility. I can construct some kind of intelligible scenario about how anger is aroused in me by experiencing these artworks, something like the way anger would be aroused in me if I had really observed an overseer whipping slaves or was present at the air raid on Guernica. What plausible story can I tell about how musical sounds stimulate anger? Is it like the cases in which people have been put in emotional states by direct stimulation of the brain, or by being administered drugs? Even these cases are controversial, since it might be argued that without the appropriate intentional objects or the normal causal histories, what is aroused here is not a bona fide emotion at all. But putting such scruples aside, at least we have some kind of physiological and neurological explanation that might seem in the ball park. Can we say the same for how the sounds of the *Grosse fuge* might directly stimulate anger—*real anger*—in us? Whatever it is that musical sounds might directly stimulate in the nature of "feelings," and I do not deny they stimulate *something*, it is so far from being identifiable as "fear" or "anger" or "joy" or "melancholy" that on the basis of such feelings alone we would never have come to describe music in those terms. And that fatal admission has already, though unknowingly, been made when it is admitted that "the feeling engendered by music is but a faint recall of the convulsive real life feeling." Indeed, it is so faint an image, so remote from the garden-variety emotions, that it provides absolutely no plausible explanation for musical expressiveness; for how or why music should be described, as it manifestly is, in terms of the garden-variety emotions.

I think it abundantly clear that "angry" is an entirely appropriate characterization at least of parts of the *Grosse fuge*. Furthermore, it is clear that if I and others are calling it "angry" on the basis of some feeling it is arousing in us, that feeling must be full-blooded anger, or the description "angry" would never have suggested itself to us at all. Finally, it is clear that if the *Grosse fuge* does arouse something like full-blooded anger in us, it must be because we recognize something in the work that can plausibly be understood to arouse full-blooded anger in us. What can that "something" be? One obvious possibility is that something represented in the music does the job, as literary "representations" do in *Uncle Tom's Cabin*, or pictorial ones in *Guernica*. Let us pursue that line of inquiry briefly.

◇ 4 ◇   In an interesting and provocative essay called "The Sentiment in Musical Sensibility," Donald Callen attempts to revive the arousal claim in direct response to my criticism of it in *The Corded Shell*. The response I would like to make to Callen is twofold. First, somewhat tangentially, I want to say something about an argument of Callen's meant to show fault in an argument of mine that "The music is sad" cannot, in any critically interesting way, be taken for a statement about the propensity of music to arouse sadness. What I want to say, needless to say, is that it is Callen's argument, not mine, that is at fault. Second, and more important, I want to say something about Callen's positive view, which might be characterized as "fictional representationalism," with regard to how he thinks music does in fact arouse emotions. For I believe it harbors a fatal flaw, as do all such "representational" accounts.

An argument that I have presented as conclusive against the arousal theory is (in Callen's words) the following:

> *If*, say, mournfulness in music were some sort of dispositional property of music to sadden us, as fragility is in a particular instance a disposition of a crystal goblet to break when dropped, then the perception of the mournful quality in the music should sadden us. Typically it does not. So expressiveness is not a power of music to move our emotions.

Callen counters as follows. He points out, first, and quite correctly, that "it is not a necessary condition of any object's having some dispositional property that the normal mode of determining that property to be present involve the activation of the disposition." And he goes on to conclude from this that if it is so, "the passive behavior of concert-goers would show only that expressiveness might be a dispositional power of music that is not always or even commonly manifested in its fullest way."[7]

This seems to me to be a non sequitur. It is, of course, not a necessary condition for being a dispositional property that the "normal" way of discovering the property is to actuate it. But it *does* seem to me to be a necessary condition for being a dispositional property, skeptical arguments aside, that if the conditions obtain under which it is supposed to be actuated, it "does its thing." To use the example of Callen's, the "normal" way I discover my stemware is fragile may not be to go around smashing the stuff. But I cannot conclude from this that if I hurl a wine glass against a brick wall with all my might and it doesn't break, it nevertheless may be "fragile" (under the normal understanding of that term vis-à-vis crockery). Likewise, even if (which I do not believe) observing the behavior of listeners were not at least *one* of the normal ways to find out whether sad music makes us sad, it would be decisive against the claim that it did if listeners, under the usual circumstances for listening, did not become sad, just as it would be decisive against the claim that a drinking glass was fragile if it withstood the charge of an adult rhinoceros.

It is important to note, apropos of this, that when we make an ascription of a dispositional property, in nontechnical language, there is an implicit assumption or set of assumptions, I would think, about what the *conditions* are under which the property will be activated. I presume that if a normal person says, in ordinary circumstances, about his sheep dog, "Laddie will respond to a whistle," he does not mean a train whistle. And I presume, likewise, that when philosophers or music theorists have claimed "The music is sad" can be explicated as "The music arouses sadness in listeners," they have intended listeners in ordinary circumstances: at the concert hall, listening to Miss Woodhouse playing the piano in the parlour, or (thanks to Mr. Edison) sitting before the phonograph. It might, for all that I know, be a true generalization that "sad" music makes listeners sad if they have been given an injection of scopolamine and had electrodes implanted in the right brain. But that would not be a confirmation of *the* arousal theory of musical expression, as I understand it.

◇ 5 ◇   This brings us, then, to the positive part of Professor Callen's thesis. For if he is to make it good, he must tell us under what conditions sad music is supposed to make us sad; and these conditions must be aesthetically acceptable—not bizarre or critically irrelevant. We must feel as though he has preserved at least the general outlines of the arousal theory as it is commonly understood. He has made a really good and valiant effort. But he has, I am afraid, come a cropper.

It is Callen's idea that music arouses emotions much in the way literary fiction does. *Whether,* and *how* fiction does arouse full-blooded emotions is, of course, itself controversial, as we have had occasion to remark before, and as Callen well knows. But if he could really show that music has at least a claim equal to fiction's in this regard, I think he would have shown a good deal.

The fact is, however, that the price we must pay to hear music fictively, and thereby have it arouse emotions in us, is to return to the worst excesses of the likes of A. B. Marx, and such "interpretations" as his well-known reading of the *Les Adieux* sonata: "Soul picture, which brings before the mind the Parting—let us assume of two lovers; the deserted—let us assume again sweetheart or wife—and Reunion of the Parted Ones."[8] Compare this to part of Callen's account of how, in general, we must hear music in the fictive mode, to enable it to stimulate our emotions. "A musical work is as a whole to be thought of as presenting the emotional life of a single organism. . . . Often one wants to identify the appearance of distinct individuals or agents in the work, inter-acting amongst themselves and sometimes with more primitive forces."[9] Not quite as bad as Marx, perhaps; at least the "agents" remain unspecified. But I don't think there is much to choose between them.

The problem for Callen is that he is between Scylla and Charybdis. If he can avoid the charge that he is inviting us to make up stories, programs, and the like, and, in general, to read into pure instrumental music figments of the Romantic imagination, this moderate line will fail to generate the cognitive content required to give music even the power of emotive arousal of "The Three Little Pigs." It is not enough, after all, simply to say the music is "expressive." On the other hand, if he gives free rein to what he seems to be suggesting in his article—namely, that "all music may be, even should be, heard programmatically"[10]—he may be able to generate the content required for emotive arousal; but we will have grounds for objecting that the conditions he demands for arousal are aesthetically, which is to say musically, unacceptable. It may be possible to get music to make us sad if we make up detailed enough stories to put in it, just as we know it can arouse the emotion if we have the right "associations." The ground rules, however, for defending the arousal theory are that the conditions we set for arousal be within the original intent of the theory, not bizarre or critically unacceptable. Now it may be less bizarre, less outré, to "make up stories" of emotional conflicts about symphonies, than to be injected with drugs and implanted with electrodes, but from the point of view of the arousal theory and its defense, they are, I submit, equally unacceptable; for they all involve going beyond what is aesthetically proper, which is to say, beyond what good musical analysis and sound musical practice will allow. We put aside forever, I hope, the kind of listening Callen's theory demands when we escaped from Sigmund Spaeth and public school "music appreciation."

◇ 6 ◇   I dare say that this put-down of fictional listening may seem rather abrupt and high-handed. So let us pursue the question a little further to see what some of the other underlying issues are here.

To begin with, I want to make it perfectly clear that I am not denying representational qualities to music *tout court*. Some works of instrumental music are frankly representational, and others narrative. Strauss's *Till Eulenspiegel* tells a story, with the help, of course, of a written program; and I see no reason in the world why the work might not, for instance, make someone sorry for Till, as *Uncle Tom's Cabin* might make us sorry for Tom— granted, that is, that fictional works really can intelligibly arouse full-blooded emotions at all. (If they cannot, of course, all bets are off.)

The issue of whether music can, in its expressive function, be thought to arouse the garden-variety emotions in listeners is the issue of whether pure instrumental music, sans text, sans title, sans program can do so: whether the *Well-Tempered Clavier* can, or Beethoven's C#-Minor Quartet. One thing the "representational" account of arousal has right. It construes music as an object of the understanding, in construing it as something in which we must recognize representations. But it does so at what to me is the absolutely prohibitive price of turning all musical works, even the paradigms of pure music, into the "crypto-programmatic." And Callen is completely out front about this, in his claim that "all music may be, even should be, heard programmatically."

Can it be? Should it be?

Of course it *can* be. It is always open to someone to make up or imagine a story that might seem to "go with" a piece of pure instrumental music, partly because music possesses expressive properties. I can, if I like, imagine the fugal opening of Beethoven's C#-Minor Quartet as a funeral procession for a fallen hero, with the entrance of each voice representing another column of mourners joining the cortege. And perhaps, if I can make the images vivid enough and specific enough, I can succeed in moving myself to sadness. All of this is possible.

Should I do it? I don't *want* to do it. Should *you* do it? Well, that's for you to decide. I do not set myself up as the defender of the pure musical faith. I admit that you *can* do it; and in so far as you and others can, it is true that Beethoven's C#-Minor Quartet can arouse sadness and other garden-variety emotions in us (if fiction can). No, on second thought, it's not *quite* true. What is true is that a combination of Beethoven's music and *your* program can arouse those emotions. For until you can give me criteria for establishing that that funeral program really is in Beethoven's work, I think I am justified in denying it. And the issue for me is not whether the C#-Minor Quartet can, suitably altered, arouse the garden-variety emotions, but whether it itself, listened to as pure musical form, albeit *expressive* form, can do so. And the representational or fictive theory of musical arousal has not shown that it can. What it has shown is that, given an active and vivid enough imagination in the listener, a piece of pure music can be made—transformed—into a programmatic work that arouses the garden-variety emotions. But since that is not the issue for me—since I do not deny that program music can arouse the garden-variety emotions—that is just, for me, an *ignoratio elenchi*.

A successful account of expressiveness in music, on the arousal model, must, I think, satisfy at least three conditions. First, it must treat the relationship of the listener to the music as the relationship of a mind to an intentional object, not the relationship of nerve-endings to a physical stimulus. Second, it must provide us a plausible account of how music can arouse full-blooded emotions, not some philosopher's or psychologist's phantoms. And third, it must show us how pure music can do this, not music with a program, whether put there by the composer or by someone else. The stimulus account fails to satisfy the first two conditions;

the representational account fails to satisfy the third. But there is another alternative, which seems to me to be the most plausible yet suggested. It seems, at least on first reflection, to satisfy all three conditions.

◇ 7 ◇   Colin Radford holds that sad music makes him sad. Surprisingly, he does not believe, across the board, that music arouses *any* emotion that it can correctly be said to possess or be expressive of. He writes: "I am an emotivist regarding sad music, but I do not wish to generalize. I do not believe, for example, that angry music may make one angry."[11]

Further, Radford does not believe that sad music is sad merely in virtue of arousing sadness in us. Rather, he thinks it is sad independent of its arousal of sadness, and identifiably so, but that, in virtue of its being sad, it in fact arouses sadness. Or, in other words, Radford believes, as I do, that music is sometimes expressive of sadness, but believes, as I do not, that music expressive of sadness arouses sadness as well, as a regular part of its expressive function. Just why someone should want to maintain that music is expressive of an emotion independent of arousing it, yet still want to hold on to the belief that it also arouses that emotion, I will conjecture about in the conclusion of this chapter. My immediate concern is what Radford's account of the arousal process is, and whether it is plausible.

But before I get to that, let me just make the following observation. If it were indeed the case that music expressive of sadness did tend to make some of us sad, but that music expressive of no other emotion tended to put listeners in that emotional state, I would not be much impressed by the singular case. It would be puzzling of course; and it would make sad music something of an anomaly. But if, for all other cases, it were true that music is expressive of the garden-variety emotions in virtue of possessing them as properties, and does not arouse them, then I do not think there would be anything aesthetically interesting about the fact that in the one case, that of sadness, the music was expressive of the emotion in the usual way, by possessing it as a property, but also, in this one case alone, tended to arouse the emotion in some as well. After all, if we can say everything musically or aesthetically significant there is to say about angry music and joyful music, hopeful music and amorous music, yearning music and exuberant music, and so on, without having to say that such music arouses these emotions, which, by hypothesis, it does not do, and if sad music is not expressive of sadness in virtue of arousing sadness, but independent of that, then the fact that in this one case the music arouses the emotion it is expressive of seems very uninteresting from the musical or aesthetic point of view (though perhaps interesting to the psychologist). And the claim that sad music makes some of us sad becomes a very uninteresting claim.

Putting this observation aside, though, and without making any commitment to how many of the emotions that it is expressive of music also arouses, let us inquire whether Radford's account of how music that is expressive of an emotion might arouse it is plausible, under the assumption that Radford thinks music is expressive of emotions in "logically" (if not "mechanically") the same way as I do: that is to say, by possessing them as perceived properties.

◇ 8 ◇   Radford's strategy, in trying to make plausible the way sad music might make us sad, is not to adduce esoteric psychological or representational mechanisms, but, rather, to remind us of some very familiar cases, like the case of music, where we seem inclined to admit that something expressive of an emotion tends to arouse that emotion in us. Thus, without really claiming to tell us how music arouses sadness by being expressive of it, he at least blunts our suspicions by getting us to see that music is not a singular phenomenon in this regard. The hoped-for result would be, I suppose, to get us to acknowledge that whatever the mechanisms might be for expressiveness arousing emotions, it is obvious that it does: too familiar a phenomenon to be denied.

Here is the way Radford puts his case. Begin with the fact, which Radford takes for granted, that "when people listen to music, i.e. music that is expressive of sadness, it may make them feel sad."[12] Now a person so aroused may be puzzled: puzzled because there is nothing to feel sad about; puzzled because there seems no reason for the emotion felt. But he or she need not feel puzzled.

Colours can also produce emotional responses, feelings, and moods. A bathroom decorated in ice blue will "feel" cold.

It will seem to "feel" or "look" warmer, if it is decorated in "warm" colours, like red, brown, or orange. Decorating a room in primrose yellow will make a room light, bright, and "cheerful." Being in it will make people feel cheerful, it will lighten their spirits. Similarly, in English climes, gray days look dull, depressing and do depress people (there is statistical evidence for this). Some colours are described as "somber" and tend to put people in "somber" moods. Are not these cases very like the case of sad music? They are both "expressive of" certain moods and feelings and help to induce them.[13]

A persuasive argument this: the most convincing I have come across to date that music expressive of the garden-variety emotions might plausibly be understood to arouse them. But it will not, I think, withstand closer scrutiny.

Let us work backward from the most clear-cut putative example of the expressive arousing emotions. English weather looks dull and depressing; and there is statistical evidence that such dull and depressing weather does depress people and dull their spirits. This seems right to me. Indeed, I was once told by a sociologist that the suicide rate goes up during long stretches of rainy weather.

Now the first suggestion that something might be amiss in the analogy here is the appeal to "statistical evidence" only in the case of the English climate. There *is* statistical evidence, no doubt, that the English climate depresses people. Is there "statistical evidence" that yellow walls will make a person cheerful? Ice blue is a cold color, orange a warm color, yellow a cheerful color. It simply begs the question at issue to take it without argument that cheerful colors make us cheerful, just as it would be to take it without argument that sad music makes us sad. Everyone knows that the opening of the second movement of the *Eroica* is sad. The question at issue is whether that means it makes us sad. There is, so far as I know, no sound statistical evidence that yellow really makes people cheerful.

Perhaps one might reply, here, that we can at least construct an analogical argument from the case of the depressing English weather to the cases of cheerful colors and sad music. Here is how it would go. English weather is expressive of depression; and statistics show that English weather tends to depress people.

Yellow is expressive of cheerfulness and (say) the minor mode of sadness. There is no statistical evidence that yellow cheers people up, or that the minor mode saddens them. But it would seem to be a fair inference, by analogy, that if A is expressive of X and arouses X, then if B is expressive of Y, and C of Z, B probably arouses Y and C probably arouses Z. Therefore, we can conclude with some degree of probability that since we know the English weather is expressive of depression, and have evidence it depresses people, it is probable that yellow makes people cheerful and the minor mode makes them sad, even though we have no direct evidence of this, knowing only that yellow is expressive of cheerfulness, the minor mode of sadness. For if the color yellow and the minor mode are like the English weather in being expressive, it is probable that they are also like it in arousing what they are expressive of. It is a form of argument not to be despised.

The problem is that there is something immediately suspect about the phrase "expressive of" when applied to the English weather. Do we really want to say that depressing weather is expressive of depression, as we would want to say that, for example, Papageno's music is, after he has lost his Papagena and is about to hang himself? I suggest it is as odd to say this as to say that sad news is expressive of sadness.

We call news sad, of course, in virtue of its unhappy consequences, either for us or for others. And it is the same for dreary, depressing weather. I am not depressed by yet another gray, damp, and bone-chilling day in London because of its "aesthetic" or "phenomenological" properties. I call it depressing because it depresses me; it does not depress me because it is depressing. And it depresses me because of its depressing consequences for my life. It will be yet another day in which I will be prevented from partaking in my favorite outdoor activities; yet another day during which my feet will be wet and cold; yet another day that my cough will linger and my nose drip; yet another day when the sun won't warm my clammy body. Cabin fever looms, and even I may become one of the sociologist's statistics. And so on. It is a no more convincing argument that sad music must make me sad because depressing weather makes me depressed than that sad music must make me sad because depressing news makes me depressed.

In short, Radford has failed to alleviate our uneasiness about the supposed sad-making propensity of things merely expressive of sadness, because he has failed to come up with a *bona fide,* uncontroversial example of anything that is both expressive of an emotion and arousing of that emotion merely in consequence of its being expressive, and not because of its practical consequences for our lives. It is clear that depressing weather depresses us, but by no means clear that it is expressive of depression; and it is clear that yellow is expressive of cheerfulness—is a cheerful color —but by no means clear that it arouses cheerfulness.

All, I think, that is left for the *property* model of emotive arousal is the bald-faced and unargued claim: it just stands to reason, is just self-evidently plain, that if something is expressive of an emotion, it must at least have some tendency, however slight, of arousing that emotion in the perceiver. I find that claim both unpersuasive and harmless, if true. It is unpersuasive to me simply because there seems to be no convincing evidence that sad music makes me, or a lot of other listeners, sad. And it is harmless because if there is a sad-making tendency at all, it must be so slight, since so little in evidence, that under normal circumstances (which are the only circumstances I am interested in), it can, for all intents and purposes, be assumed not to exist at all. A person so bowed down by grief that he is close to the edge of a breakdown might, for all that I know, be pushed over the edge if forced to listen to long stretches of music of unbroken melancholy. So be it: such bizarre cases need not detain us. What is left, I think, is to consider why the arousal theory hangs on with such tenacity, and to fill the need, which is real enough, with a viable alternative.

◇ 9 ◇   I begin with a recent characterization of my own view, as I am supposed to have expressed it in *The Corded Shell,* which, I think, is revealing.

> Some seasoned listeners, such as Peter Kivy, will not acknowledge that the feelings expressed in music have any emotive effect upon them whatsoever. Others, just as seasoned, insist that nothing could be more certain. This disagreement is striking, but it does not necessarily follow that music has an affective impact on some and not on others.[14]

I call attention to what I take to be an absolutely crucial transition in the above passage between two *very different* claims that the author apparently takes to be equivalent. In the first sentence the author says that some people—I am a case in point—claim not to be emotively affected by the emotions music is expressive of. And I take him to mean by that that some people claim not to be saddened by sad music, angered by angry music, cheered by cheerful music, and so on. But in the third sentence the author quite innocently slips into a way of talking whereby the claim that sad music doesn't make me sad, angry music angry, cheerful music cheerful . . . is represented indifferently as the claim that music does not have an "affective impact."

How surprised my friends and acquaintances would be, especially those who play music with me, to discover that I am supposed to have represented myself in print as someone upon whom music has no "affective impact." For I am known to be an extremely emotional player, and tend to gush over the music I love. What has gone wrong?

Clearly, two very different claims have been conflated here (and this is by no means a unique case in the literature): the claim that music does not arouse the garden-variety emotions in us (which I take to be true) and the claim that music is not emotionally moving—does not have an "affective impact" upon listeners—(which I take to be false). Were this an isolated instance I would not belabor the point. But it is hardly that: it is, rather, an almost universal confusion among those who write about music, and has been since at least the end of the sixteenth century. Furthermore, it quite convincingly explains the tenacity with which the view that music arouses the garden-variety emotions has hung on to the musical and philosophical consciousness, in spite of its (to me) palpable difficulties. For to give it up seems to those who hold it equivalent to giving up the notion that we emote over music; and *that* they (quite correctly) take to be absurd. Which is precisely why, I presume, it seems necessary to hold on to the view that sad music makes one sad, even when one has, as Radford has done, given up the view that sad music is expressive of sadness in virtue of that. Some sad music must arouse sadness as well as be expressive of it, or else *no* sad music would be moving—which is clearly false.

With this unjustified conflation of positions revealed, it becomes abundantly clear, then, just what philosophical need the arousal theory fills, and what can take its place. Works of art move us, works of music no less—indeed some would say and have said *more*—than the rest. I think most people, when they say that they are deeply moved by literary works—by novels and by plays—mean that they are deeply affected by the plights and situations, the human feelings, the sufferings and joys of the characters depicted therein. If you will forgive a commonplace, the reason we find *King Lear* or *Death of a Salesman* so deeply moving and a play by Oscar Wilde or Neil Simon not is because we are moved to sorrow and pity and fear—to human sympathy —by the all-too-human human beings who populate the former works.

It is natural, I suppose, to think that since music is moving, it can be moving only in something like this way: by moving us, somehow, to the kinds of emotions we are moved to by the characters in literary works—which is to say, the garden-variety emotions. But that is just not possible. And why should it be? The C#-Minor Quartet does not have a Lear or a Willy Loman to do that for us, unless we put them in ourselves. And then, of course, we don't have the C#-Minor Quartet anymore, do we?

It is high time, I would think, that we gave up this futile exercise and recognized that pure instrumental music is a different kind of art form. It moves us of course; and we need to find out how and why. But to think that our choice is between its moving the garden-variety emotions or not at all is simply to fall prey to the excluded middle.

I have written at greater length elsewhere of just how I think music moves us.[15] And I see no reason to repeat myself here. Nor, however, can I simply leave my reader in baffled suspense and (no doubt) skeptical disbelief. So I intend to conclude this chapter by giving, in the briefest possible way, at least a vague idea of my views on this regard.

◇ 10 ◇   I suppose anecdotal philosophy is not the most effective way of convincing the hard-nosed. But I think it may be the most direct way of making my point.

I was listening, recently, to a recording of Mozart's wonderful A-Minor Rondo (K. 511). I had not heard it for a long time, or, for that matter, anything else of Mozart's; and I was perhaps for that reason more than usually transfixed by the music, as if hearing it with fresh ears. A friend of mine wandered into the room and became equally absorbed. When it was over, she said something like: "It's so beautiful it almost makes you cry." I had found myself with similar feelings. It was clear that we had both been very deeply moved by what we had heard. But—and here is the crucial point—it was equally clear to both of us exactly *what* we had been moved by: *the beauty of the music*. And this is particularly significant because the A-Minor Rondo is certainly suffused with a palpable melancholy. Yet neither of us thought we were choking back tears of sorrow. It was the unutterable beauty of Mozart's music that had affected us so deeply; and it had not affected us with sorrow, though a sorrowful piece.

I am tempted to leave it at that. Music moves us by its (perceived) beauty. What more is there to say? Didn't we always really know that? Well, let me just try to anticipate some questions, based on the experiences I have had in expressing these views in public.

What *is* the emotion that musical beauty evokes? It's not anger, or sorrow, or anything like that. So what is it called?

One might reply, at the risk of sounding mysterious, that it is an emotion without a name. But what, after all, is mysterious about that? Need all of our emotions have names? Do they? If you need a name, call it musical excitement, or musical enthusiasm—or simply describe it as being moved by the beauty of music.

Am I claiming then that there is some kind of special musical emotion, like Clive Bell's special "aesthetic emotion"? Bell said: "All sensitive people agree that there is a peculiar emotion provoked by works of art." [16] Am I saying something like that about music and the emotions it arouses?

Well of course I am saying there is a "special" musical emotion, but only in the most benign, nominalistic sense. When I am moved by the beauty of music, I am experiencing "a" or "the" musical emotion, simply in virtue of my having been moved by the beauty of *music*, rather than by the beauty of something else. I am saying nothing more "metaphysical" than I would be if I said there is a special botanical emotion, namely, the emotion I get when I am moved by the beauty of a plant or flower.

Does that mean we all feel the "same" (type, not token) emotion when we are moved by the beauty of Mozart's A-Minor Rondo? And do I feel the "same" (type, not token) emotion when I am moved by the beauty of the A-Minor Rondo as when moved by the beauty of a Strauss waltz?

These are harmless questions. The answer to the second is a harmless "yes and no." And it is the same answer I would give to someone who asked me if love for a dog is the same as love for a son or daughter. Of course it is the same (type, not token) emotion: *love*. But of course it is very different to love your child and to love your mutt. And although I might try to tell you how it "feels" to love the one rather than the other, wouldn't the more direct and more common way of distinguishing these two kinds of love simply be by distinguishing their objects? Don't I pretty much tell you the whole story when I tell you that the object of my love is the creature that gives me its paw for a biscuit, or the one who lisps *When We Were Very Young* from memory? And do I not adequately distinguish my emotions when I tell you that I am moved by the intense passion and exquisite sense of balance of late Mozart in a minor key, or by the *belle epoque* charm and glitz of Strauss? One emotion, two emotions: of course.

But if we distinguish the ways in which we are moved by music by distinguishing what musical work we are moved by, so, too, do we distinguish them by what it is in a particular work that moves us at any given time. I said it is the "beauty" of the work that moves us. But, needless to say, listeners differ widely in their musical sophistication; and whereas Smith may be moved by the flowing melody of a Schubert impromptu, Jones, with Schenker-like understanding, may be moved by what she perceives to be the daring harmonic structure. Each, of course, is moved by the "same" object: the beauty of the impromptu. Yet each is also, under a different description, moved by a quite different intentional object: Smith by the beautiful melody, Jones by the beautiful harmonic structure, under some appropriately technical Schenkerian description.

Thus, the answer to our first question is that our individual emotional reactions to the same piece of music are as different as the intentional objects of our emotions; or, in other words, as different as the descriptions under which we perceive the musical beauty of the piece; or, to put it most simply, as different as what we hear.

As I have said, I have written at greater length elsewhere on the question of how music moves, and can here only refer the reader to that body of work. What I wish merely to make as clear as possible is that the denial that music arouses the garden-variety emotions is one claim, the denial that music moves the emotions of listeners an entirely different one. The former claim I believe to be true, the latter false. The second movement of the *Eroica* doesn't sadden me; and nevertheless it's sad, and nevertheless it moves.

CHAPTER XVI

Formalism and Feeling

◇ 1 ◇ When I wrote *The Corded Shell*, the last thing on my mind was what implications my views on musical expression might have for a synoptic "philosophy of music." For I had no such philosophy, nor the glimmerings of one; and I certainly had no intention of attempting to fashion such a philosophy. Indeed, it seemed brazen enough to think I had anything to say on the question of music and the emotions, the lineage of which went all the way back to Plato and Aristotle—that is to say, to the realm of the immortals. What I did have was my own musical taste, and some vagrant philosophical intuitions, all of which put together scarcely added up to a "position."

Four books later I now find myself, much to my surprise and delight, with something like a "philosophy of music." Not a philosophical "system"—but at least a general idea of how the thing should go. Much to most people's surprise who have heard my views on pure instrumental music and are familiar with my views on musical expression from reading *The Corded Shell*, I am a formalist in the tradition of Eduard Hanslick. But a formalist with a difference. For formalism is generally taken to deny that music can, in any important sense, be expressive of the emotions; whereas it was the purpose of *The Corded Shell* to defend the notion that music can be expressive, and to try to explain how it can be. Certainly, in my view, Hanslick denied that music can be expressive;[1] and such a denial is generally thought part of the formalist's creed. Which of course explains the surprise of those who know my earlier work on musical expression, and now find me defending formalism with regard to instrumental music.

But my emerging formalism is no surprise to me. For I resisted, in *The Corded Shell*, any attempt to put a semantic or representational interpretation on the expressive properties of music, denying both that music necessarily represents the emotions it is expressive of and that music is "about" the emotions it is expressive of (any more than the Saint Bernard's face is "about" sadness). And although I defended, in *Sound and Semblance*, the view that there is representational music, I was, of course, not defending the view that *all* music is representational. And it is nonrepresentational, "pure" music about which I am a formalist.

A small, but not negligible amount of instrumental and vocal music, in the modern Western tradition, is representational; and a smaller, but still not negligible amount of instrumental music in the tradition is representational and even narrative. It is arguable that all music in the modern Western tradition, where tonal, is expressive, at least to some degree. Where that music accompanies a text, or is frankly representational or narrative, expressive properties have a fairly obvious function. It needs no philosopher to tell us that a somber scene can best be represented in music by somber accents, and a happy text best accompanied by happy ones. The role of expressive properties in representation and in underscoring the sentiments of a text is clear in the main, even though the mechanisms may need spelling out.[2]

But it is where music is "pure" instrumental music, sans text or title or program, that an accounting seems necessary for the presence of expressive properties. This is true both for the arousal theory of musical expressiveness and for the cognitive, property theory, although the problem presents a different face in the one from the face it presents in the other. This problem is the subject of the present chapter.

◇ 2 ◇   I said at the beginning of the last chapter that the recent articles defending the arousal theory of musical expressiveness had one or both of two goals: to explain *how* music arouses the garden-variety emotions, and to explain *to what purpose* it does so. In the last chapter I concerned myself with the former aspect of arousal theory. It is now time to consider the latter.

How are we to understand the sense and the motivation of the question, "To what purpose are the emotions aroused by music?" The motivation, I think, is this. It is controversial whether or not music is expressive in virtue of arousing the garden-variety emotions. That being the case, one might argue that if music did indeed arouse such emotions as fear and anger and sadness, then listening to music at times would simply amount to a gratuitous infliction of pain upon the listener. For the experiencing of fear and anger and sadness—let us call them, after Jerrold Levinson, the "negative emotions"—is painful or at least unpleasant.

And it seems absurd to suppose that one would willingly, indeed enthusiastically, inflict such painful or unpleasant experiences on oneself for no further purpose of pleasure or self-interest at all. So it is an argument against the arousal theory of musical expressiveness that if the theory were true, we would have to understand listeners as gratuitously inflicting the negative emotions upon themselves. Contrariwise, it is a defense of the arousal theory to come up with a utility or pleasure to the arousal of the negative emotions by music. And that is why the possible purpose of music's arousing the negative emotions becomes an issue for the arousal theory of musical expressiveness.

Now we are past, here, the point where we will accept the simple response to the problem of negative emotions in music that Radford gives, and that we considered in Chapter XIII, namely, that there is no problem, since literature also arouses the negative emotions and no one carps about that. For if we look at the two cases more closely, we will find that the case of music is far more troublesome than that of literature. It is really the same old story of content (in literature) versus the absence of it (in music).

Now, to give a complete accounting of the role of the negative emotions in literature would necessitate, essentially, the production of a more or less complete philosophy of the subject; and that, clearly, is not an option for me here. What I can do is present some of the more common-sense explanations, with which we are all familiar, for the role of the painful emotions in literary works, the point of the exercise being to compare the ease with which such explanations can be conjured up in a literary context with their tortured musical counterparts. Here are three familiar examples.

1. It is perfectly clear that Harriet Beecher Stowe's intention in writing *Uncle Tom's Cabin* was, among others, to arouse in people some pretty unpleasant emotions: to shock and pain and outrage her readers in the interest of social and moral reform. Perhaps Abraham Lincoln exaggerated when, upon being introduced to the author, he said: "So you're the little woman who wrote the book that made this great war."[3] Certainly the author of *Uncle Tom's Cabin* did not intend to start a civil rebellion. But she did intend to start a moral one. And her instrumentality was, in part, the negative emotions aroused by her depiction of the cruelty

of the "peculiar institution." The negative emotions, in this case, have a clear consequentialist value.

2. It is frequently said that fictional works—at least the best of them—do not merely entertain us but enlighten us as well. They reveal to us our world and ourselves. But much about our world and ourselves is not pretty to contemplate. The world of *Lear* is part of our world, and of ourselves. And what it reveals to us is painful indeed in the contemplation. We cannot, however, have the knowledge without the pain. So here again, the intrinsic disvalue of experiencing the negative emotions aroused by fictional works is outweighed by the positive instrumental value of our gaining insight, through literary fiction, of life's darker side. They come with the territory.

3. For reasons that are not by any means clear, there is a deep-seated appetite within us for the hearing and (in the age of literacy) the reading of stories. It must be as old as humanity itself. And it seems without question that where there are stories capable of commanding the attention of adult human beings, there must be stories that arouse the negative as well as the pleasurable emotions. To put it as simply and as naively as possible, an interesting story must have downs as well as ups: catastrophes as well as triumphs. To live happily ever after, something unhappy must have come before. It is simply an axiom of fiction that part of our pleasure in it is the pleasure of the "rescue." And what precedes that must produce fear, anxiety, and other of the negative emotions. Thus, again, whatever intrinsic disvalue attaches to the arousing of the negative emotions in fiction is more than compensated for by the deep and abiding pleasure we take in story telling. And as the arousing of the negative emotions in fiction is a necessary condition for sustained interest, at least among adults, it has clearly positive instrumental value as a *sine qua non* for fiction and for the pleasure we take in it.

I do not, I hasten to assure the reader, claim anything for these familiar justifications of the negative emotions in literary fiction but some initial plausibility. They may all be completely wrong; and there are well-known theories of literature that would utterly reject them. The point is, that when we try the same experiment with the negative emotions in music, we don't get even this far. For music presents a stubborn problem right from the start, just because it does not, in any obvious way, offer the representational or propositional content that all three of the above accounts make use of. Let us go on, then, to see what can be done with the problem of the negative emotions in music.

◇ 3 ◇   The most thorough and persuasive attempt to provide a rationale for the arousal of the negative emotions by music is that of Jerrold Levinson. Before we get to that rationale, however, which is our present concern, we must first get a general idea of why Levinson thinks music does arouse emotions, and what the nature of those emotions is, on Levinson's view. For all of these considerations intertwine; and the plausibility (or lack of it) of Levinson's rationale for the arousal of the negative emotions cannot be considered in complete isolation from what he thinks the musical emotions are, and why he believes music arouses them (rather than merely presenting them as phenomenal properties).

Levinson's defense of the emotive arousal theory is mainly motivated, it seems to me, by the belief that music moves us, and that if that is so, there are but two alternatives: that it moves us to the garden-variety emotions, or that it moves us to some special musical emotion, in the manner of Clive Bell or Edumund Gurney. The latter view he finds *prima facie* implausible: "It just is not the case that all good or impressive music induces a single positive emotion in listeners." And that leaves the former view, that music arouses the garden-variety emotions, in sole possession of the field. "It seems to me that there are indeed compositions which can, when listened to in certain appreciatively admissible frames of mind, produce in one real feelings of both the positive and negative variety."[4]

It should already be abundantly clear that I reject this disjunctive syllogism just because I deny the disjunction of the major premise. We do not have to choose between music's moving us to anger, fear, and the like, or moving us to a special musical emotion (except in a perfectly harmless sense of the latter). There is a third alternative, as we have already seen; and although one might want to call it the view that music moves us to a special musical emotion, it is a perfectly intelligible sense of "special musical emotion," having little to do with the views of Bell or Gurney, and perfectly consistent with Levinson's quite correct contention that "the effects of different sorts of music are . . . different from one another."[5]

Another, subsidiary consideration that seems to drive Levinson to the arousal view is, baldly put, that it is just plainly evident. Levinson pictures for us a man sitting before a record player: "He appears upset, pained, and at turns a small sigh or shudder passes through his body." What can we make of such behavior except to conclude: "What he experienced can be described—at least provisionally—as intense grief, unrequited passion, sobbing melancholy, tragic resolve, and angry despair."[6]

Of course here we are playing with loaded dice. For Levinson's listener, contorted with the passions named, bears no resemblance to any living soul of my acquaintance: he is, it seems to me, purely a creature of Levinson's imagination (or perhaps of Diderot's?). If indeed such behavior and facial expression on the part of listeners were commonly observed, at least we would have some grounds for believing that music arouses the garden-variety emotions. But they are not, Levinson's image begging the question right from the start; and, as we shall see, if they were commonly observed, it would be at odds with Levinson's own view of what sorts of things the "emotions" aroused by music really are.

◇ 4 ◇   It is nontrivial that Levinson suggests we only "provisionally" describe his imagined listener as in the throes of the garden-variety emotions. For he is well aware that this cannot be literally true, and for a very plausible reason, by now familiar to readers of these pages. Music simply cannot give us the beliefs that make full-blooded emotions possible, or the objects for full-blooded emotions to take. As Levinson puts it:

> The standard emotional response to a musical work . . . is not in truth a full-fledged emotion. This is mainly because music neither supplies an appropriate object for an emotion to be directed on, nor generates the associated beliefs, desires or attitudes regarding an object which are essential to an emotion being what it is.

We are not, then, on Levinson's view, to think of the emotions aroused by music as, in all respects, the genuine article: an "'emo-

tional response' to music . . . should be understood as an experience produced in a listener which is at least the characteristic
feeling of some emotion, but which is short of a complete emotion *per se*." What the musical emotions lack, not surprisingly,
given the absence of appropriate beliefs, desires, and objects are
any practical consequences. "Angered" by music, I do not strike
out (whom am I to strike, and why?): "this weakening of the cognitive component in emotional response to music generally results in the inhibition of most characteristic behaviors and in the
significant lessening of behavioral tendencies." The objects are
gone; the beliefs are gone; the behavior is gone: the subtle distil-
late that remains is, one gathers, the raw feel. "If music inevitably
fails to induce by itself a proper, contextually embedded *emotion*
of sadness, still, some music appears fully capable of inducing at
least the characteristic feeling of sadness."[7]

This tamed kind of emotion that Levinson speaks of immediately raises questions. The first, though admittedly an *ad hominem*,
is revealing, I think, of the difficulties one is in, straightaway,
in espousing any form of the arousal theory. Recall Levinson's
imagined listener: "He appears upset, pained, and at turns a
small sigh or shudder passes through his body." What is being described here are characteristic ways in which one expresses and
gives evidence of one's negative emotions. But the expression
and evincing of emotion in gesture, vocal utterance, and facial
demeanor, no less than its expression in more active ways, such
as striking out in anger, alleviating one's depression by taking
a trip to Paris, being motivated by feelings of love to propose
marriage, are behavioral responses to full-blooded emotions with
very practical ends in view. To put it baldly, one looks pained,
one sighs to be noticed, to gain sympathy, to be helped. It is hard
to imagine looking pained, or sighing—which are, after all, in
this instance, nonverbal ways of bemoaning one's fate—if one
has, in fact, no fate to bemoan, no object of one's grief, no belief
that one is in a distressful situation. And this is so even when one
looks pained or sighs alone.

I do not think Levinson can have it both ways. Which is to say,
I do not think he can impel us to the belief that music arouses
something like the garden-variety emotions by citing sighing,
shuddering, and pained-looking listeners while, on the other
hand, insisting on these emotions being, in fact, denuded of practical consequences, due to their necessary lack both of objects

and enabling beliefs; for the sighing, shuddering, the pained look *are* the consequences of full-blooded emotions, including, necessarily, objects, beliefs, desires. I dare say it is the sighing, shuddering, pained-looking listener who must be given up, in which case, all that seems to remain to convince us that music arouses anything like the garden-variety emotions is the false choice among the alternatives of music's not being able to move us at all, moving us to a "special musical emotion" (in the bad sense of that notion), or moving us by arousing something like anger and fear and sadness and the rest.

A second difficulty with Levinson's blunted emotions, if indeed there are such, is that, at least as I imagine what they must be like, the means by which many important ones are to be distinguished evaporates in the blunting process. Here is what I have in mind. When I am nervous and anxious, before I perform (say), or give a lecture, the "raw feel," the feeling content of the emotion seems to be, most noticeably, a tightness or constriction about the chest, a kind of sinking feeling in the pit of the stomach, and a rapid heart rate. But I also have this same complex of sensations when in the grip of love and erotic expectation. This feeling complex, furthermore, is distinctly unpleasant in the former instance, distinctly pleasant in the latter. And what makes the former unpleasant, the latter pleasant, cannot, clearly, be some difference in the subjective "feels," for they are, by hypothesis, the same. Indeed, I think anyone would agree that what makes the former unpleasant and the latter pleasant must be their respective objects, desires, and surrounding belief structures. In a word, it is distinctly unpleasant to contemplate all of the possible ways I might contrive to fall on my face before the audience I am about to confront, and distinctly pleasant to contemplate the amorous and erotic scene I am about to enact with the object of my affections. What makes *the very same feeling* fear in the first instance, erotic love in the second, must be the attendant objects, desires, beliefs.

That being the case, it then becomes difficult to see what would make a feeling aroused by music the love-feeling or the fear-feeling; for music only arouses the feelings, on Levinson's view, but cannot, by hypothesis, provide the beliefs, objects, desires by which such feelings could be differentiated. A drug, after all, can produce, one presumes, tightness in the chest, a sinking feeling in the pit of the stomach, rapid heart rate—the same symptoms produced by contemplation of possible failure or expectation of sexual pleasure. But only the respective beliefs, desires, and objects can make such feelings fear or erotic love. Music, so far as I can see, can do, on Levinson's view, no more than the drug. But can it even do that? This leads us to our final difficulty.

We can, even as lay people, form an idea of how a drug could arouse the kinds of feelings and bodily sensations that might be described as what Levinson calls "the characteristic feeling of some emotion, but which is short of a complete emotion *per se*." I have no idea how music could do this; and I have never been convinced by anything I have read that anyone else has a plausible idea either. There is absolutely no evidence I know of that suggests music can or does do this, or how it might. This is not to say that it cannot or does not—only that we have no idea how it can, no evidence that it does. For all of that, it is *possible* that it can and does. And it is that *possibility* that we want to canvass. Or, rather, one implication of that possibility. For if music can arouse at least something like the garden-variety emotions, it can arouse the unpleasant as well as the pleasant ones, one would presume. And therein lies the problem we are pursuing. As Levinson puts it: "What could induce a sane person to purposely arrange for himself occasions of ostensibly painful experience?"[8]

◇ 5 ◇   Levinson enumerates no fewer than eight *possible* "rewards" (as he sometimes calls them) of experiencing the negative emotions he supposes are sometimes aroused by music. And I emphasize the word "possible" here because it will be the theme of my discussion that that is all Levinson has done. He has shown, that is to say, that experiencing the negative emotions supposedly aroused by music might possibly have certain benefits that he enumerates. But, as I shall argue in each case but one, there is not, so far as I know, a shred of evidence that listening to music really has these benefits. And if that is so, then there is not a shred of evidence that music's arousing the garden-variety emotions when we listen to it—which I deny happens, and Levinson affirms—can have these benefits either.

The first two of these possible rewards are not original with Levinson. "The first is the Goodmanian observation that emotional response facilitates our grasp, assessment, and description of the expression in a musical work"; and "the second is the Aristotelian element of catharsis."[9]

Now Goodman's point is difficult to make adequately outside of the very complex context of his own views concerning art, some of which I do not share. But if one states it broadly enough, then it seems to me completely acceptable within the context of my own views concerning how music is expressive and how music moves. Goodman writes: "Emotional numbness disables here as definitely if not as completely as blindness or deafness. Nor are the feelings used exclusively for exploring the emotional content of a work. . . . Emotion in aesthetic experience is a means of discerning what properties a work has and expresses." [10]

Translated into my own terms, I have absolutely no quarrel with this. Being *moved* by music, in my sense of that word, is bound, I would think, to draw one into the music more closely and deeply, thus revealing to a fuller extent its properties, including, of course, its expressive ones. Conversely, becoming more and more deeply engrossed in a musical work will, if it rewards scrutiny, enhance one's emotional involvement with it. In my own fashion, then, I can wholly endorse Goodman's notion that feeling and perceiving are interactive, each enhancing the other.

Catharsis, however, is another matter. It appears quite extraordinary to me that Levinson presents the supposed cathartic effect of music as received opinion, no more controversial than the gravitational red-shift or the toxicity of asbestos. "There seems no denying," Levinson confidently reports, "that dark music can be therapeutic in this way": that "the virtue of, say, a grief-response to music is that it allows one to bleed off in a controlled manner a certain amount of harmful emotion with which one is afflicted." [11]

But what, one is impelled to ask, is the source of Levinson's confidence in the catharsis principle? Is there a shred of evidence that listening to sad music makes one less sad, or better able to deal with sadness; any evidence that folks who listen to music expressive of the "dark" emotions are more emotionally healthy than those who do not? (The Nazis' love affair with Wagner always comes to mind here when entertaining such imponderables.) Levinson tells us that music allows us to bleed off harmful emotions in a manner so matter of fact as to suggest the phenomenon is as open to observation and familiar to the common man as the effect of aspirin on headaches. But we know this is not true; that the statement is, at best, highly controversial. I do not say the thing is impossible. What I would insist on is that it is empirically unsupported. What we should make of its mere possibility, and the mere possibility of Levinson's other claims about the rewards of negative musical emotions, I shall suggest as the discussion progresses.

◇ 6 ◇   Three benefits of the negative emotions in music devolve, according to Levinson, from the fact that, as we have seen, "emotional responses to music typically *have no life-implica-tions.*" As he denominates them, "these are benefits of enjoyment, of understanding, and of self-assurance."[12]

The benefit of enjoyment Levinson imagines to be a kind of savoring of the emotions' "feel" ("we can approach them like wine tasters, sampling the delights of various vintages") made possible by the lack of painful practical consequences. Of course we are on dangerous ground here, as Levinson is well aware; for it borders on the unintelligible to have a "painful" emotion without the pain. He treads a fine line:

> This is not to say that the pure feeling has nothing unpleasant about it. If in itself it did not possess a negative tone it could hardly count as a negative emotion. But in the detached context of musical response, it becomes possible for us to savor the feeling for its special character, since we are for once spared the additional distress that accompanies its occurrence in the context of life.[13]

That there may be such a phenomenon as "savoring the painful," where one feels "safe" from harm, I am inclined to grant (although it raises a host of well-known problems). That there is the kind of experience of music that Levinson invokes under that general description seems to me the remotest of possibilities. Certainly we savor the heard qualities of musical compositions, the expressive, negative as well as positive, among them; but that we reflexively, so to speak, savor our musical experiences, seems to me to be barely possible at best. Part of our experience of music is, to be sure, the savoring of expressive qualities. But we savor the qualities, not the experience, to the extent that we are musical listeners, not introspective psychologists. Somehow one thinks of someone being transfixed by his or her conscious states while listening to music as someone who has lost concentration, not someone who has achieved it. Levinson's description of emotive vintages sounds bizarre to me—not an impossible mode of musical appreciation, I suppose, but very remote from my own, and not one I would encourage in others. *Possible* is my verdict here, as elsewhere.

Levinson's second and third rewards resulting from the supposed arousal by music of the negative emotions denuded of practical consequences, beliefs, or objects return, as one might have expected, to the more fertile and familiar ground of emotional well-being, education, and improvement—so much a part, always, of the discussion of catharsis. "The second reward attaching to negative emotional response to music in virtue of its contextual freedom is that of greater understanding of the condition of feeling involved in some recognized emotion." Levinson admits that "it is notoriously difficult to say what the knowledge of how an emotion feels consists in" but assures us that, for example, "one can deepen or reinforce one's image of what it is to feel melancholy by experiencing the *Poco Allegretto* of Brahms' *Third*, or of what it is to feel hopeless passion by responding to Scriabin's c# minor Etude." [14]

But once again, when it comes to the question of what evidence there is for such claims, the inquirer comes up empty handed. The two possibilities in this regard would seem to be that people with musical experience of the kind Levinson is speaking of can tell us things about how their images of what it is to feel emotions have been deepened or reinforced, or that they will display in their emotional lives more maturity, greater ability to deal with their "dark" emotions, and so forth. In other words, they will give us, either in their verbal or other behavior, evidence of their enlightenment.

Levinson has foreclosed on the former possibility right from the start by warning us, as we have seen, that it is "notoriously difficult" (for which read "impossible") to say in what such knowledge consists, which ought to be enough to make us suspect that it does not exist at all. And with regard to the second alternative, all of us know (or ought to, by now) that, as I have said before, there is no evidence of greater emotional maturity, greater ability to deal with the negative emotions, or what have you among listeners to "serious" music. That does not mean it is not so; but it does mean that Levinson's extraordinary confidence, as expressed in such claims as "*It is clear* that such knowledge, whatever it amounts to, can be augmented by emotional experiences during or after occasions of music listening," [15] is completely unjustified, and amounts, really, to nothing more than vigorous arm waving.

"The third of the rewards announced above relates directly to a person's self-respect or sense of dignity as a human being." That is to say, "since music has the power to put us into the feeling state of a negative emotion without its unwanted life consequences, it allows us to partly reassure ourselves in a nondestructive manner of the depth and breadth of our ability to feel." [16]

As the claims for music's "therapeutic" potency escalate, so does one's admiration for Levinson's imagination, but also, alas, one's skepticism. Does the music department display more self-respect and emotional maturity than the physics department? If self-respect, as measured by "the capacity to feel deeply a range of emotions," [17] did indeed increase with musical listening, Edison would surely have been a greater benefactor to mental health than we have suspected; and the age of the phonograph would be far less the age of anxiety than it obviously is. This is a monstrously extravagant claim Levinson is making for musical listening. We surely know of no evidence at all to support it. Another remote possibility, or, rather, improbability is what, at best, we are left with.

◇ 7 ◇   The final three of Levinson's benefits are what he describes as "the rewards of imagining, through identification, that one is in the full emotional condition, while knowing throughout that one is not." [18] Which is to say, one experiences tamed emotions, without practical consequences, and so on, of the kind we have been discussing, but through a process of identification with . . . , to be discussed in a moment, one comes to imagine what one knows to be false: that one is really experiencing the full-blooded emotion, consequences and all.

How does one do that? There are actually three ways, on Levinson's view, in which it can be accomplished, corresponding to the three different "rewards."

The first method is to hear the music as the expression of some anonymous agent's emotions. "If I emphatically experience feelings of despair and anguish from a despairing or anguished piece of music and also regard the music as the unfolding expression of someone's despair or anguish, then I may begin to identify with that someone and consequently to imagine . . . that I am in actual despair or anguish."[19] So much for the emotion. Where is its reward? This lies in the fact, as Levinson sees it, that "emotion in a musical composition, because of its construction, so often strikes us as having been resolved, transformed, or triumphed over when the music is done." Thus (my example) the despair and anguish—the negative emotions—of the opening of the finale of Brahms's First Symphony are resolved in the glorious C-major theme of the last section. "By imaginatively identifying our state with that of the music, we derive from a suitable constructed composition a sense of mastery and control over—or at least accommodation with—emotions which in the extra-musical setting are thoroughly upsetting, and over which we hope to be victorious when and if the time comes."[20]

The second reward of imagining oneself, through music, as actually in the grip of a full-blooded emotion, and the method of doing so, Levinson describes as follows:

> If one begins to regard music as the expression of one's own current emotional state, it will begin to seem as if it issues from oneself, as if it pours forth from one's innermost being. It is then very natural for one to receive an impression of expressive power—of freedom and ease in externalizing and embodying what one feels. . . . The unpleasant aspect of certain emotions we imagine ourselves to experience through music is balanced by the adequacy, grace, and splendor of the exposition we feel ourselves to be according that emotion.[21]

And, finally, we may go from imagining ourselves experiencing the emotions of the music to imagining or counterfactually assuming that the composer is, and feeling, thereby, communion (in the imagination) with another human being. This sense of communion is a pleasurable, even blessed release from loneliness (and fear of solipsistic isolation?), which more than compensates for the pain of experiencing, or imagining experiencing, the negative emotions. As Levinson graphically describes this final reward and its method:

> We may sometimes as listeners adopt the Expressionist assumption—that the emotion expressed in a particular piece belongs to its composer's biography—while imagining ourselves to be possessed of the full emotion whose feeling has

been aroused within us. If we do so we are in effect imagining that we are sharing in the precise emotional experience of another human being, the man or woman responsible for the music we hear. . . . The sense of intimate contact with the mind and soul of another, the sense that one is manifestly not alone in the emotional universe, goes a long way toward counterbalancing the possibly distressing aspect of the grief, sorrow, or anger one imagines oneself to have.[22]

The previous three rewards of experiencing the negative emotions in music might be described as "instrumental": contributing to what can broadly be described as "emotional well-being," which is the ultimate payoff. The present ones might instead be described as "intrinsic": they are, to appropriate Addison's phrase, "pleasures of the imagination"; pleasures that accrue directly to experiencing music in certain emotionally imaginative ways. As such, these latter are far more difficult to grapple with, in the sense that they seem completely beyond the question of an evidential base. We could ask of the "therapeutic" rewards: Is there any evidence that listening to music provides them? Is there any evidence that those who listen to music expressive of the negative emotions enjoy better emotional adjustment than those who do not? The answer is pretty obviously "no"; and the question makes some kind of obvious sense. One can even imagine a "clinical" investigation, and a report in the *New England Journal of Medicine.*

But how does one deal with the question of evidence for whether people *enjoy* music in the ways specified by Levinson above? Of course there is ample evidence that people enjoy music expressive of the negative emotions. What kind of evidence, though, can we ask or expect for the rest of Levinson's claim? He presents us with none. One should begin, I suppose, by going through these last three, one by one, to see if they are even possible modes of musical enjoyment, let alone actual, advisable, or widespread.

◇ 8 ◇   The first of these final three hedonic modes (if I may so call them) requires the following things to happen. The music must arouse in the listener an emotion-feeling, denuded of practical consequences, and so forth: let us say "anguish," by way of example. Second, the listener must imagine the music as an unfolding expression of some agent's anguish. (In how much detail must we imagine the agent to make this all work?) Third, the listener must identify with the imagined agent, which, in turn, must (fourth) cause the listener to imagine being in that emotional state. If all of these things eventuate, then the unfolding of the music will, at least in some cases, result in the imagined anguish of the listener being (imaginatively) resolved: when, that is, the music "resolves" (say) from anguished diminished chords, chromaticism, minor tonality into sunny, diatonic major harmonies. The listener can then derive satisfaction from this resolution to compensate for the painfulness of the negative emotion—the anguish, in this case—by patting himself or herself on the back and thinking: "That was my emotion, that is how I dealt with it, that is what became of it."[23]

I confess to finding this fantastic; woven out of whole cloth. But putting my initial disbelief and astonishment aside, is this a possible mode of responding to music? And, if so, will responding in this way do the job for Levinson: that is, provide the pleasure for the painful emotions?

I am somewhat at a loss to assess possibility here. But I suppose one should give Levinson the benefit of the doubt. If someone can play fifty games of chess at one go, or compose an opera while engaged in conversation with friends at table, then I dare say someone is capable of the various kinds of emotive imagining Levinson describes. What I myself would say to a listener engaged in such an orgy of imaginings would be: "Get back to the music; you have lost concentration."

As to whether, if possible, such a mode of responding to music would do the job, two difficulties immediately obtrude. To begin with, in this mode of responding, the hedonic pay-off cannot occur until the anguish of C minor resolves to the triumph of C major. That is to say, on Levinson's view, the pleasurable compensation for the negative emotions comes at the end, where the negative emotions are triumphed over by the music and, so the account has it, by the imagination of the listener. Only then can the accounts be balanced, and the listener be in the black, on the pleasure side of the ledger. But this does not seem to square with experience—at least with mine. For I am quite thoroughly enjoying the anguished part of the music all the while: I do not have to await the C-major finale to have my debt in pain paid off in pleasure. My way is pleasure all the way: Levinson's way seems to be "It feels so good when it stops." To this Levinson might reply that the "pleasure along the way" of which I speak is provided for by some of his other "rewards": this, after all, is only one of eight. The point is well taken: but what would at least have to be the case, if this "reward" is to be believable, is that there is always a marked *surge* of pleasure at the end, when negative emotions are resolved to positive ones; and *more* of a surge than when positive are resolved to negative (for the pleasure must result not merely from musical resolution, if Levinson's theory is to be sustained, but from musical resolution of negative into positive emotions). I do not observe this to happen, nor do I think it has been observed.

Furthermore, it seems perfectly clear to me that I can enjoy music expressive of the negative emotions without going through any of these imaginative contortions that Levinson has described —and that goes for the lot, not merely the ones under discussion now. I enjoy music expressive of anguish without imagining that I have the emotion, without imagining that some nameless agent does, without imagining that the composer does, without imagining that the music expresses my emotion, without imagining that I have triumphed over it (since there is nothing for me to triumph over), without imagining communion with another soul, without being emotionally reassured, and so on. Nor, I think, can it be reasonably argued that I am simply not aware of all of this going on. For all of the rewards of this emotive imagining, so far as I can see, seem to follow from actually being conscious of having imagined certain things to be the case: being conscious of triumphing over my emotions, being conscious of communion with another soul, and so on. I can't very well pat myself on the back for an imagined emotional life I am not conscious of. Thus my final verdict here, as elsewhere, is that Levinson may have presented a possible mode of responding to music, but not a necesary mode for the enjoyment of the negative emotions in music; and has failed, in every case, to present any evidence for his claims.

And much the same thing, I think, can be said for the remaining modes of response. The second one, Levinson assures us, is "simpler" than the first; and, therefore, one can perhaps more readily grant, straightaway, that it is at least a possible way of responding to music, although not, in my view, any more desirable. I myself would find it quite possible, though distracting, to imagine music as expressing in imagination my own emotional life. It can also be said for this second mode of response, as for the third, that it is immune to the first difficulty suggested above. For the reward comes in the process of listening, rather than at its close. "The sense one has of the richness and spontaneity with which one's inner life is unfolding itself [in the music], even where the feelings involved are of the negative kind, is a source of indescribable joy."[24] And this coincides with the way in which I perceive that we enjoy the negative emotions. That is to say, we enjoy them along the way, not (necessarily) at some climactic payoff at the end; although, needless to say, I am not in accord with Levinson as regards the source of this enjoyment, which I take to be purely musical.

But, as in the previous case, it appears to me that, although it may be possible to get enjoyment out of music by imagining it as an expression of your emotions, and taking in "the richness and spontaneity with which one's inner life is unfolding itself," I find it hard to believe that it, or all of Levinson's modes of responding put together (if *that* is possible), is a necessary condition for enjoying sad or anguished or angry music. It seems utterly alien to my own listening experiences, which are so centered on the music, and to those experiences (in so far as I know them) of others whose musical tastes I most admire. A possibility, nevertheless, it remains, so far as I can make out; although *how much* enjoyment it can result in (and that goes for Levinson's other modes of responding as well) is questionable. I find it hard to believe it adds up to the degree of pleasure that I take in the negative emotions of the acknowledged masterpieces.

Finally, it does, I am sure, remain a possible way of responding to music to make the imaginative or counterfactual assumption that one is listening to the expression of the composer's emotions. (Indeed, many people probably *believe*, never mind imagine, that that is the case.) And, if that is so, it *may* be possible for people to take some pleasure in this imagined communion with another soul. I find that possibility—that is, the possibility of the pleasure—pretty remote, and the pleasure, if it should possibly accrue, pretty negligible: hardly a drop in the bucket of pleasure I take, for example, in the opening movement of Mozart's great G-Minor Quintet. But who can say that some lonely people, or people suffering from some kind of solipsistic *Angst*, do not find it comforting to imagine that they are hearing Mozart pouring out his anguished soul in K. 516? Perhaps that is their only way of responding. And who am I to take it from them? Bad sex, after all, is better than none, so the saying goes. There are, however, better ways of responding and no evidence, so far as I know, that one cannot enjoy music expressive of the negative emotions without recourse to Levinson's elaborate machinery of imaginative identification with agents, composers, the music itself, and imaginative experience of the negative emotions themselves. And, indeed, the whole notion of imagining oneself to be anguished or angry or mournful demands some scrutiny; for it is not altogether clear what the difference is between imagining you are afraid and being afraid.

◇ 9 ◇   We say that hypochondriacs' illnesses are "in the imagination," which is to say, they don't really have them. Now what of the fear (say) that is "in my imagination," when I am listening to music? Is it like a hypochondriac's imagined illness? If so, then I believe I am afraid; for hypochondriacs certainly believe they are ill. And one then wonders what the difference might be between imagining one is afraid and being afraid. We have a clear idea what the difference is between imagining you have a brain tumor and really having one; for in the latter case there really is that horrible, lethal thing growing in your skull. The question is, is there conceptual space, within the concept of emotion, for that distinction to be drawn? Is my imaginary fear, as opposed to my real fear, intelligible? While I am imagining I am fearful, am I not *fearful*, with all that implies?

Compare "He has an imaginary illness," "He has an imaginary pain," "He has an imaginary emotion." I would suggest that "He has an imaginary pain" can mean only "He has a pain caused by something imaginary," perhaps caused by his imagined brain tumor. But the pain is real; and I suggest, further, that "He has an imaginary emotion" is, *prima facie*, more like "He has an imaginary pain" than "He has an imaginary illness." It must mean something like "He has an emotion caused by his imaginings," perhaps caused by his imagining some of the things Levinson has suggested we can imagine when listening to music. But the emotion is real: real fear, real anger, real anguish. And that being the case, it raises all of the problems that the arousing of real emotions raises, principally, why we should want to have painful (real) emotions raised in us by music, if we can avoid it.

Notice, we cannot give Levinson's old answers here, based on the notion that these are tamed emotions, without the nasty practical accoutrements; for, by hypothesis, they are not: they are the real thing. Thus it would appear that Levinson's last three "rewards" of the negative emotions in music may raise more questions than they answer. Their reliance on the notion of "imaginary emotion" makes them as problematic as that notion itself. I do not claim its unintelligibility is a certainty. I do claim that it raises that distinct possibility. We had better be more sure than Levinson leaves us, about exactly what it would be like to have imaginary fear or anger or anguish, as opposed to the "real thing," that did not just amount to real fear or anger or anguish caused by an imaginary object or state of affairs, before we accept, even as possibilities of musical response, these concluding benefits that Levinson supposes the negative emotions in music to bestow.

◇ 10 ◇   Where then does this leave us with regard to Levinson's attempt to justify the purported arousal of the negative emotions by music? Perhaps I am paying both of us too extravagant a compliment in suggesting it: but it seems to me that, in a sense, Levinson is playing Leibniz to a kind of musical problem of evil, and I am playing his Voltaire.

If Leibniz can be thought of as having showed us how it is not contradictory to believe the usual Christian dogma about the omniscience, omnipotence, and goodness of God, in full knowledge of the Lisbon earthquake, by demonstrating it is *possible* that this is the best of all possible worlds, then Levinson has perhaps shown how one can, without contradiction, believe that music is sometimes expressive of the painful emotions, moves us by arousing them, and is pleasing as well, by showing it is *possible* that one might reap enjoyment from the emotively painful. Indeed, Levinson has, it seems to me, given the strongest, most compelling explanation to date of how the arousal of painful emotions *might* have sufficiently pleasurable payoffs to compensate for the pain.

But if one thinks it only the remotest possibility, given the deplorable state of the world in which we live, that this is the best that omnipotent and morally perfect rationality could achieve, one is impelled toward atheism or (as some of Voltaire's statements seem to suggest) at least to the denial of omnipotence.[25] The musical counterpart of atheism, in response to the "musical problem of evil," and the realization that even the most clever and imaginative attempts to defend the pleasure in the pain present us with only the most remotely possible scenarios, without a shred of supporting evidence, is the denial that music arouses the garden-variety emotions at all.[26] That, of course, is the option I have elected.

The driving force impelling one to the view, as paradoxical as it is, that music arouses the garden-variety emotions, including the painful ones, is, as I have argued here, and elsewhere, the twin beliefs (or, better, certainties) that music is expressive of the garden-variety emotions, including the painful ones, and that listening to music, at times, anyway, is a wonderfully moving experience, even when the music moving one is expressive of the painful emotions. For if the only possibility one envisages, to make sense of music's power to move, is that music moves us to the emotions it is expressive of, then it follows that music sometimes moves us to the negative emotions, and does so, optimally, on just those occasions when we would expect it also to be the most pleasurable—that is, when it is very good music. Simply put: the better the music, the more moving and the more enjoyable; the better the music expressive (say) of anguish, the more intensely moving and the more enjoyable the music; the more intensely moving the music, the more intense the feeling of anguish aroused in the listener; and so (paradoxically) the more painful the music (since anguish is a painful emotion), the more intensely enjoyable the music. Hence, the musical problem of evil, or, how the intensely painful can also be enjoyed.

But once one sees that it is the fallacy of "no third thing" to argue that either music arouses the painful emotions or music expressive of the painful emotions cannot be moving (which is absurd), then the musical problem of evil simply solves itself without recourse to elaborate and only barely intelligible explanations, for which there is no positive evidence at all, of how being moved to the painful emotions by music might have pleasurable payoffs overriding the painful ones. Anguished music can be moving, of course; but it does not move us to anguish. And in that recognition the "problem" of the negative emotions in music, the musical "problem of evil" dissolves.

◇ 11 ◇ But is there perhaps a musical "problem of evil" for my view as well? The problem for the arousal theorist is how having painful emotions can be enjoyable. Is there not an analogous problem, for those who think that the expressiveness of music consists in phenomenological properties heard in it, of how perceiving painful emotive qualities in music can be enjoyable? Why in the world should I *want* to hear the anguish in Brahms's First Symphony?

Let me begin by suggesting that there are two questions lurking here. The first question is whether the perceiving of painful emotions in music is itself a painful experience. If you answer that question in the affirmative, then you do indeed have the musical problem of evil all over again. For you will be compelled to ask why people should choose to have the painful experience of perceiving the painful emotions in music, when they can perfectly well avoid doing so.

Well, I would think it perfectly clear that the answer to the first question is an emphatic negative. There is no more reason to believe it is a painful experience to perceive sadness in a symphony than to perceive it in the face of a Saint Bernard. If I am under the misapprehension that dogs express their emotions with their faces, then I might indeed be saddened by the further misapprehension that the sad face of the Saint Bernard now confronting me betokens a sad Saint Bernard. But when I realize that dogs express their emotions with their tails, a Saint Bernard with a "sad" face and a madly wagging tail will have no tendency to make me sad. Why should it? The face may amuse me, or fascinate me; I may be taken with its handsome markings. There is no reason in the world, however, to think that because it is "phenomenologically" sad it should infect me with that emotion. Thus far, then, there seems to be no problem of negative emotions, no musical problem of evil, for the "phenomenological" view of musical expressiveness.

The question can, however, be pressed further. For one can reasonably ask for an account of why pure music possesses expressive properties at all. Or, to put it another way, what is it that we enjoy in perceiving the expressive properties of pure music? Surely they cannot be extraneous baggage.

The force of this question, however, is very different from that of the previous one: it scarcely has the force of paradox, for we are not asking how something can be both desirable and undesirable, both pleasurable and painful, but merely how something that we have no a priori reason for believing to be either one or the other has a role to play in our enjoyment of music.

But in a sense, the answer to this question must be philosophically very disappointing. For there is no interesting answer, in the sense of *the* answer, any more than there is an answer to *the* question of why a C-major chord in the root position is enjoyable in music. You may indeed ask why *this* C-major chord in the root position is so wonderful, so moving, so pleasurable in *this* particular musical composition. That however, is a question to be answered by the music critic or analyst, not the philosopher; and it is to be answered by showing what role, function, purpose that particular chord has in that particular place, in that particular composition—relative, of course, to a complete interpretation or analysis or understanding of the whole movement or work of which that particular chord is a part. This, needless to say, is true of any musical quality; and what I want to urge here is that expressive qualities of pure music just are *musical* qualities, not semantic or representational ones, and that, therefore, the explanation of why any expressive quality occurs in a musical passage, if it has any explanation at all, has a formally musical one.[27]

Now if I am right about this, then something very interesting follows for the practice of musical analysis; namely, that a new kind of musical analysis is called for: what I shall call (until something better comes along) "emotive formalist" criticism. Analysis (or interpretation) of pure instrumental music tends to be of three kinds: (1) it is purely formalistic, in which case it eschews expressive qualities as either nonexistent or (at least) irrelevant; (2) it is mixed, in which case the expressive qualities are treated as semantic or representational (or a little bit of both), and thus, although embedded perhaps in the formal structure, not formal structure themselves (Cone and Newcomb are good examples of this); or (3) rarer today among "respectable" critics but, of course, dominant during the nineteenth century, purely emotive, in which case, being either semantic or representational or both, it pretty much reduces instrumental music to the crypto-programmatic. What I am suggesting is a wholly new alternative.

From what has gone before it must be clear to the reader that I totally reject semantic and representational construals of expressiveness in music. I am a self-described (and self-invented) "emotive formalist," which is to say that like the traditional formalist, I take pure instrumental music to be pure musical form and quality. But, unlike my formalist predecessors (at least so far as I know), I take expressive properties to be some of the properties of musical form and sensuous surface. To be sure, I thoroughly endorse pure formal analysis that pays no attention to expressive properties, just so long as it is clearly understood that such analysis is not telling the whole formalist story. What I am urging, however, is that another kind of musical analysis be explored: an analysis that accepts a musical formalism expanded to contain, within its catalogue of sensuous and formal properties, expressive ones too. It is an analysis that will interpret to us not merely the formal, syntactical, and sensual properties of music as they are usually understood by the unreconstructed formalist, but those properties, where appropriate, that possess expressive color as well. It is an analysis that will not tell us emotional stories, or paint us emotional pictures, but an analysis that will convey to us the formal, sensual, syntactic roles of expressive properties, where they occur, and where they have such roles to play. I have only vague glimmerings of what such an analysis would be like. But I believe it both possible and required—required if we are ever going to understand fully a piece of *expressive* music in formalist terms, which are the only terms that do justice to its musical purity. Formal analysis without expressive analysis is incomplete; formal analysis with expressive analysis in semantic or representational terms is false. I don't think there has ever been formal analysis true to the expressive properties of music *and* true to itself.

◇ 12 ◇   Where do we go from here? Perhaps the best way to answer that question is to come to some realistic estimate first of where, at present, we are.

It seems to me, to begin with, a near certainty that music is recognized as expressive, where it is, in virtue of our hearing expressive qualities in it, not in virtue of having the emotions it is expressive of aroused in us. This is a result that analytic philosophy (broadly conceived) has made particularly firm, in recent years, and was made convincingly, I would think, as far back as the work of Carroll C. Pratt and Susanne K. Langer.

I am equally certain, mainly because of work by analytic philosophers of psychology since and including Anthony Kenny on the nature of the emotions, that it is a near absurdity to think that music can arouse the full-blooded, garden-variety emotions in any but "weird" contexts, completely irrelevant to aesthetic appreciation. And this certainty, along with the knowledge that music is, for me, a deeply moving experience, and must be for others as well, has convinced me that music moves us not, as has been thought since at least the end of the sixteenth century, by arousing the emotions it is expressive of (or something like that), but through our being moved by its beauty (and all that its beauty contains and implies).

With these conclusions established, for me, beyond any reasonable doubt, two paths of future research present themselves. One lies in the direction of spelling out just what roles expressive properties of music play in pure instrumental compositions, given they are not dispositional properties of arousal, as so many have thought, but phenomenal properties of the music itself. Are they semantic properties? Representational? Do they refer? I have denied all three and argued for what I have called an "emotive formalism." But the conclusion that emotions are "in" the music, not the listener, is certainly compatible with other possibilities, and all of these must be canvassed more thoroughly than I have done, by those more sympathetic to those views, if we are to reach any firm conclusions. I look forward to what others will do in this direction, as well as to pushing ahead myself.

A second path of research that I envisage may surprise some of my readers, for it is the very path pursued in *The Corded Shell*. The conclusions of that book concerning *how* music comes to be expressive are not on my list of settled doctrine. They remain for me, as I know they do for others, highly questionable.

Whenever I re-read *The Corded Shell*, I am convinced by my own arguments. Whenever I listen to a piece of complex expressive music, I am convinced that neither I nor anyone else understands how it is possible for the expressiveness to be in the music at all. It is there: of that I am sure; but how, in what manner remains to me a divine mystery.

Much more wants to be done to answer the question of how music is expressive. It is still, in spite of all the work that has been expended on the "property" theory of musical expressiveness in recent years, an entirely open question.

But, in conclusion, although I see it as an open question, I also see it as a question whose answer must be bounded by what I consider as the inviolable "purity" of pure instrumental music. It is particularly easy for philosophers, who have cleverness and ingenuity bred in the bone, to come up with intriguing explanations of musical expressiveness that, in the end, reduce pure music to some form of representation or emotive fiction. Indeed, since it is as yet unclear just why we should have any deeply abiding interest in the purely sensuous, syntactic, and formal structure of musical sound, we are often told, with evangelical fervor, that to view music as such trivializes it, and makes our enthusiasm for it unintelligible.

This self-righteous attitude simply begs the most important question at issue. As philosophers of art, we must take it as a given datum that human beings *do* have a deep, emotional, and abiding interest in pure musical syntax and structure. This is a datum to be explained, not explained away. And until we explain it, there remains something mysteriously intriguing and deeply puzzling about human nature.

Notes, Bibliography,
and Index

Notes

NOTES TO I

1. Robert Schumann, *Music and Musicians: First Series*, trans. Fanny Raymond Ritter (8th ed.; London: William Reeves, n.d.), pp. 264-265.
2. *Memoirs of Hector Berlioz*, trans. Ernest Newman (New York: Tudor, 1932), p. 321.
3. Donald Francis Tovey, *Essays in Musical Analysis: Volume I, Symphonies* (London: Oxford University Press, 1935), pp. 32 and 86.
4. Edmund Gurney, *The Power of Sound* (London: Smith, Elder, 1880), p. 339.
5. Grosvenor Cooper and Leonard B. Meyer, *The Rhythmic Structure of Music* (Chicago: University of Chicago Press, 1960), p. 65.
6. Joseph Kerman, *The Beethoven Quartets* (New York: Alfred Knopf, 1967), pp. 175-176.
7. Arnold Isenberg, "Critical Communication," *Aesthetics and Theory of Criticism: Selected Essays of Arnold Isenberg*, ed. Callaghan, Cauman, Hempel, Morgenbesser, Mothersill, Nagel, and Norman (Chicago and London: University of Chicago Press, 1973), p. 162.

NOTES TO II

1. I am indebted for this distinction to Alan Tormey's book, *The Concept of Expression: A Study in Philosophical Psychology and Aesthetics* (Princeton: Princeton University Press, 1971), Chap. II. I am indebted, too, to Professor Tormey's book for teaching me to think clearly about the concept of expression.
2. J.W.N. Sullivan, *Beethoven: His Spiritual Development* (New York: Vintage Books, 1960), pp. 138-139.
3. Ibid., p. 36.
4. Cf. for example, Sidney Finkelstein, *How Music Expresses Ideas* (New York: International Publishers, 1976).
5. For an illuminating and thorough survey of the varieties of artistic "expression," the reader is enthusiastically referred to Guy Sircello's book, *Mind and Art: An Essay on the Varieties of Expression* (Princeton: Princeton University Press, 1972), Chap. I, passim.

NOTES TO III

1. Manfred Bukofzer, *Music in the Baroque Era* (New York: Norton, 1947), p. 25.
2. Ibid.
3. Ibid., p. 26.

4. Ibid., p. 25.
5. Letter to G. B. Doni, in Oliver Strunk, *Source Readings in Music History* (New York: Norton, 1950), p. 364.
6. Strunk, *Source Readings in Music History*, p. 374.
7. Ibid., p. 371.
8. Ibid., p. 378.
9. Quoted in Leo Schrade, *Monteverdi: Creator of Modern Music* (New York: Norton, 1950), p. 239.
10. Strunk, *Source Readings in Music History*, p. 364.
11. Ibid., p. 382.
12. *Roger North on Music*, ed. John Wilson (London: Novello, 1959), p. 292.
13. Ibid., pp. 111 and 110.
14. Francis Hutcheson, *Inquiry Concerning Beauty, Order, Harmony, Design*, ed. Peter Kivy (The Hague: Martinus Nijhoff, 1973), p. 81.
15. Cf. O. K. Bouwsma, "The Expression Theory of Art," *Philosophical Analysis*, ed. Max Black (Ithaca: Cornell University Press, 1950), pp. 82-83.
16. Richard Wollheim, *Art and Its Objects: An Introduction to Aesthetics* (New York: Harper and Row, 1968), p. 22.
17. Bouwsma, "The Expression Theory of Art," p. 100.
18. See above, notes 10 and 11.
19. For a detailed account of Reid's views on artistic expression, see my "Thomas Reid and the Expression Theory of Art," *The Monist*, LXV (1978).
20. Thomas Reid, *Essays on the Active Powers of the Human Mind*, III, ii, 6; *Works of Thomas Reid*, ed. Sir William Hamilton (8th ed.; Edinburgh: James Thin; London: Longmans, Green, 1895), Vol. II, p. 574.
21. Reid, *Essays on the Intellectual Powers of Man*, VIII, iv; *Works of Thomas Reid*, Vol. I, p. 504.
22. Thomas Reid, *Lectures on the Fine Arts*, ed. Peter Kivy (The Hague: Martinus Nijhoff, 1973), p. 49.

NOTES TO IV

1. Charles Avison, *An Essay on Musical Expression* (3rd ed.; London, 1775), pp. 3-4.
2. Wilson Coker, *Music and Meaning: A Theoretical Introduction to Musical Aesthetics* (New York: Free Press, 1972), p. 149.
3. Daniel Webb, *Observations on the Correspondence between Poetry and Music* (London, 1769), pp. 1-2.
4. Ibid., pp. 2-3.
5. Susanne K. Langer, *Philosophy in a New Key* (New York: Mentor Books, 1959), p. 181.

6. Webb, *Observations on the Correspondence between Poetry and Music*, pp. 4-6.
7. Ibid., p. 6.
8. Ibid., pp. 7-8.
9. Ibid., pp. 9-10.

NOTES TO V

1. Hans Lenneberg, "Johann Mattheson on Affect and Rhetoric in Music," *Journal of Music Theory*, II (1958), pp. 51-52. I have in general relied on Lenneberg's excellent translation; but I have not scrupled to make changes where I thought appropriate.
2. Langer, *Philosophy in a New Key*, p. 207. Cf. Carroll C. Pratt, *The Meaning of Music* (New York: McGraw-Hill, 1932).
3. René Descartes, *The Passions of the Soul, Philosophical Works of Descartes*, trans. E. S. Haldane and G.R.T. Ross (New York: Dover, 1955), Vol. I, p. 349. It is worth pointing out that although Mattheson adopted Descartes' emotive doctrines, and was a "Cartesian" in this respect, he did not, in my view, share Descartes' musical opinions. For Descartes, at least in his early *Compendium Musicae* (c. 1618), explicitly endorsed the "arousal" theory of musical expression, writing there that the "aim [of music] is to please and to arouse various emotions in us." See René Descartes, *Compendium of Music*, trans. Walter Robert (American Institute of Musicology, 1961), p. 11, passim.
4. Lenneberg, "Johann Mattheson on Affect and Rhetoric in Music," p. 51.
5. Ibid.
6. Quoted in Newman Flower, *George Frideric Handel: His Personality and His Times* (New York: Charles Scribner's Sons, 1948), pp. 301-302.
7. Manfred Bukofzer, "Allegory in Baroque Music," *Journal of the Warburg and Courtauld Institutes*, III (1939-1940), p. 21. This is not to say that Mattheson did not believe that music can be "moving"; but, unfortunately, some of the passages in which he says so have been taken to suggest, I think mistakenly, that he is talking about particular passions being moved or aroused. I doubt that is the case: most of such passages can, on careful reading, be brought into conformity with the interpretation of Mattheson I am developing here. On this see, for example, *Der vollkommene Capellmeister* (Hamburg, 1739): II, ii, 40.
8. Langer, *Philosophy in a New Key*, pp. 186-187.
9. Arthur Schopenhauer, *The World as Will and Representation*, trans. E.F.J. Payne (Indian Hills, Colorado: The Falcon's Wing Press, 1958), Vol. I, p. 257.

10. Ibid., Vol. I, p. 261.
11. See Richard Kramer, "Notes to Beethoven's Education," *Journal of the American Musicological Society*, XXVIII (1975), pp. 94-97.

NOTES TO VI

1. Langer, *Philosophy in a New Key*, p. 202.
2. Eduard Hanslick, *The Beautiful in Music*, ed. Gustav Cohen (New York: The Liberal Arts Press, 1957), p. 29.
3. Langer, *Philosophy in a New Key*, p. 194.
4. Nelson Goodman, *Languages of Art* (Indianapolis and New York: Bobbs-Merrill, 1968), pp. 85-86, passim.
5. See Harold Osborne, "The Quality of Feeling in Art," *Aesthetics in the Modern World*, ed. Harold Osborne (New York: Weybright and Talley, 1968): "But the moods are not highly structured as works of art are structured. So far as I can observe, my feeling of sadness or elation is as nearly structureless as anything I know" (p. 114).
6. I am grateful to Martin Bunzl for pressing me on this point, and forcing me to provide some kind of answer.
7. Cf. Wilson Coker, *Music and Meaning*: "We can notice that the production of sound by voice or the orchestral wind and stringed instruments requires a certain effort. And to move in a given direction from a fixed pitch by a large interval normally is to use more energy for that pitch displacement than is required to move in the same direction from that pitch by a smaller interval. . . . So we tend to regard the displacement of pitch by larger intervals as more forceful than the displacement of smaller intervals, other things being equal" (pp. 43-44).
8. Nelson Goodman, *Ways of Worldmaking* (Indianapolis and Cambridge: Hackett, 1978), p. 106.

NOTES TO VII

1. Thomas Mace, *Musick's Monument* (London, 1676), p. 234.
2. Wollheim, *Art and its Objects*, p. 28.
3. I am grateful to Seymour Feldman for raising this objection, and for suggesting the reference to Maimonides.
4. On this see, Ernest Nagel's review of *Philosophy in New Key* in *Journal of Philosophy*, XL (1943), pp. 324 and 327; and Monroe C. Beardsley, *Aesthetics: Problems in the Philosophy of Criticism* (New York: Harcourt, Brace, 1958), pp. 335-337.
5. I am indebted to James Bogen for pressing me vigorously on this point.
6. For the pros and cons of this question, see: V. A. Howard, "On Representational Music," *Nous*, VI (1972); Richard Kuhns, "Music as a Representational Art," *British Journal of Aesthetics*, XVIII

(1978); Roger Scruton, "Representation in Music," *Philosophy*, LI (1976); J. O. Urmson, "Representation in Music," *Philosophy and the Arts*, Royal Institute of Philosophy Lectures, Vol. VI (London: Macmillan, 1973).

7. Dennis W. Stampe, "Toward a Causal Theory of Linguistic Representation," *Contemporary Perspectives in the Philosophy of Language*, ed. French, Uehling, and Wettstein (Minneapolis: University of Minnesota Press, 1978), p. 87.

NOTES TO VIII

1. I am not intending to suggest by this that there was no thought given in the Middle Ages or Renaissance to the proper setting of text to music; only that in the *Camerata*, and what directly led up to it, we have a special confluence of theoretical and practical interest in musical expressiveness as a measure of propriety in the relation of tone to text.

2. Edward J. Dent, *Mozart's Operas* (2nd ed.; London: Oxford University Press, 1960), p. 112.

3. Hanslick, *The Beautiful in Music*, p. 34.

4. Ibid., p. 32.

5. Deryck Cooke, *The Language of Music* (London: Oxford University Press, 1959), p. 83.

6. John Dewey, *Art as Experience* (New York: Milton Balch, 1934), p. 239.

NOTES TO IX

1. Walter Kaufmann, *The Rāgas of North India* (Bloomington: Indiana University Press, 1974), p. vi.

2. Ibid., p. 10.

3. Curt J. Ducasse, *Art, the Critics, and You* (New York: Bobbs-Merrill, The Library of Liberal Arts, 1955), pp. 53-54.

4. Kaufmann, *The Rāgas of North India*, p. 281.

5. Ibid., p. 1.

6. This is not to say that intervals smaller than the half-step do not figure in western musical culture. The string player, we know, distinguishes, for example, between the pitch of A-sharp and B-flat; and the well-tempered tuning must augment and shave perfect intervals. But the part played is not structurally apparent: it performs no aesthetic function, but a technical one (which, to be sure, has aesthetic consequences). What we hear are half-steps, made "right," sometimes, by the performer or tuner making distinctions finer than that.

7. Bach's authorship of these fugues is in question; but I like to give

my bird the benefit of the doubt, and continue to call it the "Bach-bird."

8. Part of my line of argument here was suggested by an unpublished paper on the origins of polyphony by Richard Norton.

NOTES TO X

1. Johann Adam Hiller, "Abhandlung von der Nachahmung der Natur in der Musik," *Historisch-kritische Beyträge*, ed. Friedrich Wilhelm Marpurg, Vol. I (Berlin, 1754), pp. 515-543. I am grateful to William Waite, of Yale University, who, in my student days in musicology, first called my attention to Hiller's essay.

2. *Historisch-kritische Beyträge*, Vol. I, p. 520.

3. Ibid.

4. Ibid., p. 521.

5. For an account of this theory, and some of its more recent adventures, see: Peter Kivy, "Charles Darwin on Music," *Journal of the American Musicological Society*, XII (1959), and "Herbert Spencer and a Musical Dispute," *The Music Review*, XXIII (1962).

6. *Historisch-kritische Beyträge*, Vol. I, p. 526.

7. Ibid., p. 523.

8. Ibid., p. 525.

9. Ibid., p. 524.

10. James Beattie, *The Philosophical and Critical Works*, Vol. I (Hildesheim and New York: Georg Olms, 1975), p. 463.

11. Ibid., p. 465.

12. Alan Tormey, *The Concept of Expression*, pp. 133ff.

13. Ibid., p. 17.

14. Ibid., p. 136.

15. Ibid., p. 138.

16. In commenting on this point, Nelson Goodman has suggested, rightly, I think, that the tables can sometimes be turned: that an emotively vague text might be given greater specificity by a musical setting with a more particular emotive cast than the text. So, for example, in setting the Queen of the Night's texts in *Die Zauberflöte*, Mozart gives them an "hysterical" tone with his music that they by no means possess in themselves.

NOTES TO XI

1. Avison, *An Essay on Musical Expression*, p. 4; Webb, *Observations on the Correspondence between Poetry and Music*, p. 28.

2. Cf. P. F. Strawson, "Aesthetic Appraisal and Works of Art," *Freedom and Resentment, and Other Essays* (London: Methuen, 1974), pp. 178-188.

3. Albert Schweitzer, *J. S. Bach*, trans. Ernest Newman (New York: Macmillan, 1950), Vol. I, p. 395. My italics.

4. Charles Hartshorne, *The Philosophy and Psychology of Sensation* (Chicago: University of Chicago Press, 1934), pp. 176-177.

5. H. C. Robbins Landon, *Haydn: Chronicle and Works, Volume IV: The Years of "The Creation," 1796-1800* (Bloomington: Indiana University Press, 1977), p. 68.

6. Ibid., p. 66.

7. Guy Sircello, *A New Theory of Beauty* (Princeton: Princeton University Press, 1975), p. 43.

8. Ibid., p. 18.

9. Ibid., pp. 94-95.

10. Ibid., p. 96.

11. Ibid., p. 99.

12. For the classic account of these eighteenth-century theories, see: Samuel H. Monk, *The Sublime: A Study of Critical Theories in Eighteenth-Century England* (Ann Arbor: University of Michigan Press, 1960).

13. Joseph Addison, *The Spectator*, ed. Alexander Chalmers (New York: D. Appleton, 1879), Vol. V, p. 34 (Paper 412—the second of the series "On the Pleasures of the Imagination").

14. Immanuel Kant, *Critique of Aesthetic Judgement*, trans. James Creed Meredith (Oxford: The Clarendon Press, 1911), p. 90.

NOTES TO XII

1. For a recent defense of this view, see A. J. Ayer, *The Problem of Knowledge* (Harmondsworth: Penguin Books, 1961), Chap. 5.

2. Ludwig Wittgenstein, *The Blue and Brown Books* (New York: Harper Torchbooks, 1965), p. 25.

3. Michael Scriven, "The Logic of Criteria," *Journal of Philosophy*, LVI (1959), pp. 859-860.

4. Sircello, *Mind and Art*, pp. 245-246.

5. Ibid., pp. 246-247.

6. Ibid., p. 248.

7. Ibid.

8. See the work of Eckman.

9. On this, see also, Peter Kivy, "Aesthetic Aspects and Aesthetic Qualities," *Journal of Philosophy*, LXV (1968).

10. For a more general version of this argument, see Peter Kivy, "Aesthetics and Rationality," *Journal of Aesthetics and Art Criticism*, XXXIV (1975).

NOTES TO XIII

1. On this, see Peter Kivy, "Something I've Always Wanted to Know about Hanslick," *Journal of Aesthetics and Art Criticism*, XLI (1988).

2. In, principally, *The Corded Shell: Reflections on Musical Expression*, Part I herein; and *Music Alone: Philosophical Reflections on the Purely Musical Experience* (Ithaca: Cornell University Press, forthcoming), Chaps. VIII and IX.

3. Colin Radford, "Emotions and Music: A Reply to the Cognitivists," *Journal of Aesthetics and Art Criticism*, XLVII (1989), p. 72.

4. Colin Radford, "How Can We Be Moved by the Fate of Anna Karenina?" *Proceedings of the Aristotelian Society*, Supplementary Volume, LXIX (1975).

5. See, for example, Kendall Walton, "Fearing Fictions," *Journal of Philosophy*, LXXV (1978).

6. Radford, "Emotions and Music," p. 72.

7. I think Richard Wollheim is presenting a version of the "fusion" theory for expression in painting. On his latest version of this approach, see his *Painting as an Art* (Princeton: Princeton University Press, 1987), pp. 80–95.

8. Hartshorne, *The Philosophy and Psychology of Sensation*, p. 243.

9. Ibid., pp. 244–245.

10. Ibid., p. 112.

11. Ibid., p. 193.

12. Malcolm Budd, "Appropriate Feelings," *Times Literary Supplement*, 3 July 1981, p. 762. My italics.

13. Plato, *The Republic*, trans. John Llewelyn Davies and David James Vaughan (London: Macmillan, 1950), p. 92n.

14. Ibid., p. 92 (399).

15. It may surprise some, as it did me, to discover that speculation about the expressiveness of music did not die out in the middle ages, only to be revived by the Humanists in their rediscovery of Plato and the *Poetics*, but was quite in evidence when the musical setting of texts was discussed. On this see Don Harrán, *Word-Tone Relations in Musical Thought: From Antiquity to the Seventeenth Century* (American Institute of Musicology: Hänsler-Verlag, 1986).

16. See Wollheim, *Painting as an Art*, Chap. II.

17. On this see Kivy, *Music Alone*, Chap. I.

NOTES TO XIV

1. Anthony Newcomb, "Sound and Feeling," *Critical Inquiry*, X (1984), pp. 618–619.

2. For my own views on this regard, see Peter Kivy, *Sound and Semblance: Reflections on Musical Representation* (Princeton: Princeton University Press, 1984).

3. Newcomb, "Sound and Feeling," p. 620.

4. Ibid.

5. Ibid., p. 632.

6. Edward T. Cone, "Music and Form," *What Is Music?: An Introduction to the Philosophy of Music*, ed. Philip Alperson (New York: Haven, 1988), p. 141.

7. See Peter Kivy, *Osmin's Rage: Philosophical Reflections on Opera, Drama, and Text* (Princeton: Princeton University Press, 1988), Chaps. VII and X, et passim.

8. Newcomb, "Sound and Feeling," p. 626.

9. Ibid., p. 627.

10. Anthony Newcomb, "Those Images That Yet Fresh Images Beget," *Journal of Musicology*, II (1983), p. 232. My italics.

11. Ibid., p. 244.

12. For Arthur Danto's view, see *The Transfiguration of the Commonplace: A Philosophy of Art* (Cambridge, Mass.: Harvard University Press, 1981).

13. See Edward T. Cone, "Schubert's Promissory Note: An Exercise in Musical Hermeneutics," *Nineteenth-Century Music*, V (1982); and Anthony Newcomb, "Once More 'Between Absolute and Program Music': Schumann's Second Symphony," *Nineteenth Century Music*, VII (1984).

14. Cone, "Schubert's Promissory Note," pp. 235–239.

15. Ibid., pp. 239–240.

16. Ibid., p. 240.

17. Ibid.

18. Ibid., p. 241.

19. Newcomb, "Sound and Feeling," p. 630.

20. Quoted in ibid., p. 631.

21. See, especially, Stanley Fish, *Is There a Text in This Class?* (Cambridge, Mass.: Harvard University Press, 1980), Chaps. 15 and 16.

22. On this see, Peter Kivy, "Fish's Consequences," *British Journal of Aesthetics*, XXIX (1988).

23. Newcomb, "Sound and Feeling," p. 629.

24. Ronald de Sousa, *The Rationality of Emotion* (Cambridge, Mass.: MIT Press, 1987), p. 145.

25. Sigmund Spaeth, *Great Symphonies: How to Recognize and Remember Them* (Garden City: Garden City Publishing, 1936), pp. 39–40. I am grateful to Richard Taruskin for pointing out this bizarre passage to me in his review of *The Corded Shell*, in *The Musical Quarterly*, LXVIII (1982). My reply to his point in the review is the same as my reply to Sigmund Spaeth and the wine club's reply to Mr. Bibulous.

26. Newcomb, "Sound and Feeling," p. 629.

27. Ibid., p. 634.

Notes to XV

1. John Nolt, "Expression and Emotion," *British Journal of Aesthetics*, XXI (1981), p. 145.
2. Nolt considers a related example, but goes in a different direction with it, which I do not wish to trace out here. See, on this, Robert Stecker, "Nolt on Expression and Emotion," *British Journal of Aesthetics*, XXIII (1983).
3. Stanley Speck, "'Arousal Theory' Reconsidered," *British Journal of Aesthetics*, XXVIII (1988), p. 45.
4. Ibid., p. 46.
5. See Kivy, *Music Alone*, Chap. III, et passim.
6. Nolt, "Expression and Emotion," p. 47n.
7. Donald Callen, "The Sentiment in Musical Sensibility," *Journal of Aesthetics and Art Criticism*, XL (1982), p. 382. I am grateful to the editor of the journal, Donald Crawford, for permission to reprint here sections 4 and 5 of this chapter, which are a revised version of my note in reply to Donald Callen.
8. Quoted in Kivy, *Sound and Semblance*, p. 216.
9. Callen, "The Sentiment in Musical Sensibility," p. 386.
10. Ibid., p. 387.
11. Radford, "Emotions and Music," p. 69.
12. Ibid., p. 70.
13. Ibid.
14. Speck, "'Arousal Theory' Reconsidered," p. 41.
15. On this see Peter Kivy, "How Music Moves," in *What Is Music?*; and Kivy, *Music Alone*, Chap. VIII.
16. Clive Bell, *Art* (New York: Capricorn Books, 1958), p. 17.

Notes to XVI

1. My interpretation of Hanslick on this regard is not altogether uncontentious. On this see, Peter Kivy, "What Was Hanslick Denying?" *The Journal of Musicology* (forthcoming). And cf. Geoffrey Payzant's translation of Hanslick, *On the Musically Beautiful: A Contribution towards the Revision of the Aesthetics of Music* (Indianapolis: Hackett, 1986), translator's preface.
2. On the former, see Kivy, *Sound and Semblance*, Chaps. VII and IX; on the latter, Kivy, *The Corded Shell*, Chapter X of Part I herein.
3. James M. McPherson, *Battle Cry of Freedom: The Civil War Era* (New York and Oxford: Oxford University Press, 1988), pp. 89–90.
4. Jerrold Levinson, "Music and Negative Emotion," *Pacific Philosophical Quarterly*, LXIII (1982), p. 329.
5. Ibid.
6. Ibid., p. 327.

7. Ibid., p. 332.
8. Ibid., p. 327.
9. Ibid., pp. 337–338.
10. Goodman, *Languages of Art*, p. 248.
11. Levinson, "Music and Negative Emotion," p. 338.
12. Ibid.
13. Ibid., p. 339.
14. Ibid., pp. 339–340.
15. Ibid., p. 339. My italics.
16. Ibid., p. 340.
17. Ibid.
18. Ibid.
19. Ibid.
20. Ibid., p. 341.
21. Ibid.
22. Ibid., p. 342.
23. Ibid., p. 341.
24. Ibid.
25. See the entry "Power, Omnipotence," in *Voltaire's Philosophical Dictionary*, no translator credited (Cleveland and New York: World Publishing, 1943), pp. 240–244.
26. There is, as well, a musical counterpart to the denial of omnipotence, in, for example, Charles Avison's insistence that music arouses only the *"social and happy passions"* (*Essay on Musical Expression*, p. 4).
27. I have argued this point at greater length than I have time for here in *Music Alone*, Chap. IX.

Bibliography of Works Cited

Addison, Joseph. *The Spectator*. Edited by Alexander Chalmers. 6 vols. New York: D. Appleton, 1879.

Avison, Charles. *An Essay on Musical Expression*. 3rd ed. London, 1775.

Ayer, A. J. *The Problem of Knowledge*. Harmondsworth: Penguin Books, 1961.

Beardsley, Monroe C. *Aesthetics: Problems in the Philosophy of Criticism*. New York: Harcourt, Brace, 1958.

Beattie, James. *The Philosophical and Critical Works*. Vol. I. Hildesheim and New York: Georg Olms, 1975.

Bell, Clive. *Art*. New York: Capricorn Books, 1958.

Berlioz, Hector. *Memoirs*. Translated by Ernest Newman. New York: Tudor, 1932.

Bouwsma, O. K. "The Expression Theory of Art." *Philosophical Analysis*. Edited by Max Black. Ithaca: Cornell University Press, 1950.

Budd, Malcolm. "Appropriate Feelings," *Times Literary Supplement*, 3 July 1981.

Bukofzer, Manfred. "Allegory in Baroque Music." *Journal of the Warburg and Courtauld Institutes*, III (1939–1940).

————. *Music in the Baroque Era*. New York: Norton, 1947.

Callen, Donald. "The Sentiment in Musical Sensibility," *Journal of Aesthetics and Art Criticism*, XL (1982).

Coker, Wilson. *Music and Meaning: A Theoretical Introduction to Musical Aesthetics*. New York: The Free Press, 1972.

Cone, Edward T. "Music and Form," *What Is Music?: An Introduction to the Philosophy of Music*. Edited by Philip Alperson. New York: Haven, 1988.

————. "Schubert's Promissory Note: An Exercise in Musical Hermeneutics," *Nineteenth-Century Music*, V (1982).

Cooke, Deryck. *The Language of Music*. London: Oxford University Press, 1959.

Cooper, Grosvenor, and Meyer, Leonard B. *The Rhythmic Structure of Music*. Chicago: University of Chicago Press, 1960.

Danto, Arthur. *The Transfiguration of the Commonplace: A Philosophy of Art*. Cambridge, Mass.: Harvard University Press, 1981.

Dent, Edward J. *Mozart's Operas.* 2nd ed. London: Oxford University Press, 1960.

Descartes, René. *Compendium of Music.* Translated by Walter Robert. American Institute of Musicology, 1961.

———. *The Philosophical Works of Descartes.* Translated by E. S. Haldane and G.R.T. Ross. 2 vols. New York: Dover, 1955.

de Sousa, Ronald. *The Rationality of Emotion.* Cambridge, Mass.: MIT Press, 1987.

Dewey, John. *Art as Experience.* New York: Milton Balch, 1934.

Ducasse, Curt J. *Art, the Critics, and You.* New York: Bobbs-Merrill, Library of Liberal Arts, 1955.

Finkelstein, Sidney. *How Music Expresses Ideas.* New York: International Publishers, 1976.

Fish, Stanley. *Is There a Text in This Class?* Cambridge, Mass.: Harvard University Press, 1980.

Flower, Newman. *George Frideric Handel: His Personality and His Times.* New York: Charles Scribner's Sons, 1948.

Goodman, Nelson. *Languages of Art.* Indianapolis and New York: Bobbs-Merrill, 1968.

———. *Ways of Worldmaking.* Indianapolis and Cambridge: Hackett, 1978.

Gurney, Edmund. *The Power of Sound.* London: Smith, Elder, 1880.

Hanslick, Eduard. *The Beautiful in Music.* Translated by Gustav Cohen. New York: The Liberal Arts Press, 1957.

———. *On the Musically Beautiful: A Contribution towards the Revision of the Aesthetics of Music.* Translated by Geoffrey Payzant. Indianapolis: Hackett, 1986.

Harrán, Don. *Word-Tone Relations in Musical Thought: From Antiquity to the Seventeenth Century.* American Institute of Musicology: Hänsler-Verlag, 1986.

Hartshorne, Charles. *The Philosophy and Psychology of Sensation.* Chicago: University of Chicago Press, 1934.

Hiller, Johann Adam. "Abhandlung von der Nachahmung der Natur in der Musick." *Historisch-kritische Beyträge.* Edited by Friedrich Wilhelm Marpurg. Vol. I. Berlin, 1754.

Howard, V. A. "On Representational Music," *Nous,* VI (1972).

Hutcheson, Francis. *Inquiry Concerning Beauty, Order, Harmony, Design.* Edited by Peter Kivy. The Hague: Martinus Nijhoff, 1973.

Isenberg, Arnold. "Critical Communication," *Aesthetics and Theory of Art Criticism: Selected Essays of Arnold Isenberg*. Edited by William Callaghan, Leigh Cauman, Carl Hempel, Sidney Morgenbesser, Mary Mothersill, Ernest Nagel, and Theodore Norman. Chicago and London: University of Chicago Press, 1973.

Kant, Immanuel. *Critique of Aesthetic Judgement*. Translated by James Creed Meredith. Oxford: The Clarendon Press, 1911.

Kaufmann, Walter. *The Rāgas of North India*. Bloomington: Indiana University Press, 1974.

Kerman, Joseph. *The Beethoven Quartets*. New York: Alfred Knopf, 1967.

Kivy, Peter. "Aesthetic Aspects and Aesthetic Qualities." *Journal of Philosophy*, LXV (1968).

————. "Aesthetics and Rationality," *Journal of Aesthetics and Art Criticism*, XXXIV (1975).

————. "Charles Darwin on Music," *Journal of the American Musicological Society*, XII (1959).

————. *The Corded Shell: Reflections on Musical Expression*, Part I herein.

————. "Fish's Consequences," *British Journal of Aesthetics*, XXIX (1988).

————. "Herbert Spencer and a Musical Dispute," *The Music Review*, XXIII (1962).

————. "How Music Moves," *What Is Music? See* Cone, "Music and Form."

————. *Music Alone: Philosophical Reflections on the Purely Musical Experience*. Ithaca: Cornell University Press, forthcoming.

————. *Osmin's Rage: Philosophical Reflections on Opera, Drama, and Text*. Princeton: Princeton University Press, 1988.

————. "Something I've Always Wanted to Know about Hanslick," *Journal of Aesthetics and Art Criticism*, XLI (1988).

————. *Sound and Semblance: Reflections on Musical Representation*. Princeton: Princeton University Press, 1984.

————. "Sound Sentiment: A Reply to Donald Callen," *Journal of Aesthetics and Art Criticism*, XLI (1983).

————. "Thomas Reid and the Expression Theory of Art," *The Monist*, LXV (1978).

————. "What Was Hanslick Denying?" *The Journal of Musicology* (forthcoming).

Kramer, Richard. "Notes to Beethoven's Education," *Journal of the American Musicological Society*, XXVIII (1975).

Kuhns, Richard. "Music as a Representational Art," *British Journal of Aesthetics*, XVIII (1978).

Langer, Susanne K. *Philosophy in a New Key*. New York: Mentor Books, 1959.

Lenneberg, Hans. "Johann Mattheson on Affect and Rhetoric in Music," *Journal of Music Theory*, II (1958).

Levinson, Jerrold. "Music and Negative Emotion," *Pacific Philosophical Quarterly*, LXIII (1982).

Mace, Thomas. *Musick's Monument*. London, 1676.

McPherson, James M. *Battle Cry of Freedom: The Civil War Era*. New York and Oxford: Oxford University Press, 1988.

Mattheson, Johann. *Der vollkommene Capellmeister*. Hamburg, 1739.

Monk, Samuel H. *The Sublime: A Study of Critical Theories in Eighteenth-Century England*. Ann Arbor: University of Michigan Press, 1960.

Nagel, Ernest. Review of Langer, *Philosophy in a New Key*, *Journal of Philosophy*, XL (1943).

Newcomb, Anthony. "Once More 'Between Absolute and Program Music': Schumann's Second Symphony," *Nineteenth-Century Music*, VII (1984).

———. "Sound and Feeling," *Critical Inquiry*, X (1984).

———. "Those Images That Yet Fresh Images Beget," *Journal of Musicology*, II (1983).

Nolt, John. "Expression and Emotion," *British Journal of Aesthetics*, XXI (1981).

North, Roger. *Roger North on Music*. Edited by John Wilson. London: Novello, 1959.

Osborne, Harold. "The Quality of Feeling in Art." *Aesthetics in the Modern World*. Edited by Harold Osborne. New York: Weybright and Talley, 1968.

Plato. *The Republic*. Translated by John Llewelyn Davies and David James Vaughan. London: Macmillan, 1950.

Pratt, Carroll C. *The Meaning of Music*. New York: McGraw-Hill, 1932.

Radford, Colin. "Emotions and Music: A Reply to the Cognitivists," *Journal of Aesthetics and Art Criticism*, XLVII (1989).

———. "How Can We Be Moved by the Fate of Anna Karenina?"

Proceedings of the Aristotelian Society, Supplementary Volume, LXIX (1975).

Reid, Thomas. *Lectures on the Fine Arts*. Edited by Peter Kivy. The Hague: Martinus Nijhoff, 1973.

————. *Works*. Edited by Sir William Hamilton. 8th ed. 2 vols. Edinburgh: James Thin: London: Longmans, Green, 1895.

Robbins, Landon, H. C. *Haydn: Chronicle and Works, Volume IV: The Years of "The Creation," 1796–1800*. Bloomington: Indiana University Press, 1977.

Schopenhauer, Arthur. *The World as Will and Representation*. Translated by E.F.J. Payne. 2 vols. Indian Hills. Colorado: The Falcon's Wing Press, 1958.

Schrade, Leo. *Monteverdi: Creator of Modern Music*. New York: Norton, 1950.

Schumann, Robert. *Music and Musicians: First Series*. Translated by Fanny Raymond Ritter. 8th ed. London: William Reeves, n.d.

Schweitzer, Albert. *J. S. Bach*. Translated by Ernest Newman. 2 vols. New York: Macmillan, 1950.

Scriven, Michael. "The Logic of Criteria," *Journal of Philosophy*, LVI (1959).

Scruton, Roger. "Representation in Music," *Philosophy*, LI (1976).

Sircello, Guy. *Mind and Art: An Essay on the Varieties of Expression*. Princeton: Princeton University Press, 1972.

————. *A New Theory of Beauty*. Princeton: Princeton University Press, 1975.

Spaeth, Sigmund. *Great Symphonies: How to Recognize and Remember Them*. Garden City: Garden City Publishing, 1936.

Speck, Stanley. "'Arousal Theory' Reconsidered," *British Journal of Aesthetics*, XXVIII (1988).

Stampe, Dennis W. "Toward a Causal Theory of Linguistic Representation," *Contemporary Perspectives in the Philosophy of Language*. Edited by Peter A. French, Theodore F. Uehling, Jr., and Howard K. Wettstein. Minneapolis: University of Minnesota Press, 1978.

Stecker, Robert. "Nolt on Expression and Emotion," *British Journal of Aesthetics*, XXIII (1983).

Strawson, P. F. *Freedom and Resentment, and Other Essays*. London: Methuen, 1974.

Strunk, Oliver (ed.). *Source Readings in Music History*. New York:

Norton, 1950.

Sullivan, J.W.N. *Beethoven: His Spiritual Development*. New York: Vintage Books, 1960.

Taruskin, Richard. Review of Peter Kivy, *The Corded Shell: Reflections on Musical Expression*, *The Musical Quarterly*, LXVIII (1982).

Tormey, Alan. *The Concept of Expression: A Study in Philosophical Psychology and Aesthetics*. Princeton: Princeton University Press, 1971.

Tovey, Donald Francis. *Essays in Musical Analysis: Volume I, Symphonies*. London: Oxford University Press, 1935.

Urmson, J. O. "Representation in Music," *Philosophy and the Arts* ("Institute of Philosophy Lectures," Vol. VI). London: Macmillan, 1973.

Voltaire, *Voltaire's Philosophical Dictionary*. No translator credited. Cleveland and New York: World Publishing, 1943.

Walton, Kendall. "Fearing Fictions," *Journal of Philosophy*, LXXV (1978).

Webb, Daniel. *Observations on the Correspondence between Poetry and Music*. London, 1769.

Wittgenstein, Ludwig. *The Blue and Brown Books*. New York: Harper Torchbooks, 1965.

Wollheim, Richard. *Art and Its Objects: An Introduction to Aesthetics*. New York: Harper and Row, 1968.

———. *Painting as an Art*. Princeton: Princeton University Press, 1987.

Index